CHRISTENDUMB

CHRISTENDUMB

A Tongue-in-Cheek History of Christianity

Eric W. Gritsch

CASCADE *Books* • Eugene, Oregon

CHRISTENDUMB
A Tongue-in-Cheek History of Christianity

Copyright © 2013 Eric W. Gritsch. All rights reserved. Except for brief quotations in critical publications or reviews, no part of this book may be reproduced in any manner without prior written permission from the publisher. Write: Permissions, Wipf and Stock Publishers, 199 W. 8th Ave., Suite 3, Eugene, OR 97401.

Cascade Books
An Imprint of Wipf and Stock Publishers
199 W. 8th Ave., Suite 3
Eugene, OR 97401

www.wipfandstock.com

ISBN 13: 978-1-62032-538-4

Cataloging-in-Publication data:

Gritsch, Eric W.

    Christendumb : a tongue-in-cheek history of Christianity / Eric W. Gritsch.

    xii + 172 pp. ; 23 cm. Includes bibliographical references.

    ISBN 13: 978-1-62032-538-4

    1. Church history. I. Title.

BR145 .G835 2013

Manufactured in the U.S.A.

"You are the salt of the earth. But if the salt _becomes DUMB_, how can its saltiness be restored? It is no longer good for anything, but is thrown out and trampled under foot."

—Matthew 5:13[1]

"For everything there is a season, and a time for every matter under heaven: a time to weep and a time to laugh."

—Ecclesiastes 3:4

---

1. Underlined emphasis added from the Standard German translation based on Martin Luther "*wird dumm*" and the Greek *moranthe*: third person singular, aorist passive, conditional subjunctive, meaning, "if salt were to be made foolish (insipid), how might it be salted?" The verb is used as a metaphor for "has lost its taste" (modern English translation), literally "dumbed down" or "become dull," connoting both taste and mentality. Matthew used the verb *moraine* to highlight the contrast between the "wise" and the "foolish" in the parable of the ten virgins (Matt 25:2)—five were "foolish" (*morai*) and five were "wise" (*phronimai*)—again in Matt 10:16: "wise as serpents"). I am grateful for a comprehensive grammatical instruction by the biblical scholar Wayne Rollins, a friend and former colleague, and the comments of another former colleague and New Testament scholar, Michael Gorman.

Contents

Prologue | ix

Chapter 1: Mission Impossible?, c. 7–700 CE | 1

    Memory, Momentum, and Misery | 1
    Greed and Creed | 19
    When in Rome . . . | 33
    A Fuzzy Fusion | 39

Chapter 2: Edifice Complex, 700–1400 CE | 47

    An East-West Wall | 47
    Skyscrapers, Bunkers, and Sand Boxes | 58
    Silos of Doctrine | 74
    Pay, Pray, and Obey | 85

Chapter 3: Loose Ends, 1400–2010 CE | 97

    Retardation and Reveille | 97
    Mazy Means and Ways | 120
    Faith on the Rocks | 133
    Back to the Future | 152

A Serious Epilogue | 161

Timetable | 167

Bibliography | 171

Prologue

I PRESENT A SWIFT trek through the history of two millennia of Christianity, wrapped in wit, with a twist of satire and a dosage of gallows humor. Its title uses the word-play "dom-dumb"[1] as a pun, echoing the saying of Jesus in the Sermon on the Mount about Christian witness as "salt."[2] to alert readers to the Christian flaws and foibles in history, prompting the question, "How dumb does it get?" The facts are very convincing: disagreements galore about doctrine and life; massive hostile schisms between Eastern (Greek Orthodox) and Western (Roman Catholics), as well as between northern Roman Catholics and Protestants; Christian mission as proselytism, often drenched in sweat, blood, and tears; and nasty quarrels about two holy mysteries, such as the Trinity and the Eucharist.

Christian theology views the historic dumbness of Christians as part of a basic human flaw—an "original" and "inherited sin" manifested in a self-righteousness as the enduring temptation to be "like God" (Gen 3:5).[3] One is free from this temptation only after death in a never-ending future with God, promised by Jesus Christ. Such freedom must guide life in this world, nourished by prayer, embodied in love of neighbor, and guarded by vigilance—echoing the proverbial wisdom, "Eternal vigilance is the price

---

1. "-dom—*suffix* [from the Latin *fixum*, an adverb of *figere*, 'attached') denoting a state or condition" like "institutionalized Christianity"—the church, Christendom. "Dumb—unable, to speak, most typically because of congenital deafness; it has been overwhelmed by a newer sense, meaning 'stupid' to such an extent that the use of the first sense is now almost certain to cause offense." *The New Oxford American Dictionary*, 2nd ed. Erin McKean (Oxford: Oxford University Press, 2005). Hereafter cited NOAD.

2. See above, 2 n.1. Salt preserves and makes food attractive. It was the payment ("salary") for Roman soldiers. Christians are to be the spice of life in this world offering a foretaste of eternal in the world, to come.

3. Explicated above, 186–89.

Prologue

of liberty"[4] and recalling the tried and true warning, "Those who cannot remember the past are condemned to repeat it."[5]

In a half-century of teaching, I have encountered a steady increase of historical and theological amnesia whenever Christianity is a topic, be it in informal conversation or in formal teaching events. More often than not, the amnesia makes pious, but ignorant Christians retreat to a naïve "fundamentalism" or "traditionalism." Adherents to the former are usually Protestants who believe "in the strict and literal interpretation of the Bible, including its narratives, doctrines, prophecies, and moral laws." Adherents to the latter are usually Roman Catholics who believe "that all moral and religious truth comes from divine revelation [through a hierarchy of clergy topped by the papal office], human reason being incapable of attaining it."[6] It could be said that "Fundamentalism" is "unblessed ignorance." In regard to "traditionalism," the renowned American church historian Jaroslav Pelikan hit the nail on the head when he said that "tradition is the living faith of the dead, traditionalism is the dead faith of the living."[7]

Great numbers of Christians follow noisy and theatrical preachers, also known as "Televangelists," pumped up to an addictive and expensive feel-good religiosity, often mixed with moral mandates regarding sex and politics. In the 1960s, the sad condition of Christian leadership was satirically presented under the title *How to Become a Bishop Without Being Religious*.[8] But critical wit gave way to naive "ignoramuses" who talk about Christianity without being aware of its complex, indeed controversial, history in its institutional form, the church. There are also romantic "Ecumeniacs" who propose a scheme for overcoming divisive issues and create Christian unity at the drop of their hat. But great expectations often reveal only self-deceptions, echoing the ancient Roman proverb (based on

---

4. Attributed to Thomas Jefferson but not found in his works. Quotation from 1852 by Wendell Philipps, abolitionist, traced to John Philpot Curran, Irish politician, speech of 1790. Quoted in *John Bartlett's Familiar Quotations*, ed. Justin Kaplan (New York: Hatchet, 2002): "The condition upon which God has given liberty to man is eternal vigilance."

5. George Santayana, *The Life of Reason, or, The Phases of Human Progress* (New York: Scribners, 2006), 284.

6. NOAD.

7 Jaroslav Pelikan, *The Vindication of Tradition* (New Haven: Yale University Press, 1984), 65.

8. Charles M. Smith, *How to Become a Bishop Without Being Religious* (New York: Doubleday. 1965).

Prologue

Aesop's Fables from the sixth century BCE), "The mountains were in labor but delivered only a mouse."

In my own denominational camp, I have heard ignorant Lutherans spout their favorite slogan, "I am justified by faith alone without the merits of 'good works'" (echoing Martin Luther's adaptation of Rom 3:28). An annoyed educated Lutheran responded with ironic wit: "You don't need to be justified by faith alone because you don't do 'good works' anyway!" Or, as a frustrated parish pastor put it: "when Christ comes at the end of the world to usher in 'new heavens and a new earth' [2 Peter 3:13] I will hear the seven last words from my parishioners, "We never did it like this before.'"

The history of the Christianity reflects the story recorded in World War II at the Italian front when an Italian infantry commander ordered his company to storm from an alpine ridge against American troops below. Waving his pistol, he yelled, "Follow me!" The entire company responded "Bravo, Bravissimo," clapped their hands but did not follow him. He died a lonely death, cheered from behind by a bunch of cowards who ignored his command.

The story is a parable for the long trek of Christian history. Singing "Onward Christian soldiers, marching as to war," or "Lift high the Cross, the love of Christ proclaim," Christians have quarreled among themselves, crusaded against enemies, and made a mockery of "Christian love." Most of them have a zeal for glory rather than for the cross. It is an irony of history when proud cathedrals are ornamented with humble crosses, when "let us pray" becomes "let us bray," and the "kiss of peace" is a "hiss of tease." The founder of Christianity has been cheered from behind for centuries by the earthly "church militant" assuming to be the "church triumphant." Triumphalism has outflanked humbleness. The meantime between Christ's first and second advent has become a mean time. Many Christians are no longer patient pilgrims but desperate refugees or determined storm troopers hurrying to the promised kingdom, leaving a lot of refuse on the road. And yet, there are always believers who neither rush nor stay on the sidelines as "God's frozen people." They simply keep moving, adjusting to the flow of time, always ready and not surprised by the Last Day as "the little flock" (Luke 12:32) that suffers with Christ before being glorified by him (Rom 8:17).

There are about 2.2 billion Christians in a world population of about 6.5 billion.[9] But a reality check quickly shows that the "dumb" state of affairs

---

9. Martin E. Marty, *The Christian World. A Global History* (New York: Modern Library, 2007), 4.

Prologue

has not changed. Individuals and groups still compete for exclusive power, no longer with sword or ban, but with a hypocritical spirituality that tries to sideline dissenters. Old quarrels are revived, and unity for a common witness in the world remains a dream. Well-researched historical narratives become boring because irritating facts are repeated.[10]

I present my narrative in the context of familiar pious symbols and images: three chapters (symbolizing the Trinity), each intoned by a passage from Holy Scripture and covering seven centuries (symbolizing the seven days of creation); and four sections within each chapter (symbolizing the four gospels). I am providing footnotes for elucidation; and an appendix with a time-table, a brief bibliography of quoted sources, and an index.

All biblical quotations are from *The New Revised Standard Version of the Holy Bible*. Whatever a reader wants to know about Christian history is available in the one-volume edition (1343 pages!) of *The Cambridge Dictionary of Christianity*, ed. Daniel Patte (Cambridge: Cambridge University Press, 2010). Those who have the patience of Job, the curiosity of a cat, and the stamina of a marathon runner are directed to seven volumes of *A People's History of Christianity Series: The Lived Religion of Christians in the First Two Thousand Years*, ed. Denis R. Janz (Minneapolis: Augsburg Fortress, 2010). Perfectionists can combine sight and sound by plowing through the door-stopper *A History of Christianity: The First Three Thousand Years* by the Oxford historian Diarmaid MacCulloch whose work of 1161 pages is a summary of a BBC DVD documentary narrated by him in 2010 and available as a "home movie." Finally, there is "googling" on the Internet. I present all the material found in a lengthy text book. But I have followed the proverbial wisdom transmitted in my native German, "Brevity is the soul of wit" (*In der Kürze liegt die Würze*).

I am grateful to my wife Bonnie for proof-reading and helpful comments. My good friend and former editor, Dr. Norman Hjelm, read the manuscript and offered good advice The Day of St. Luke, author of the first history of the church, *The Acts of the* Apostles, October 18, 2012.

EWG

---

10. When I began my graduate theological education in 1950 I, too, was bored to tears by a standard German *Handbook of Church History* (*Handbuch der Kirchengeschichte*), constructed by the German Protestant scholar Karl Heussi (1877–1961) to cram facts for exams. See Eric W. Gritsch, *"Professor Heussi? I Thought You Were a Book!" A Memoir of Memorable Theological Educators (1950–2010)* (Eugene, OR: Wipf & Stock, 2009). I was reminded of the famous line of the detective Joe Friday (played by Jack Webb), "Just the facts, ma'am," in the popular radio and TV series *Dragnet* (1940s to the 1980s).

1

Mission Impossible?
c. 7–700 CE

> "All authority in heaven and on earth has been given to me. Go therefore and make disciples of all nations, baptizing them in the name of the Father, the Son and the Holy Spirit, and teaching them to obey everything I have commanded you. And remember, I am with you always, to the end of the age."
>
> —Matthew 28:18–20

Memory, Momentum, and Misery

There is only very meager reliable evidence about the beginning of Christianity. The first "church history" is presented in the New Testament by a physician-turned-historian, Luke, a companion of the apostle Paul. The narrative has two parts: 1) the activity of Jesus ("The Gospel According to Luke") and 2) the impact of his teaching, mainly through Paul ("The Acts of the Apostles"). Only he and Matthew record the birth of Jesus. But both offer contradictory accounts. Matthew (2:1) places Christ's birth in he reign of the Jewish king Herod (73–4 BCE); the story is adorned with a popular tale about "wise men" (a mild translation of the Greek *magoi*, "magicians," Matt 2:1–12). They date from an ancient priestly caste in Persia who were also known as astrologers. Dictionaries deduce from the three gifts the number "three" and give them the names of Balthasar, Casper, and

Melchior.¹ Luke adorns his account with shepherds and angels (2:8–20), speaks of the reign of the Roman emperor Augustus (63–14 BCE), and notes the census commanded by the Syrian governor Quirinius in 14 CE (2:1–2, 8–20). This timeframe puts the birth of Jesus between 4 and 14 CE. But Matthew has the family escape to Egypt when King Herod ordered the massacre of all male babies (2:13–18). After Herod's death, Joseph moved the family to Nazareth (2:19–23). The Dutch painter Peter Paul Rubens (1577–1640) titled his depiction "the massacre of holy innocents," the designation in the liturgical calendar (December 28). Scholarship cannot reconcile the two contradictory Gospel accounts. Both Gospels have Jesus born in a Bethlehem "manger" (from the Latin *mandere*, "to chew")—"a long open box or trough for horses or cattle to eat from."² Literary sources form rhe second-century mention a cave as the location of the home and manger of "the holy family" in Bethlehem. Excavations show that such a location was in the ground floor of a house, often also serving as a stable which looked like a cave. Helena, the mother of Constantine I and the first tour guide to the Holy Land chose such a site for building the Church of the Nativity.³

Non-Christian sources convey a few lines about the appearance of "Christians." They are mentioned by the Roman historian Cornelius Tacitus (c. 55–c.120) as scapegoats for the destructive fire in Rome in 64 ordered by Emperor Nero. Tacitus believed that Christians were innocent of the charge, but called their faith a pernicious superstition. The Jewish historian Flavius Josephus (c. 37–100) refers to a "wise man," Jesus, who had a following, "the tribe of Christians." This meager evidence could have motivated Ebenezer Scrooge's critique of Christmas as "humbug," the Santa Claus hoopla designed for an annual shopping spree from October to January; with a commercial "Black Friday" in Advent mocking the "Good Friday" in Lent.

The story of Mary's pregnancy through the "overshadowing" of the Holy Spirit (Luke 1:35) created a "Mariology," motivating a church without female priests to make her a "co-redeemer" in her son's work of salvation. As such, she is celebrated, indeed worshiped, as a Virgin Mother who remained a virgin (despite clear evidence of other children in Matt 13:55).

1. "Three Wise Men" in NOAD.
2. NOAD.
3. Built 327–333, destroyed by fire in 339, and rebuilt by Justinian I in 565, the church is maintained by teams of monks, Greek Orthodox and Roman Catholic, with occasional reports about violations of the use of assigned architectural space, resulting in minor physical violence (using brooms as weapons).

Mission Impossible?

Did Joseph father them with another wife, enjoying the divinely approved Jewish polygamy? In 1854, a solemn dogma of her "immaculate conception" was promulgated, followed in 1950 by the dogma of her "assumption" into heaven (bodily reception after death, not just a rational "assumption"), and a declaration of her perpetual virginity ("ever-virgin") by the Second Vatican Council in 1964. The "Ave Maria" (a prayer adapted from the greeting of Mary by an angel in Luke 1:28) is imbedded in spirituality and in music. The "Hail Mary" has become "a desperation long pass [in the American football game] to try to score late in the game, typically unsuccessful."[4] Her son Jesus, fathered by God, not Joseph, cannot be described like other figures in history because there are no records showing what he looked like, his height and weight, etc. The "quest for the historical Jesus" (the title of many publications) has found no reliable answers. But ignorant Fundamentalists still speculate about the historical Jesus ("What kind of car would he have driven?"). What is remembered about him in "Scripture" and "tradition" does not satisfy historical research.

"Scripture" is a collection of sixty-six books (thirty-nine in the Old Testament and twenty-seven in the New Testament). The history of their origins and collection reads like a murder mystery, spanning a time period from the lawgiver Moses in the fourteenth century BCE to the apostle Paul in the first century CE. The "canonical" (from the Greek *kanon*, "rule," indicating "authority") books were distinguished from "apocryphal" (from the Greek *apokryphos*, "hidden") ones; they were regarded as being not genuine. The "canon" of Scripture became a "cannon" used against heretics! The Old Testament was the "Bible" of Jesus and his disciples. Some of them believed that the Old Testament was "scripture inspired by God" (2 Tim 3:16), foreshadowing the Protestant biblical "Fundamentalists" of today. The original Greek text says "wafted by God" (*theopneustos*), translated in Latin editions of the Bible as "divinely inspired (*divina inspirata*). Since the third century BCE the Old Testament was read in a Greek translation by Jews in Egypt and, when the Christian movement began, by Christians. The translation became known as "The Septuagint" (from the Latin *septuaginta*, "seventy," abbreviated LXX) because it was believed to have been produced by seventy translators ("seven" being a holy number). The New Testament was created by culling writings from a wide variety of publications attributed to authors of gospels, sermons, epistles, and other texts. The *Gospel of Thomas*, for example, portrays Jesus as a wonder-working teenager. But the criteria

4. NOAD. CDC.

for selecting authentic texts are not clear. Moreover, a substantial collection of writings, neither canonical nor apocryphal, was preserved under the peculiar title *Apostolic Fathers*. They should have been called "Apostolic Sons" since they were part of the second generation of Christians. The most famous "son" was Ignatius of Antioch (c. 35–107)[5] who, like the apostle Paul, sent letters to various congregations including to one in Rome. But unlike Paul, he was a bureaucrat advocating a hierarchy of offices, headed by bishops who must guard the Eucharist as the "medicine of immortality," the antidote for dying. He took it before he was martyred.[6] But he snubbed the claim of popes to be in an "apostolic succession" beginning with Peter.

"Tradition" was first defined in the fifth century during a nasty and recurring quarrel about the relationship between human freedom and divine election. The renowned "church father" Augustine defended the doctrine of "original sin" against the teaching of the British monk Pelagius who, shocked by morals in Rome, claimed that humans did not lose their original freedom to accept or reject divine salvation. He foreshadowed the popular contemporary question of missionaries, "Do you accept Jesus Christ as your personal savior?" Augustine would never ask for a decision because he taught that this freedom to decide was lost when Adam and Eve used it to disobey God and fell in to sin. Accordingly, redemption can only come through God's election in the "Son," Jesus Christ.[7] A rather obscure French monastic theologian, Vincent of Lerins (near Nice), sided with Pelagius and, in the context of a summary of his views, spoke of "tradition." But the "definition" says little, if anything, with a pomposity later common in many ecclesiastical declarations: tradition is "what has been believed everywhere, always, by all," based on the Bible as the ultimate authority when interpreted according to the "ecclesiastical and catholic [ecumenical] sense." This phrasing assumes a global "sense" that makes little, if any, sense in the face of a controversy that divided Christians. Its non-sense was preserved and used by the Latin Christianity in the West, embodied by Roman Catholicism which insists that "Sacred tradition and sacred Scripture are to be accepted and venerated with the same sense of loyalty and reverence."[8]

---

5 "C." (from the Latin *circa*, "about") indicates an uncertain historical date.

6. Ignatius, "Letter to the Ephesians," 20.

7. See below, p. 42.

8. The Second Vatican Council (1892–1965) on "Divine Revelation" (*Dei Verbum*), par. 9; "Vincent of Lerins," *The Catholic Encyclopedia*. Hereafter cited NCE.

Mission Impossible?

The New Testament presents a life of Jesus as a migrating teacher who summarized his message in the "good news of God": "the time is fulfilled, and the kingdom of God has come near; repent, and believe in the good news" (Mark 1:15). He was one of at least six children, four brothers and "sisters" (not numbered) in a family in Nazareth (Mark 6:3). But he was presented by John the Baptist as "Christ" (from the Greek for "anointed one," or "Messiah"). The daughter of King Herodias, made John literally lose his head (Matt 3:3); the event has been the source of art and music, exemplified by Richard Strauss's opera "Salome" (1905); she is portrayed as seductive and cunning. Herod succumbed to her charms and, believing that John was resurrected, has him beheaded (Mark 6:16).[9]

The history of Christianity begins with its mission linked to the twelve "apostles" of Jesus (from the Greek *apostolos*, "someone sent," "a messenger"). Their commission by Jesus looks like the popular TV series *Mission Impossible*: a seemingly hopeless assignment that was pulled off by nothing less than totally unexpected means and ways—"miracles." The apostles were not equipped for going everywhere and converting people to Christianity. The brothers James and John, called "sons of thunder," substituted megalomania for mission and had their mother beg Jesus to make them big guns in the kingdom of heaven. But he stole their thunder by telling them that there would a cross before the glory (Matt 20:20–23). And there is the infamous "Judas kiss," signaling the betrayal and death of Jesus by the disciple Judas Iscariot who committed penitential suicide by hanging himself, or died under peculiar circumstances (Matt 26:14–16; 27:3–5; Acts 1:18).

The first disciples of Jesus exhibited more doubt and fear than faith. When Jesus seemed godlike in stilling a storm, they were amazed and he called them men of "little faith" (Matt 8:26–27). When Mary Magdalene told them that Jesus had been resurrected, they would not believe it (Mark 16:9–11). Thomas believed only what he saw and touched (John 20:20–25). Peter mouthed his admiration for Jesus as the "Messiah" and "Son of God," earning the title "rock" as the foundation of the future church (Matt 16:16–18). But Peter refused to pay the cost of discipleship and chickened out, swearing an oath, "I do not know this man [Jesus]," forgetting the crowing of a cock Jesus had predicted as the symbol of betrayal (Matt 26:74–75;

---

9. The account of the death of John does not mention Salome, the daughter of Herod II and wife Herodias whose name was also applied to Salome (Mark 6:22). Another Salome is a disciple of Jesus and an eyewitness of his crucifixion and resurrection (Mark 15:40 and 16:1).

John 13:36–38).[10] But earlier he boasted that he would die for Jesus and offer his whole body to be washed, not just his feet. But Jesus told him that some would never be clean, hinting at Peter's betrayal (John 13:9–11). The resurrected Jesus asked him three times to be a reliable shepherd who would have to die for his sheep (John 21:15–19). When Peter was puzzled about a mission to Gentiles, especially Roman pagans, he had a dream: a net was lowered from heaven filled with animals Jews do not eat, such as reptiles and birds. A voice ordered him (three times!) to kill and eat them. Finally Peter got it; he was to go and be with a Roman military officer, Cornelius, who was to be baptized with his family and staff (Acts 10:1–33). The apocryphal *Acts of Peter* portray him as a coward and slow learner. The story is told how he fled from persecution of Christians by Emperor Nero in 64 in Rome and saw an apparition of Jesus on the road. He asked the Lord, "Where are you going?" (*quo vadis* in Latin). Jesus replied, "I am going to Rome to be crucified again," implying that he was taking the place of Peter. Peter quit petering out and returned to Rome to be crucified—upside down.[11] But "Scripture" defies the "tradition" of cowardice. The first church historian, Doctor Luke, pictured him as a brave leader in *The Acts of the Apostles*: he preached in the streets, healed a crippled beggar in the Temple Square of Jerusalem, argued with Jewish theologians, spent time in prison, and was in the cadre of leadership (Acts 2:14–36; 3—4:22; 5:17–42; 15).

Only a converted, well-trained "Pharisee" (from the Aramaic for "separated one"—ultra-conservative in doctrine and life-style), Paul of Tarsus (Acts 21:39), met the charge of mission head-on. He was compelled to do so because he was literally stopped by the resurrected Jesus on a road to Damascus where he intended to wipe more Christians off the map, "breathing threats and murder" (Acts 9:1). Jesus made him fall to the ground, and he was temporarily blind, with nothing to eat or drink for three days. Then he was commissioned to be a missionary (Acts 9:1–19). The story was big news in Jerusalem. It took some time to trust him. But Paul became the class act of the Christian mission, the only theologian in the apostolic band in Jerusalem. His letters to his congregations, especially the one in Rome,

---

10. The cock replaced the cross on top of Protestant churches in some "Catholic" countries (like Austria) as a polemical reminder that the pope, as alleged successor of Peter, continued the betrayal of Christ.

11. The *Acts of Peter* are part of the New Testament apocrypha. The story became well known through the best-selling novel *Quo Vadis* by the Polish writer Henryk Sienkiewicz in 1895. He received the Nobel Prize for Literature in 1905, and the novel was made into a popular move, *Quo Vadis*, in 1951.

offered the first comprehensive Christian world view. He also helped negotiate a compromise between Gentile and Jewish Christians with respect to kosher laws (Acts 15:1–21). He may have persuaded the "council" of the apostles to write the most appropriate minutes of any Christian meeting: "it seemed good to the Holy Spirit and us to impose on you [the Gentiles] no further burden than these essentials" (Acts 15:28)—a brief list of recommendations avoiding offenses of Jewish customs, such as eating the blood of slaughtered animals—quite different from later missionary zealots who want to impose their "Christian" culture on others. Paul also objected to call Christianity a "new" covenant. He unequivocally affirmed the validity of the "old" divine covenant with Abraham and Moses, calling for a peaceful co-existence between Jews and Christians, a situation that must be honored as a "mystery" grounded in the "unsearchable judgments" and "inscrutable ways" of God (Rom. 11:25; 33). But soon many Christians ignored, indeed rejected, Paul's view of Jewish-Christian relations and, like pompous theological wiseacres, began an ardent "mission to the Jews" and, when Jews stuck to their faith, inaugurated an enduring anti-Semitism ending in the Holocaust staged by Adolf Hitler during World War II (1941–1945). Yet Paul also was a child of his time in his mandates for Christian life, even though he spoke of "new rules." Women should be subject to men, especially in marriage, the husband being "the head of the wife just as Christ is the head of the church" (Eph. 5:22–24), or just as slaves are subject to their masters. But men should be loving lords, reflecting the Lord (Eph 5:22–24; 6:5–9). Not to be married was Paul's preference—later as a mandate for being a priest in Roman Catholicism, with a compromise in Eastern Orthodoxy which allows clerical marriage but not for bishops. Consequently, most bishops are either young bachelors or old widowers. His rationale for marriage was later adopted by "Puritans" of all stripes: marriage prevents the sowing of wild oats (1 Cor 7:8–9). Divorce, though granted by Jesus for men whose wives commit adultery (Matt 19:9), is the sin of women (1 Cor 7:8–10). "Mixed marriages" between Christians and non-Christians should not lead to divorce (1 Cor 7:12–15), only when one partner cannot stand the other any more (1 Cor 7:15). But marriage is a "mystery" of two becoming "one flesh," symbolizing the mystery of the relationship between Christ and the church. Since the Greek term "mystery" (*mysterion*) is translated as "sacrament" in Latin Bibles, Paul's text became a proof-text for the "sacrament of marriage."[12] But women cannot preside at worship and must

---

12. "Sacrament of Marriage" in NCE.

be silent (1 Cor 14:34–35). So women are "sacramental" but cannot be ordained in some churches; and ordained men are prohibited from enjoying one of the seven sacraments they alone can celebrate—two of the many "holy contradictions" in church history, leading to some confusion about human sexuality. Paul picks the sin of a man living with his father's wife as an example of abuse; he must be punished by being banned from the community (1 Cor 5:1–13).

During his missionary journeys Paul went to many places in the Greek Roman world, protected to some extent by being born a Roman citizen (Act 22:28). It saved him from some severe encounters with Jewish persecutors (Acts 22:22–26). He, like Peter in the tale about his crucifixion, felt that he saw the world upside-down. "I have been crucified with Christ, and it is no longer I who live, but it is Christ who lives in me" (Gal 2:20). This is the talk and the walk of faith in Christ that make human achievements look foolish. With a gallows humor Paul described such faith and its style of life as foolish. Christians are like fools, or court-jesters. "Has not God made foolish the wisdom of the world?" (1 Cor 1:20). "We proclaim Christ crucified, a stumbling block to the Jews and foolishness to the Gentiles" (1 Cor 1:23). In the image of the world, apostles are "fools for the sake of Christ" (1 Cor 4:10). They deliberately "rush in where angels fear to tread" because they are on the way to a future where they will have the power "to judge angels" (1 Cor 6:3). With such talk Paul wanted to show the paradox of God's seemingly contradictory action—to be simultaneously divine and human in Jesus. This view of divine contrariness dominates his theology and work as a pastor. He needed it because his congregations, established while being on the run, exhibited annoying issues. As the "pastor" in the decadent "sin city" Corinth, he encountered members who "spoke in tongues" (1 Cor 11:10), engaged in fornication (1 Cor 5), and got drunk with Eucharistic wine (1 Cor 11:21). He traveled with a physician, Luke, the author of a "Gospel" and "Acts of Apostles"; with Barnabas, a "Levite": (assistant in Jewish worship services); and with a young disciple, Timothy, whom Paul "had circumcised because of the Jews" (to hide the fact that he had a Greek father and a Jewish mother) (Acts 16:3). After a sensational healing, an excited crowd thought that Barnabas was the chief Greek god Zeus and Paul his speaker, Hermes (Acts 14:11–12). In Ephesus Paul caused a riot staged by defenders of Greek polytheism (Acts 19:21–41). In Athens he was rebuffed by the intellectual elite (Acts 17:16–34). He may have been martyred in Rome, although final reports describe him there as living in peace, teaching "without hindrance" (Acts 28:31). When Paul's apostolicity was questioned, because he was not one of the original apostles in the company of Jesus, he offered a boastful litany of misery that was his plumbline, as it were, for what it means to go with the flow of divine contrariness and experience, the vicissitudes of history in the mean, meantime between Christ's first and second coming.

> But whatever anyone dares to boast of—I am speaking as a fool—I also dare to boast of that. Are they Hebrews? So am I. Are they Israelites? So am I. Are they descendants of Abraham? So am I. Are they ministers of Christ? So am I. I am talking like a madman—I am a better one; with far greater labors, far more imprisonments, with countless floggings, and often near death. Once I received a stoning. Three times I was shipwrecked; for a night and a day I was adrift at sea; on frequent journeys, in danger from rivers, danger from bandits, danger from my own people, danger from Gentiles—danger from false brothers and sisters; in toil and hardship, through many a sleepless night, hungry and thirsty, often without food, cold and naked. And, besides other things, I am under daily pressure because of my anxiety for all the churches (2 Cor 11:21–28).

Paul continued a momentum of mission that had begun fifty days after Easter, at Pentecost (from the Greek *pentecost*, "fiftieth" day after Passover) when the Holy Spirit, experienced as wind and fire (Acts 2:2), drove the twelve apostles from their hiding place in Jerusalem into the streets. It was a missionary event, never repeated: what the disciples proclaimed was understood by everyone in the city, including foreigners who had come to celebrate the Jewish "Harvest Festival" (commemorating the exodus from Egypt)—the first simultaneous translation of Christian preaching (without technology)! "Each one heard them speaking in the native language of each" (Acts 2:6). When the news about the event spread, outsiders accused the apostles of being drunk (Acts 2:13). But three thousand were baptized (Acts 2:41) and formed the first megachurch. Fired up, the new believers established a utopian community: they sold all their possessions and gave the proceeds to the apostles who distributed funds "to each as any had need" (Acts 4:35); and they conducted daily Eucharistic services in private homes: and daily life became a doxology—"praising God and having the goodwill of all the people" (Acts 2:47). The media viewed them as a Jewish sect founded by Jesus. They were first called "Christians" in Antioch (Acts 11:26).

Christendumb

The momentum of mission caused some panic on the part of Jewish authorities. When the apostles were arrested, an angel told them in prison to continue and, miraculously, they were found preaching again the next day (Acts 5:19–21). At an official hearing they told the Jewish Supreme Court, "We must obey God more than any human authority" (Acts 5:29)—a declaration in an apostolic succession of Christian political ethics more impressive than the "apostolic succession" of bishops and popes. The declaration was appreciated only by one lawyer among the Pharisees at the Court, Gamaliel, who counseled against a verdict of death. His wise words became immortal, repeated innumerable times by defenders of religious liberty: "if this undertaking is of human origin it will fail; but if it is of God, you will not be able to overthrow them [the apostles]—in that case you may even be found fighting against God!" (Acts 5:38–39).

Internal problems revealed the dark side of any human venture. A greedy couple, Ananias and Saphira, tried to cheat the church out of money and dropped dead, accused of having offended the Holy Spirit (Acts 5:1–11)—an effective biblical text for "Stewardship Sunday"! Stephen, the first of seven deacons called to organize a daily distribution of food to the poor, especially widows, was arrested, tried, and stoned to death (Acts 6–7). As the first martyr, he is celebrated in many countries on the day after Christmas, St. Stephen Day—in the context of a holiday jocularity because it is the day when the carnival season begins. But already at the beginning of the Christian movement, its spiritual power, manifested in healings, attracted unsavory business. A magician named Simon converted and offered to buy the wonder-working power of the Holy Spirit. But when threatened by the apostles with divine punishment he apologized (Acts 8:18–24). "Simony" became known as the "buying and selling of ecclesiastical privileges, for example pardons or benefices (permanent church appointments)."[13] It was part and parcel of succumbing to "pride, pomp and circumstance."[14] It foreshadowed the buying and selling of ecclesiastical offices; today, political candidates do something similar when they raise money to advertise their ambitions, trying to "buy" an office.

The early momentum of mission soon became misery through persecution and martyrdom. For decades, great numbers of Christians were

---

13. NOAD.

14. An appropriate description of the church and its "triumphalism" through a close alliance with secular power (pope and emperor). The British composer Edward Elgar (1837–1934) used the phrase from William Shakespeare's play "Othello" (Act III, Scene III).

literally biting the dust to entertain crowds in ancient Roman amphitheaters, killed by wild animals, often lions. This misery is highlighted by the tale of Emperor Nero who burned Rome in 64 to make room for new buildings, blaming Christians for the disaster and martyred many. Other Roman emperors continued the persecution for more than a century (180–313). To them, Christians were dangerous heretics because they refused to believe in the deities of the state religion, Roman gods, and especially the "divine" emperor. But Christians prayed for secular authorities as divinely instituted guardians of law and order (Rom 13:1–7). Only tyrannical government should not be obeyed (Acts 5:29), and it cannot take the place of God, exemplified by Roman emperors. So when ordered to worship the state gods, most Christians refused, even when dragged to pagan altars by soldiers. Some obeyed by burning incense at the Roman altars without, however, changing their faith in Christ. It was a compromise between fear and faith. The clergy became the target of persecution, and many were executed. Nevertheless, Christianity expanded in the East, especially in Asia Minor and in Egypt. In the West, a congregation existed in Rome; small Christian groups could be found in Southern Italy, North Africa, and Southern France. The church became anchored in martyrdom as the best "witness" (from the Greek *martyros*). Such a stance eventually stopped the persecution because it strengthened the faith of the victims. Soon martyred members of the church, the "communion of saints," were honored as special "saints" of the earthly church, the "church militant"; they were viewed like soldiers who died in battle, "baptized by fire" and transferred to the heavenly church, the "church triumphant." Prayers to these saints became popular as superstitious sources of help for issues in earthly life. The stories of their death were read in worship services. The model was Polycarp (c. 69–155), the bishop, of Smyrna (on the western coast of Asia Minor, now the Turkish city of Uzmir) who was said to have been a disciple of the apostle John, a disciple of Jesus. In his eighty-sixth year he was burned at the stake. After him, martyrdom (from the Greek *martys*, "witness," Acts 1:8) was viewed as the ultimate witness linked to the resurrection of Jesus. The African "church father" Tertullian (c. 160–220) coined the popular phrase "The blood of the martyrs is the seed of the church."[15]

There were controversies between rigorists and lax Christians who compromised, indeed denied, their faith under pressure, be it hard by

15. *Apology* 50 (From the Latin *apologia*, "defense," not "apology") in vol. 3 of *The Ante-Nicene Fathers*, 55.

physical persecution or soft by the pagan surrounding culture. The first most radical rigorists, Christian nuts, as it were, were the "Montanists" in the middle of the second century (c. 150), named after Montanus who claimed in ecstatic language to be a prophet initiating the final phase of history, the rule of the Holy Spirit. He traveled with two prophetesses, Prisca and Maximilia, in Asia Minor. The trio claimed to be divinely inspired with specific rules for Christian life: fasting, no second marriage, and volunteering for martyrdom; they behaved "as if they had eaten the Holy Spirit, feathers and all."[16] They began their propaganda in Asia Minor and spread to North Africa and Italy, with a group in Rome. There were literary feuds between Montanus and mainline theologians. After the death of Montanus and his two prophetesses, Montanists abandoned their predictions about the end of the world and concentrated on abstention from sex and on fasting. Tertullian became their most famous member.

Another group spread the notion, popular now and then in the history of Christianity, that believers should not create an institution, the church, because anything "earthly" is evil. Christians can only survive through a "secret knowledge" (*gnosis* in Greek). Such knowledge consists of a maze of mystical ideas, governed by the notion of a total separation of the material world from faith in Christ's immaterial kingdom. Mystical concentration on secret Gnostic formulae assured salvation from the sinful material world. Around 150, one of the Gnostics, Marcion, a wealthy Roman shipowner, called for the rejection of the Old Testament as the revelation of a "material" god, an enemy of the "Father of Christ." Gnosticism, too, was condemned as a heresy—the beginning of a favorite way of the organized church to deal with opposition. Here begins a tendency that is typical of defenders of mainline Christians, namely, to assume that the Holy Spirit prefers bureaucrats rather than "free spirits," dubbed "charismatics" from the Greek *charisma*, "Spirit"). The bureaucracy began when leaders of the church tried to preserve unity by means of a hierarchy of offices, reflecting the military tradition of a chain of command: "bishops" (from the Greek *episcopos*, "overseer"), "presbyters (from the Greek *presbyteros*, "elder"), and "deacons" (from the Greek *diakonos*, "servant" or "waiter"). The first three offices became ordination ranks, granting the power to celebrate the Eucharist. Cyprian (c. 200–258), the bishop of Carthage in North Africa,

---

16. Adapted from a saying of Martin Luther about a fictional exhibit of medieval relics, including "two feathers and an egg from the Holy Spirit." Gritsch, *The Wit of Martin Luther*, 29.

defined the unity of the church as a hierarchical organization led by bishops in apostolic succession from the apostle Peter to the bishop of Rome, the "father of fathers," as it were (*papa*, in Latin, "pope").

Montanists and Gnostics were the first of many groups to establish hard and fast rules for living in the world with one foot in heaven. But limping is frustrating when one tries to run, and sooner or later a radical eschatological (end-time) lifestyle, or a rationalistic dualism, falls to the ground, revealing utopian speculations rather than realistic choices of living. Whether they are refugees from "secular" civilization, like monks and other deserters found in deserts, or romantic reformers of Christendom, like theocrats and other faith healers of society, they fail in the face of earthly imperfection.

The young established church was severely tested during the height of persecution by Roman emperors, particularly intense under the rule of Emperor Diocletian (284–305). Spiritual cowardice became an issue when rigorists refused to take communion from the ordained, especially bishops, who had fled from persecution, avoiding the supreme Christian testimony. In 312, rigorists in Carthage, North Africa, elected their own bishop, Donatus, to replace a bishop who communed lapsed Christians. The mainliners rejected the hard-liners and permitted the communion of lapsed Christians. But Donatism survived until the sixth century, and Gnosticism, of one variety or another, re-appeared every so often like mole-hills in the Christian landscape. The rationale for the decision to commune lapsed church members is like a permanent ghost haunting the church through the centuries: the Eucharist (from the Greek *eucharistia*, "thanksgiving") and sacraments in general are valid when they are properly celebrated: the reality of the Eucharist rests on the exact repetition of the words Christ used at the final Passover Meal (the "Words of Institution" beginning with "This is my body," 1 Cor 11:24–26) The sacraments are not invalidated by the moral behavior of the celebrant because the spiritual power resides only in the sacrament and is released "by the act itself" (*ex opere operato* in Latin). This view was made a dogma by Pope Eugenius IV in 1439. An ironic by-product of the dogma is the impact of the use of the Latin words for "This is my body" (*hoc est meum corpus*) in the medieval Mass as a formula used by magicians, "hocus pocus." It is surmised that these two Latin words were heard but not understood by the simple, uneducated medieval worshippers. They usually were too far away from the altar to see what the priest did, being seated in distant pews or standing in the rear of

Christendumb

the sanctuary. At the precise moment when the priest said the Latin words, an altar bell indicated that the priest had pronounced the "magic" formula that brought the Eucharistic Christ to the altar. TV viewers may recall the words of the comedian Groucho Marx, "Say the secret word, down comes the duck."[17] It is also ironic that the modern definition of "hocus pocus" conveys the exact opposite of the original meaning—"meaningless talk or activity, often designed to draw attention away from and disguise what is actually happening."[18] Exclusion from the Eucharist has remained a mark of spiritual segregation (in the Roman Catholic Church as the "true" church without any equal), or as punishment of members labeled "sinners" (a practice popular among Protestant "Puritans" and their descendants).

Church leaders became known as "Church Fathers" (no "Church Mothers" allowed)—"early Christian theologians (in particular during the first five centuries) whose writings are regarded as especially authoritative."[19] They tried to overcome the misery of spiritual sins by theologizing about a "catholic" church (from the Latin *catholica*, "common"). The bishop of Antioch, Ignatius (c. 35–107), was the first to do so, saying that the universal church is united by bishops, presbyters, deacons, and the Eucharist. Other theologians argued that Christianity was the only valid religion, "unique" unlike anything. They tried to "prove" that Christ as the eternal "word" (*logos* in Greek) is the beginning and end of all wisdom. This is their "apology" (from the Greek *apologia*, "defense")—not an excuse for, but a defense of Christ in whom everyone and everything came into being (John 1:3). Justine Martyr (c. 110–c. 165) was the classic apologist who became a migrant theologian in the dress of a philosopher, arguing for the truth of Christianity with Greeks and Jews. Tertullian, a converted Roman citizen from Carthage, North Africa, was the first apologist to write in Latin. He also was a rigorist who joined the radical "Montanists."[20]

Cultural differences, rooted in ancient Greece in the East and in Rome in the West, created the first of many schools of theology. In Alexandria, Egypt, the first Eastern school of theology was founded by a catechist named Clement (c. 200) and made famous by his student Origen (c. 185–254),

---

17. Said at the award of money won in the popular quiz-show in the 1950s "You Bet Your Life." The money was delivered by a descending toy duck resembling Groucho Marx.
18. NOAD.
19. NOAD.
20. Below, 22.

a native of Egypt. He put the school on the map, with another school in Caesarea (a significant Roman port in Palestine, now on the Mediterranean side of Israel). He wrote, edited, and collected hundreds of works; making him one of the most prolific writers in Christian history—estimates run from 800 to 6,000 publications. Assisted by many students, he published the Hebrew text of the of Old Testament texts, with a transliteration of it in Greek letters, and Greek translations in parallel six columns, the *Sextuple* (*Hexapla* in Greek). His most significant work is *First Principles*, the first of many systematic summaries of doctrine, noted for unsystematic, indeed arrogant, treatment of topics, covering the whole country-side of the Christian faith as unmatched "truth." According to Origen, only Jesus embodied whatever is meant by "God," the power where all bucks have to stop. Origen was so far out that some church bureaucrats condemned him in order to avoid confessing that they did not understand him—a reaction quite popular among sissy minds. Other officials disliked his odd behavior: he wanted to be a martyr and, in lieu of being missed from the list, he did the next worst thing and castrated himself in literal obedience to Matthew 19:12 ("there are eunuchs who have made themselves eunuchs for the sake of the kingdom of God").[21] In his old age he was imprisoned during the persecution ordered by the Roman emperor Decius in 250 and, weakened by torture and confinement in a dungeon, he died a few years later. Consistent in being far out, he also advocated the notion that in the end everything and everyone will be reconciled with God through Christ, even the devil (based on Col 1:20: "through him [Christ] God was pleased to reconcile to himself all things, whether on earth or in heaven"). This view, later dubbed "universalist," was rejected because it neglected the popular notion of a "day of judgment" (Matt 12:36)—a popular fear factor driving sinners to expensive repentance. There is only one other church father who was castrated, Peter Abelard. It was the punishment for having an affair with a student, Heloise, resulting in the birth of an illegitimate son.[22] Their lives disclose the esoteric variety of Christian history.

A counterpart to the Greek theologian Origen in the East was Irenaeus in the West (c. 130–200). He was bishop of Lyons, France, and is known for a "systematic theology" that was to refute the misery of heresy,

---

21. This "dumb" action waa repeaped by the theologian Peter Abelard and the Russian sect of the "Scopts." See pp. 73 and 84.

22. Below, 81.

especially "Gnosticism."²³ While traditional in the arrangement of topics (God, creation, church, sacraments, etc.), Irenaeus depicted salvation as a "recapitulation" of sinful humankind to its original "Image" of God (Gen 1:27): Christ transmits the Holy Spirit through sacraments as the power that unites humans again with God making them again incorruptible as was Adam before the fall into sin. The Virgin Mary represents the new Eve, cooperating with the Holy Spirit in the process of salvation. Irenaeus also called for obedience to bishops, especially the Roman bishop, and to the authority of the Bible. But he did not yet know the "canonical" New Testament.

These first "systematic" theologians tried to proselytize Greek and Roman minds by calling attention to Christ as the "word" (*logos*, in Greek), the foundation of everything that is. But this stance created issues regarding the relationship between divine and human elements in the "logos," Christ, because he was of human "flesh" (John 1:14). The perennial issue of "faith" and "reason" raised its ugly head, exposing a schizophrenic side of theology—the attempt to "explain" the "truths of faith." Consequently, some theologians thought that Christ was human endowed with divine "power" (*dynamis* in Greek). But, like dynamite, this notion only blew up the rationalist construction. Other theologians contended that Christ was human with a divine "appearance" (*modus* in Latin). This stance, too, never even reached the point of being outmoded. "Adoptionists" assumed that Jesus was adopted as the Son of God in his baptism (Mark 1:11). The most controversial "Christology" was offered by a native of Lybia, teaching in Rome, Sabellius (c. 215). He postulated that the one God had three "masks" (*morphai*, in Greeek), analogous to Greek actors who wore masks on stage. This kind of intellectual theater went over like a lead balloon and was quickly condemned as nonsense. But there is hardly any rationalist gymnastics that theologians have not tried to build ecclesiastical muscles.

Impatient missionaries soon blamed their lack of success on "Antichrists" who deny the "truth" of Jesus' divinity (1 John 2:22).²⁴ Moreover, spiritual impatience spawned speculations about the imminent return of Jesus. They saw "signs" of it pointed out by their Lord, such as the destruction of the temple in Jerusalem, wars, and natural disasters like earthquakes,

---

23. Below, 22–23.

24. The "Antichrist" may be anyone claiming to be Christ (Matt 24:5: "many will come in my name, saying, 'I am the Messiah'"). He also appears as an apocalyptic figure of the end-time, an opponent of change favored by anti-establishment "reformers."

wars, and persecution (Matt 24:1–14): fraudulent "saviors" (like the Gnostics), political unrest (in Jerusalem and Rome), and natural disasters. The link of such signs to the Last Day has been labeled "millenarianism"—"the belief in a future (and typically imminent) thousand-year age of blessedness beginning with or culminating in the Second Coming of Christ."[25] Millenarians use Psalm 90:4 as "proof-text" that a thousand years are like a day and use this formula in their chronological calculations about the end of the world. Example: the last book of the Bible assumes a conflict between Christ and Satan for "forty-two months" (Rev 13:5) and, using the formula that a day equals a thousand years, a fanatic Italian monk, Joachim of Flora (c. 1132–1201), predicted the end of the world for 1260 and lifted up the monastic vow of poverty, combined with an ascetic life style, as penance for the accumulation of wealth in the church. When Rome opposed such views, the monks called the pope the "Antichrist." The final prayer in the Bible begins with "Amen" (from the Greek *amen*, "so be it") to express the end as a beginning, "Amen. Come Lord Jesus!" (Rev 22:20). But frustration about the future and fear of ever more brutal persecution made the newly baptized groups go underground, assembling in unpopulated places or in underground cemeteries, called "catacombs" from the Latin *cata tombos*, "among the tombs"). Worship became known as an "arcane" event (from the Latin *arcanus*, "secret"). Weekly services were conducted on "the third day" after the resurrection of Jesus (Matt 17:23), the "Day of the Lord," later called "Sunday," adopted from the veneration of the Roman sun god Mithras. It was staged before sunrise and after sunset, symbolizing an imminent eternal future and offering some security from being arrested and martyred. Stories of "saints," Bible readings, preaching, and Eucharistic celebration made up the services. Some churches added foot-washing, continuing the ceremony Jesus had performed before his death (John 13:1–20). There was singing, perhaps consisting of biblical texts, such as Eph 5:14: "Sleeper, awake! Rise from the dead, and Christ will shine on you." Prayers may have been short, such as "Come Lord Jesus" (Rev 22:20). Participants often took a "solemn oath" (from the Latin *sacramentum*) to remain faithful and moral in mutual love. "Sacrament" also came to mean the a liturgical action in the church, like baptism and Holy Communion, by which God saves from sin through Christ. In the worship service the Eucharist was usually followed by a meal, with singing, also known as "Agape"— not "open-mouth-gaping" but "loving" (from the Greek *agape*, "love"). A

---

25. NOAD.

Christendumb

"holy kiss" marked such love, also shown in the bringing of the Eucharistic bread and wine to those who were absent. By 150, Sunday worship consisted of two parts, the first marked by a liturgy of the "word" (Scripture reading, preaching, praying, and singing); the second by a "a visible word," the liturgy of the "sacrament," Holy Communion.[26] Only baptized members participated, including infants because the Eucharist was viewed as "necessary for salvation." In the thirteenth century, only "adults" (defined as a seven-year-old) could commune after going to Confession.[27] Visitors were dismissed after the first part. The second part became known as "Mass" based on the "dismissal" of unbaptized visitors (from the Latin *mittere*, "sending away"). Wednesday and Friday became days of fasting, a competition with Jewish fasting on Monday and Thursday. A "church year" was constructed with the seasons of Advent, Christmas/Epiphany, Lent, Easter, and Pentecost. The first Christmas celebration on December 25 occurred in 336 in Rome, replacing the pagan Roman celebration of the winter solstice. The East favored Epiphany on January 6 as the celebration of Christ's birth, linked with the odd story of the "wise men" as representatives of unbaptized Gentiles. The use of decorated Christmas trees goes as far back as ancient Egypt when pharaohs decorated evergreens to celebrate life.[28] Christian life and discipline became centered on penance because the delay of the endtime increased "sins" related to lax behavior. Sinners who repented were first readmitted to the first part of worship, then to the second part with Holy Communion. But compromises prevailed, driven by the enduring human desire for pleasure and entertainment. Some Christians went to church on Sunday morning and to a pagan circus in the afternoon.

The extension of the interim through the delay of Christ's Second Coming and the expansion of the Christian movement increased its institutional diversity. Still limited to the Middle East and parts of southern Europe, different political social, and moral conditions prevailed among simple

26. The designation "visible word" stems from St. Augustine (354–430), Tract 80:3 (on John 15:3: "you have already been cleansed by the word I have spoken to you") in vol. 7.344 of the *Nicene and Post-Nicene Fathers*, 7, 344. "Liturgy," from the Geek *leiturgia*, "public worship," or "work of the people."

27. Below, 40.

28. Legend links the origin of the Christmas tree to St. Boniface (c. 672–754), a British monk who converted Germanic tribes on the continent. He substituted a pagan holy oak-tree with green fir to celebrate the birth of Christ. The first Christmas tree appeared in 1441 in Estonia, then was seen in the Germanic regions in the sixteenth century (another legend attributed it to Martin Luther), in 1832 in England, and in 1850 in the United States. Boniface, below, 54.

"cultural" and elitist "cultured" Christians. Leaders began to distinguish between "orthodoxy" (from *orthodoxos*, "correct teaching"), "heterodoxy" (from *heteros*, "different"), and "heresy" (from the Greek *hairesis*, "contrary teaching"). After three centuries, there was an institutional church marked by a confession of faith in baptism, a collection of texts called "Scripture," and an episcopacy as the source of "authoritative teaching" (*magisterium* in Latin, "the office of the master"), with a link to an "apostolic succession" of bishops, headed by the bishop of Rome who claimed to have "succeeded" the apostle Peter in his "office." But institutionalization created more fear than hope regarding eternal life in the future. Faith became entangled with merit and reward; citizenship in the future kingdom of God had to be earned. The confession of sins, penance, determined how many "good, works" needed to be done to earn salvation. It was part of worship centered in Holy Communion. The simple mandate to "love your neighbor as yourself" (Matt 24:39) became complicated. The missionary momentum became an institution—safe, but not very sound.

Greed and Creed

The conversion of Emperor Constantine I, "the great," transformed Christian misery into might. The story is told by his protégé and court historian Eusebius (c. 263–339) who became bishop of Caesarea. Always praising his boss, the emperor, Eusebius "recorded" a "miracle" that could be a good side-show of the Hollywood version of Jesus, *The Greatest Story Ever Told* (1965). But the tale about Constantine would be in stark contrast to the grand, pious cinematographic portrait of Christ. For any realistic film about the first Christian emperor would be part of the Hollywood tradition of greed, violence, and murder: he eliminated other contenders to the throne in ruthless battles; he had his second wife and oldest son put to death; and he used his baptism on his death-bed to arrive purified "on the other side" since baptism forgives sins and the "sacrament of extreme junction" had not yet been inaugurated. He intended not to die with any post-baptismal sins and thus avoid divine punishment. "The road to hell is paved with good intentions."

According to Eusebius, Constantine won his final battle for the throne after he saw "a most marvelous sign" while praying in his military headquarters in the early afternoon: "A cross of light in the heaven, above the sun and bearing the Greek inscription 'Conquer by this sign' (*touto nika*)."

Christendumb

All the soldiers saw the same sign. While Constantine pondered the experience during the night, he had a vision: "in his sleep the Christ of God appeared to him with the same sign and commanded him to make a likeness of that sign and use it as a safeguard in all engagements with his enemies."[29] Constantine made it into a monogram and emblem which he had put on his military banners. It depicted the first two letters of the name "Christ," PX, the letter "P" ("R") being intersected with "X" ("CH"), still shown today on liturgical vestments and other symbols of "salvation." The emblem was called "labarum."[30] Constantine used this heavenly sign to beat the hell out of his opponent Maxentius at the Milvian bridge in Rome—the first time Christ was invoked by the military, beginning a tradition of "crusades" and raising enduring questions about the true meaning of the cross. Should it be used as a symbol of war? After all, Jesus had told his disciples, "I have not come to bring peace but the sword" (Matt 10:34); and, on the other hand, Paul told his congregations to make every effort "to maintain the unity of the Spirit in the bond of peace" (Eph 4:3). Eusebius himself admitted that the story of Constantine's conversion was "hard to believe, had it been related by any other person"; but the emperor assured him that it was true, and the military victory proved that the sign was right. Since Eusebius was a "court historian" employed by the emperor, he embodied the truth of the German proverb, "Whose bread I eat his song I sing." Here begins the enduring problem of war and peace, ranging from Christian "crusades" and "military chaplaincy" to "conscientious objection" and pacifism. Bearing the cross with peaceful humility and using it with violent pride is an indelible ironic mark of Christianity. Even the armies of agnostic or atheistic rulers, such as Adolf Hitler, echoed a "Christian" culture on their belt-buckles with the inscription "In God We Trust." Ever since Constantine, the cross was crucified in one way or another.

Almost overnight Christianity became the favored religion of the empire with the essential fixings so common later: baptism, Sunday worship, and catechesis with rules for a Christian life. Other religions were tolerated until 380 when Emperor Theodosius I prohibited them. The elevation of Christianity to a state religion was regulated by "Canon Law," church

---

29. Eusebius, *Ecclesiastical History*, "The Life of Constantine" in vol. 1 of the *Nicene and Post-Nicene Fathers*, 489-91. Constantine's sword" is a symbol of Christian abuse in James Carroll, *Constantine's Sword: The Church and the Jews—A History*. The film "Constantine's Sword" was directed by Oren Jacob (Vista, CA: Storyville Films, 2008).

30. Unclear origin. Perhaps from the Latin *labare*, "to totter," to wave" (a flag?). Known exclusively as Constantine's symbol.

regulations from cradle to grave. Emperor Justinian (c. 443–565) put them all together in a "code," and this "Justinian Code" became the standard legislation in the empire, known as the "body of Canon Law" (*corpus iuris canonici* in Latin) in the Byzantine empire, created by Constantine who moved East and made the ancient city of Byzantium into a "new Rome" called "Constantinople." In 1170, the "Corpus" of laws was adopted in the West as Roman Catholic "Canon Law."

Constantine had a mausoleum built in the new capital of the empire. It was housed in the Church of the Apostles, where he rested from his strange Christian labors as if he were the thirteenth apostle. Moreover, this ferocious Christian ruler insisted in being honored as the "Prince of Peace," a title reserved for the coming Messiah in the Old Testament (Isa 9:6). His mother Helena inaugurated pilgrimages to the "Holy Land," soon advertised by greedy travel agents who entertained curious tourists with invented stories about holy places and events.

A document, known as "The Donation of Constantine," appeared in the ninth century, probably in Rome, and in the fifteenth century was proven to be a forgery, making an amazing claim: the bishop of Rome, "Pope" Sylvester I (c. 314–325) was Constantine's Sunday School teacher, he cured Constantine of leprosy, and he baptized the emperor just before he died. Constantine rewarded the pope with a testamentary "donation" stipulating that he had power over all bishops in the world and jurisdiction over Italy and "the Western world," that is, all of Europe. Moreover, he had the privilege of appearing in public showing imperial insignia, such as a golden crown and a purple cloak. The document was said to have been signed by Constantine and deposited in the tomb of St. Peter in Rome. But there is no reliable historical evidence for Peter's presence there. Any denial of the violation of the "Donation" was punished.

Anyone familiar with the language and culture of the age of Charlemagne (742–815) can identify the "donation" as a crude forgery, designed to secure papal power. But it took centuries to do that since any criticism of church and state exacted a high price, usually the end of life by burning at a stake. Nevertheless, the adoption of Christianity by Emperor Constantine constitutes one of the two most significant events in Christian history regarding the relationship between church and state. In 313, the first converted emperor initiated a fusion of church and state, viewing the bishop of Rome as "pope" of Christendom; and in 1791, the government of the United States issued the First Amendment, declaring the separation of church and state.

Christendumb

Constantine should be better known as the politician who was responsible for providing the principal ecumenical creed, the Nicene Creed of 325. When intensive theological controversies threatened Christian unity, Constantine assembled about three hundred bishops in Nicaea, near Constantinople, to save the unity of the young church. The attending bishops represented the Greek, Eastern part of the church; the Western, Latin part was represented by two presbyters sent by the bishop of Rome. The rage (*rabies* in Latin) of theologians had infected the "body of Christ" and threatened its sanity, and just as rabies spreads through human saliva, so did mouthy Christians spread confusion about faith in Christ. The issue was worship, centered in the invocation of God as "Father, Son, and Holy Spirit." Logical Greek minds tried hard to transform such Trinitarian doxological talk into a theological rationale. But that is as impossible as to live with rabies. Still, theologians tried anyway. So the controversy became tied to the question of the relationship between Christ's divinity and humanity, his two "natures"—a hot potato that has never really cooled off in two millennia of Christianity. Its seed appears in the notion that Christ was the "word" that had become "flesh" (John 1:14). Arius, a theologian and presbyter in Alexandria, Egypt, contended in 318 that the "Word" (*logos* in Greek), Christ, as "Son of the Father," was different in "being" (*ousia* in Greek) from God because he was the first creature, not co-eternal with the Father. This "Arian" assertion denied that Jesus was of "the same nature" (*homousios* in Greek) as God. Consequently, Arians proposed to describe the Trinity with the phrase "one being and three sub-beings" (*hypostases* in Greek).

The opponents of the "Arians" viewed such talk as a spiritual poisoning of the established worship of the Trinitarian God, "Father, Son, and Holy Spirit." Constantine agreed with them and demanded that an "orthodox" (from the Greek orthodoxos, "true," "sound") dogma of the Trinity must assert the equality of the three persons. He introduced a phrase, perhaps suggested by a "court theologian," which, like an anti-rabies shot, would overcome the life-threatening division in the church. It was the formulation, "the Son is of one being (*homousios* in Greek) with the Father." The Council adopted the formula as part of the Nicene Creed, perhaps threatened by Constantine not to cover the bishops' travel expenses, or other, worse punishments. But theological hotheads continued the controversy, arguing that the "Son" could be "like," "similar," or "unlike" the "Father," using such verbal hair-splitting like ammunition against opponents. Some fought over one letter, the letter "I" in the word "homousios: if it is spelled "homo – I – ousios" it means "like" the "Father." Legend has it that monks used their cinctures (from the Latin *cincture*, "girdle," usually a rope holding up a cloak) in the streets to beat people into affirming or dropping the letter "I" in their affirmation of the Trinity. Much ado about nothing! The controversy continued after the Council of Nicaea[31] even though "Arians" had been condemned as heretics. But they were tolerated during the reign of Emperor Julian (331–363), "the apostate," an idiosyncratic nephew of the first Christian emperor Constantine. Although baptized, he was attracted to Greek philosophy and mystery cults. He also became convinced that Christian controversies had so divided the church that it should no longer be the religion of the empire. So he returned to Greek "paganism" and, with a satirical twist, tolerated all Christian parties, hoping that they would destroy each other. He had his lackeys run the royal bureaucracy; while he turned to research and writing in the context of a private ascetic life. Succeeding emperors legislated a uniform, anti-Arian Christianity summarized in the Nicene Creed of 325. In 534, Emperor Justinian I made the denial of the Nicene dogma of the Trinity punishable by death, even though he himself had an affair with a dancing girl who belonged to a sect that denied the Trinity. He embodied the proverb, "People who live in glass houses should not throw stones."

Controversies about the Trinity have never ended because there are only insufficient hints in the New Testament, usually used as a popular Trinitarian greeting (2 Cor 13:13). Theologians in the East, led by the Greek bishop and his school of theology in Alexandria, Egypt, Athanasius (c. 296–373), defended the Nicene Creed for almost a half-century. His name was also used as the author of the "Athanasian Creed," a long summary of a Trinitarian creed which, however, was composed in Latin by an unknown Gallic (French) author in the ninth century. The creed is almost never used in worship because it contains complex language and is too long to fit into an efficient liturgy. What is fraud today was fact then. Important popular writings were attributed to renowned church fathers until the fifteenth century when "Humanists" developed the field of literary criticism.[32]

---

31. The first of the Seven Ecumenical Councils which are acknowledged by most churches as authoritative summaries of the faith. Texts in vol. 14 of the *Nicene and Post-Nicene Fathers*, Series II.

32. Below, 126.

Christendumb

The Trinitarian controversies contradict the proverbial "truth" that "Variety is the spice of life." There was so much theological spice that Christian mouths were burned by its heat. Theologians in the West expected help from Ambrose (c. 338–397) who was bishop of Milan, Italy, an icon of Catholic orthodoxy. He was a friend of Emperor Theodosius and is remembered as a great liturgist and composer of hymns. But he built dogmatic consensus through sermons and political lobbying, not through rationalizing. A popular liturgy, the "Ambrosian Rite," has been wrongly attributed to him (its origin is unknown). An old Roman creed, the "Apostles' Creed," was used in the liturgy of baptism since the third century and became part of the creedal tradition in Rome but was not formally adopted until the twelfth century. This creed does not contain controversial phrases trying to explicate the Trinity.

But busy minds could not rest. New formulations of old concepts appeared like old doggy bones of contention—dug up, cleaned, and chewed again. A trinity of theologians, Basil of Caesarea (c. 330–379) his brother Gregory of Nyssa (c. 330–c. 395O), and his friend Gregory of Nazianzus (c. 330–389) constructed a dogma of the Trinity in which all three "persons" are equal, interpenetrating each other, the Holy Spirit being the "advocate" of the "Father" (John 15:26). The three theologians were known as the "Cappadocian Fathers" because they worked in Basil's hometown Cappadocia (the Greek name for Caesarea). The town was the source for the horses of the emperor—giving rise to the rare satirical bilingual designation of "history" (*Geschichte* in German) in the form of a pun as Horsegeschichte and Heilsgeschichte ("salvation history"). But the Cappadocian definition of the Trinity as "one being and three persons" did not end the controversies about the Trinity. The Syrian theologian Apolinarius of Laodicea (c. 310–90) used Greek anthropology to solve the riddle of God's incarnation in Jesus: the divine "logos" had human "flesh" (*sarx* in Greek) and a human "spirit" (*psyche* in Greek). But this formulation asserts the full divinity of Jesus but not his full humanity. The Cappadocian trio attacked Apolinarius as a heretic, supported by Athanasius and other defenders of the Nicene Creed. In 381, the Second Ecumenical Council of Constantinople condemned Apolinarius. But his disciples kept the controversy going. Moreover, the relation of the Holy Spirit to Christ also created hot debates. The church in the West, claiming to be "catholic" (from the Greek *katholikos*, "common," "universal") adopted a solution by augmenting the text of the Nicene Creed with the notion that the Holy Spirit proceeds from the Father "and from the Son" (*filioque* in Latin), based on John 20:22 where Jesus "breathed" on the disciples and said, "Receive the Holy Spirit" as the power to forgive sins. In the west, a synod in Toledo, Spain, adopted the formula in 589. But the church in the East, "Greek Orthodoxy," never adopted it, claiming that only a true ecumenical council (like the first one in Nicaea in 325) can change the creed. The addition remains a bone of contention still today.[33]

With zealous logic, the controversies about the "two natures" of the Son moved to questions about the mother, Mary. Did she give birth to a divine or a human being? If divine, she needed to be a virgin untainted by sin and sex; if human, her immaculate being was gone. The two ancient prominent schools in Antioch, Syria, and Alexandria, Egypt, fought over this issue when a graduate of Antioch, Nestorius, taught that Mary could not be honored as "Mother of God" (*theotokos* in Greek) since Jesus was only human on earth. Other graduates joined him, fighting graduates from the school in Alexandria. One of them, Eutyches (378–455), denied the doctrine of Christ's "two natures," accepting only one nature, generating another party name, "Monophysites" (from the Greek *monos*, "alone," or "one," and *physis*, "nature"). The "Nestorians" were condemned and Emperor Theodosius II sent Nestorius into exile in 435. Eutyches lobbied for a council favoring a compromise: Christ had one, divine nature before he became man and two natures after his birth on earth. A council met in Ephesus in 449, dominated by Alexandrians, supported by a mob and soldiers, and marked by mutual condemnations. The bishop of Rome, playing the role of the cool outsider, "pope" Leo I, compared the council to "highway robbery"; it is known in the annals of church history as an invalid "robber council." The Fourth Ecumenical Council of 451 restored the honor of Mary as "Mother of God." But Nestorians spread in Persia; Roman Catholic missionaries discovered Nestorian churches in China in 1625, recalling the German proverb, "Ill weeds grow apace" (*Unkraut verdirbt nicht*).

Another controversy arose over the substitution of "nature" with "will" (*thelema* in Greek). "Monothelets" (from the Greek *mono*s, "one") argued that Jesus had only one will. They were condemned by the Sixth

---

33. Greek Orthodox theologians agree that the Holy Spirit is given through the Son (John 20:22), but only as part of the Father's power of creation and redemption. The Son does not have the same power as the Father because of his human nature. Such hairsplitting argumentation is not very persuasive. A hush-hush attitude prevailed until 809 when the first "holy Roman emperor," Charlemagne, had the formula adopted at a synod in Aachen, Germany. But popes hesitated until 1014 to approve the formula as a part of the Nicene Creed.

Ecumenical Council at Constantinople in 681. The controversies disclose the need to distinguish between "doxology" and "theology": the former is anchored in worship as praise for what God did in Christ; the latter tries to construct a rational summary of faith in Christ as a way to bridge cultural differences, especially between Greek and Latin ways of life and thought. But trans-cultural formulations are always problematic. They can cause culture shock, indeed culture wars that try to impose one way of life on another. On the other hand, cult or liturgy can faithfully preserve religious affirmations. Sometimes it is better to sing or to intone rather than to syllogize. It would be odd, indeed foolish, to baptize in the name of "one being and three emanations" instead of "in the name of the Father, the Son and the Holy Spirit." Centuries later, even this formulation was attacked by "feminists." They substituted "Mother" for "Father" or used Trinitarian functions as titles—"creator, redeemer, sustainer." In the eighteenth century, some Lutheran "Pietists" tried to be cute like small children and used pet names, "papa, little lamb (Son), mama (Holy Spirit)."

The first six Ecumenical Councils at Nicaea (325), Constantinople I (381), Ephesus (431), Chalcedon (451), Constantinople II (553), and Constantinople III (681) created and summarized the familiar doxological assertions about the Trinity. They are solemnly repeated in worship services, usually after the reading of the selected Gospel text. The praise of God was codified for future generations as a wedge against "logical" Trinitarian explanations.

Constantine and his successors realized the dream of Christian theocrats to create a Christian world, beginning with the immediate political environment (today, a "Christian America") and export the dream to the rest of the world. Other dreams were not permitted and, if dreamers tried to realize them, they faced persecution, indeed death. The emperor was the head of church and state. He controlled the church through imperial and regional synods chaired by bishops in the West and by patriarchs in the East. Ordination into the priesthood meant loyalty to the emperor. Only men were ordained, and they were to be celibate.[34] Sexual activity was said

---

34. Celibacy was a strict requirement for religious orders; priests were exempt from it until the fourth century. In the East, Greek Orthodox priests were permitted to marry, but bishops had to be single—making them either rather young or quite old, pending the lack or length of a marriage. In the West, Roman Catholic priests had to be celibate. But strict enforcement was not enacted until the Second Lateran Council of 1139. Ordination took place at age twenty-five. Women were not ordained before the twentieth century and still are not in the Catholic Church and in other churches, such as the Lutheran

to cripple cultic purity—an old religious superstition. Another superstition was continued, namely, the "tonsure," shearing the hair on the top of the head to indicate an otherworldly, holy estate; the practice began with the priests of the Egyptian goddess of fertility. It is an oxymoron of mythology that priestly and monastic tonsures symbolized fertility in Egyptian religion and virginity in Christianity.

Membership in the church began with legislated baptism which was rich in ceremony: renunciation of evil and affirmation of Christ; the blessing of the water; immersion repeated three times, anointment with scented oil oil, recitation of the Apostles' Creed and the Lord's Prayer, candles, and special dress, usually a white garment. Infant baptism became popular after the fifth century as a convenient way of increasing church membership. Baptism was combined with Holy Communion and Confirmation in the East. Accordingly, infants were communed because all three "sacraments" are necessary for salvation from "original sin;" infants are born with it and need the strength for spiritual survival provided by the "holy meal" of the Eucharist. In the West, infant communion was abandoned. Participation in Holy Communion was allowed only after auricular confession and the rite of Confirmation at age seven (defined as the "age of discretion," being an "adult").[35] Life was regulated by the norms of the Bible, the episcopacy, three creeds (Apostolic, Nicene, and Athanasian), catechesis, and Canon Law. Worship services were enhanced by processions, fasting at specific seasons (like Lent), and festivals, especially Christmas and Easter. Prayers to deceased saints, veneration of relics, and pilgrimages to the Holy Land and other locations kept believers busy.

Shortly after becoming "Christian," the legendary Roman Empire fell victim to the onslaught of northern and eastern European tribes. Historians dubbed the event *Völkerwanderung* (from the German "migration of peoples"). Germanic and Slavic groups in the north and east of Europe stormed south between the third and the eleventh centuries (Franks, Goths,

---

Church-Missouri Synod.

35. Mandated by the Fourth Lateran Council in 1215. "The Fourth Lateran Council," NCE. In the East, the combination of Baptism, Communion, and Confirmation remained unchanged. "Infant Communion" was eventually introduced by Protestant churches, for example, The Evangelical Lutheran Church in America, in 1997, after a debate. See *The Use of the Means of Grace*, 26–27. Infants become Greek Orthodox in a ceremony that begins with baptism by sprinkling with water or immersion, then continues with Holy Communion by consuming a mixture of bread and wine with spoon, and ends with Confirmation by being anointed with scented oil on hands and feet.

Lombards, Vandals, Huns, and others). The Gothic king Alaric conquered Rome in 410, and Attila the Hun invaded Italy in 452, followed by violent "vandalizing" by the Vandals in 456. The Roman bishop Leo I impressed both of them as a religious leader with supernatural powers. He was also an experienced diplomat, who faced the superstitious invaders with his religious demeanor and succeeded in persuading them to move on. The Goths settled in Gaul (now France) and Spain; Attila the Hun withdrew from northern Italy to the region north of the Danube. But the glory of ancient Rome ended in 476 when the last emperor, dubbed "little Augustus" (*Romulus Augustulos*), was deposed. Leo I used his "victories" as evidence of divine authority given to him as the global shepherd of the church. It is an irony of history that converted Germanic tribes adopted the "heresy" of Arianism, denying any illogical Trinitarian theology and thus believing only in the divinity of Jesus.

Three church fathers tried hard to preserve orthodoxy in new ways: Jerome, Augustine, and Chysostom. Jerome (c. 340–420) worked closely with popes, traveled widely in the church at large, and is best known for translating the Bible from Hebrew (Old Testament) and Greek (New Testament) into Latin, known as the "Vulgate" of 405 (from the Latin *vulgare*, "to be common" and deteriorate to "being vulgar"). Improved work on biblical texts proved the Vulgate to be too vulgar in its accuracy; but it endured in the improved translation of the King James Version of 1611. Jerome became an ordained ascetic monk spending his declining years in a monastery in Bethlehem. In his prime, he mingled with noblemen in Rome as their spiritual guide, advised the pope, and defended orthodoxy based on the Bible and the ecumenical creeds. Women liked Jerome. An aristocratic widow, Paula, accompanied him to Bethlehem and presided over a convent near his monastery—a Platonic relationship that obeyed the biblical injunction, "Honor widows who are really widows" (1 Tim 5:3).

Aurelius Augustine (354–430), a native of Thagaste, Africa (now Algeria) became one of the most influential theologians in the West—perhaps the first "bishop of color." His best-selling autobiography, *Confessions*, is a classic tale of conversion from sinful youth to redeeming old age: He was a wild bachelor committed to the "lusts of the flesh" and to experiments of the mind, ranging from membership in secret pagan cults to fathering an illegitimate "love child" named Adeotatus (from the Latin *a deo datus*, "a gift of God"). He was like a fatherless young drug addict in our cities today, with a grieving, devout Christian mother, Monica, who prayed for a miracle. It happened in the form of a sudden conversion at age thirty-three, the age of Jesus when he was crucified. Augustine heard a child's voice, saying, "Pick it up and read it." He opened the Bible and read Rom 13:13–14 (an urgent appeal to renounce "the desires of the flesh" and to "put on the Lord Jesus Christ"). He was baptized and spent some time in a retreat, living by the "rule of Augustine." It was approved by Pope Alexander IV in 1256 for a strict, "mendicant" (from the Lation *mendicare*, "begging") order. Augustine engaged in literary battles against the "Donatists" and the "Pelagians," followers of the British monk Pelagius (died c. 420). His stance reflects another enduring controversial issue, besides the Trinity, namely, the relationship between human freedom and divine grace. Can humans decide whether or not to be saved, or is their salvation strictly a matter of divine election? Pelagius taught that humans can decide to be saved just as Adam and Eve decided to sin. Their sin is not "original" or "inherited"; babies are born without it. Pelagius was the first town-crier calling for "freedom of conscience" and "religious liberty." Using a musical paradigm, he could be linked to the popular egotistic song of Frank Sinatra (1915–1998), "My Way" (in contrast to the saying of Jesus "I am the way" [John 14:6]). But the church kept the doctrine of original sin and divine election for salvation. Augustine won, and "Pelagianism" was condemned at the Second Council of Orange in 529. Casuistic minds did some hairsplitting later, known as "Semi-Pelagianism": the human will initiates salvation by asking for it, and the Holy Spirit completes the process by supplying the power to be accepted—a peculiar view of divine intervention! One theologian, the renowned reformer John Calvin (1509–1564), complicated the issue with a doctrine of "double predestination" that emanates divine cruelty: God elects some for salvation and others for damnation.[36] This doctrine raises the question of how one knows whether one is saved or condemned. The answers are choosy and juicy, exemplified by Puritan minds who imagine heaven populated with people who have given up much while hell is filled with those who have given in to too much. The Swedish Lutheran theologian, Krister Stendahl, reheated the Donatist controversy in 1961 when he contended that St. Paul, St. Augustine, and Martin Luther (an Augustinian monk) are the guns for the destructive trajectory of a "guilty conscience" by viewing divine law as a "disciplinarian" (Gal 3:24) who demands a price of human penance no one can afford, sending anxious minds on an unending guilt trip. Yet "law," Stendahl pointed out, ("Torah" in the Old Testament) is

---

36. See below, 145.

part of divine grace. The Jewish psychoanalyst Sigmund Freud (1856–1939) made his living in treatments of guilt imbedded in human sexuality. Stendahl called for a rejection of this Freudian culture of guilt and presented his arguments against it in an explosive lecture at a meeting of the American Psychology Association in 1961, titled "The Apostle Paul and the Introspective Conscience ofthe West."[37] But Augustine did bequeath a burden on women who as mothers were marked by the "original sin of the flesh," giving sex a bad name.

John Chrysostom (c. 347–407), known as the bishop with a "golden mouth" (from the Greek *chrysostomos*), had his headquarters in Constantinople but was well known as a preacher on biblical texts in the cathedral in Antioch for eleven years. Contemporaries describe him as being honest, ascetic, and tactless; he was straight in his talk; he was eager to become a martyr; and he did not mind offending opponents. Above all, he used his "golden mouth" to issue a steely anti-Semitic hate, calling for the extermination of Jews as the killers of Christ. He offended the imperial court with his critique of pomp and circumstance. But when he was deposed, public reaction quickly ended the punishment. His continued his critique of the "pagan" life-style of the rich and famous and was punished with exile. He died in Caucasian Armenia (now southern Russia)—a man fit to be tied and put on trial for being an angry man.

Christian pride and prejudice, disguised as a defense of the original "gospel," had transformed the stories about Jesus into creeds and legalistic rules. This development weakened the Christian mission which, in its Jewish setting, was based on story-telling, well illustrated by the New Testament parables. When a "smart" lawyer asked Jesus, "Who is my neighbor?," Jesus answered the question with the parabolic story of the "good Samaritan" (Luke 10:25–37). When the telling of stories diminishes, indeed dies out, religion and culture have lost power and grow dark like a room without comforting lit candles.

Institutionalization, pushed by emperors, kings, and bishops, created the future features of ecclesiastical orders. It became popular to distinguish between an order of "clergy" (from the Greek *kleros*, "order"), consisting of those who were "ordained," and the "laity" (from the Greek *laos*, "people"). The notion that all the baptized are "priests" (1 Pet 2:5) was soon silenced, making way for calling "ordination" a special "sacrament" besides baptism. "Clericalism" raised its ugly head and would soon become the spiritual

---

37. *The Harvard Theological Review* 56 (1963) 199–215.

parallel to the secular power of the capitalist captains of industry, dubbed "CEOs" (Chief Economic Officers). Moreover, bishops competed with each other for superior authority and wealth.

In the midst of all the theological confusion, some minds recalled two formulations of the bishop of Carthage, North Africa, Cyprian (c. 200–258), an expert in Roman Law, a staunch defender of the episcopate, and a revered martyr: 1) "There is no salvation outside the [institutional] church;" and 2) "He can no longer have God for his Father who has not the church for his mother."[38] They became persuasive sound bites to define the church as the institution of salvation.

A revival of the philosophy of Plato (c. 427–347 BCE) in Egypt and Syria by an not well-known philosopher, Plotinus (c. 205–244), who taught in Rome, created a movement known as Neoplatonism. Plato focused on invisible ideas rather than on "realities" observed in nature, as Aristotle did. Plato's basic "idea," is the concept of a "soul" (*psyche* in Greek) that depicts a "breath of life" linked with the "mind" (*nous*, in Greek) and connects humans with immortality. Christian theology began to use this philosophical speculation as a convenient way to link heaven and earth. Superstitious minds contended that, when someone dies, the soul leaves the body through the mouth (usually open during the final moment to catch breath). In modern parlance, the concept of an assumed soul could be substituted by the scientific discovery that designates a unique particular human life, the DNA—"DeoxyriboNucleic Acid, a self-replicating material present in nearly all living organisms as the main constituent of chromosomes. It is the carrier of genetic information."[39] The soul is "I," without any duplication. Plotinus taught that there is a "chain of being" consisting of souls linked to God as the "absolute soul" uniting physical and metaphysical elements, such as earthly love (*eros* in Greek) and heavenly love (*agape* in Greek). The notion of an "immortal soul" cannot be found in the Bible.[40] The "soul" is "I," without any duplication. Plotinus taught that there is a "chain of being" consisting of souls linked to God as the "absolute soul" uniting physical and metaphysical elements, such as earthly love (*eros* in Greek) and heavenly love (*agape* in Greek).

38. "On the Unity of the Church," in *The Ante-Nicene Fathers*, 4, 21.

39. NOAD.

40. In the Old Testament it is the "wind" of God creating the earth (Gen 1:2) and the "breath of life" in the human creature (Gen 2:7). In the New Testament "soul" is derived from the Greek *pneuma*, "breath" (Eph 4:4) and means the unique identity of a person. Related is the designation "enthusiast," one who is "in God" (*entheos* in Greek).

Neoplatonism started the Christian mystical tradition. It was wrongly attributed to Dionysius "the Areopagite," one of a few converts in the crowd in Athens addressed by Paul (Acts 17:34). Writings with his name began to appear in the fifth century in Spain and, since the author could not be identified, they were called "Pseudo-Areopagite" until the sixteenth century. The writer introduced favorite concepts: a celestial hierarchy of angels reflected in the ecclesiastical hierarchy of deacons, presbyters, and bishops; the purification of the soul leading to perfect union with God; and a dialectic between darkness and light. To be "mystical" means "to close the eyes or lips," or "to initiate" (from the Greek *myein*)—to shut out the intrusion of the external world in order to be able to concentrate on specific notions that might provide unusual insights. That is why mystics are odd and clever.

Some Christians became disgusted with the "glory" of state religion, disclosing greed and pride rather than faith and humility. They became loners, called monks (from the Greek *monos*, "living alone"). The first monks simply left the "world" with its sinful distractions and temptations. They were driven by biblical injunctions calling for perfections through total separation from earthly possessions and hatred of worldliness (Matt 19:21; 1 John 2:15). The Egyptian desert seemed to be an ideal place: rough and rumored to be a place where Satan lived. Some monks went there to encounter him. Legendary imagination depicted them as odd recluses with visions of fighting Satan. Saint Anthony's story became popular: he lived in an empty tomb, then in an old castle, and finally died at age one-hundred-five in 356 on the rocks, as it were, that is, in a rocky mountain formation. All kinds of people flocked to him for meditation and advice. He was a "hermit," deserted in the desert (from the Greek *eremos*, "desert"). Wild stories were told about other "desert fathers" known as "pillar saints" or "stylites" (from the Greek *stylos*, "pillar"). They were said to have lived for years on the top of pillars, even hung on a contraption between them. Tourists gawked at them, and travel agents spread "miracle" stories about them. Their veracity may be measured by the contemporary world record for "pole-sitting": 196 days, 13 hours, and 13 minutes by Daniel Baraniuk in Gdansk, Poland, on May 15, 2002. Eventually, some of the monks would live together in a "cloister" (from the Latin *claustrum*, "enclosed space"), establishing a discipline of combining "prayer and work" (*ora et labora* in Latin)—the two pillars of monastic life, with added vows of chastity, poverty, and obedience to the head of the monastery, the "abbot" (from the Greek *abbas*, "father"). Military experience may have played a role in the establishment of monastic communities since the founder of the first cloister in Tabessini was the Egyptian monk Pachomius (290–346), a former soldier.

The church had outlived Greek and Roman "paganism" (from the Latin *paganus*, "villager"), a derogatory term to depict lowbred people in the countryside—perhaps because most Christians lived in cities. In contrast to the first Christian generation, made up of fishermen and other "ordinary," indeed poor, people, Christians constituted a higher class of society because the church had been politically adopted by and adapted to secular power and greed. Even its first creedal formulations were made possible by Emperor Constantine I who called, chaired, and financed the Council of Nicaea. He provided needed doctrinal changes and ordered them to be adopted without any opposition. Political greed provided an ecumenical creed.

When in Rome . . .

The center of the Christian mission began to move from Jerusalem to Rome after the destruction of the Jewish temple in 70 by a Roman army as punishment for a Jewish revolt. Other Christian centers, Antioch in Syria, Alexandria in Egypt, and even Constantinople did not have the same attraction. The apostles Peter and Paul had been in Rome; rumors spread that they had been martyred there. Two epistles attributed to Peter were put into the New Testament, there also is an apocryphal *Gospel of Peter*. But there was no Roman primacy in the church even though Constantine honored the bishop of Rome as a useful partner in building a uniform society. The Roman bishop Damasus I (366–384) began talking about an "apostolic see" (from the Latin *sedes*, "seat," a cathedral as the residence of bishops and archbishops). The pope addressed bishops of other churches as "sons" rather than as "brothers." His successor Siricius (384–399) was the first to send out formal messages, called "decretals," imitating the imperial way of communication. Innocent I (401–417) claimed to be the judge in controversies as "governor of God's Church" (*rector ecclesiae Dei*); his decisions affected "all the churches of the world." Boniface I (418–422) introduced the title "vicar of Christ."

It was the "lion" (*leo* in Latin) Leo I (440–461) who was the first real "pope." The title, meaning "father" (from the Greek *pappas* and the Latin *papa*), was used in the East for bishops and is still applied to Roman

Catholic priests. But Emperor Valeran III increased the power of the title by making Leo the caretaker of the church whenever squabbles threatened to disturb the peace. In the fifth century, a phrase appeared, attributed to St. Augustine and used to define such "papal" caretaking: "Rome has spoken, the case is closed" (*Roma locuta, causa finita* est). Leo advertised himself as the "primary" bishop based on the merits of Peter as the "rock" of the church (Matt 16:18). He added two more proof-texts to solidify his "papal" authority (John 21:15–17 and Luke 22:32). The three texts became "Scripture" as the foundation for "tradition." An additional "proof" was invented in 445 (probably arranged by Leo): the Latin translation of the Greek Canon 6 of the Council of Nicaea in 325 appeared with the title "On the Roman Ecclesiastical Primacy" (*de primatur ecclesiae Romanae*), beginning with the statement "The Roman Church always had primacy." Emperor Valentinian III enforced the fraudulent claim of Canon 6 by an edict in the same year it appeared. When the Council of Chalcedon in 451 rejected the fraudulent claim, Leo used his political power to remove his eastern counterpart, the patriarch of Alexandria. But the Council declared in its "Canon 28" that the bishops of Rome and Constantinople had equal power. Incorrigible and unperturbed, Leo insisted that he alone was "Christ's deputy" (*vicarious* Christi) on earth. Later, Pope Gregory I (590–604) mixed arrogance and humility by calling himself "servant of servants," and he criticized the bishop of Constantinople for not being humble by using the title "Ecumenical Patriarch." The incident is one of many, exemplifying the enduring apostolic question addressed to Jesus, "Who is the greatest in the kingdom of God?" (Matt 18:10). "Greatest" becomes "humblest" in the minds of church leaders who compete with each other throughout the ages for the best way to be humble. This competition for humility is one of the many ugly scandals of Christianity. It is also a classic oxymoron—a figure of speech in which apparently contradictory terms appear in conjunction (e.g. *faith unfaithful kept him falsely true*, from Greek "*oxymoron*, neuter used as a noun of *oxymoros*, 'pointedly foolish,' from *oxus*, 'sharp' + moros, 'foolish.'"[41]). Pope Gelasius I (492–496) played for even higher stakes, insisting that the emperor must be guided by the pope who is not subject to any human authority.

The successors of Leo I fortified his papal claims. Symmachus I (498–514) declared that the pope cannot be judged by any human court. He also was the first pope to wear a papal dress, the "pallium—a [white] woolen

---

41. NOAD.

vestment, consisting of a narrow, circular band around the shoulders with short lappets hanging from front and back."[42] Popes resided in the "Vatican," the name of a hill in Rome on the left bank of the river Tiber where Emperor Nero (54–68) had built his circus. Peter was supposed to have been crucified and buried there. So Emperor Constantine I had the "shrine of St. Peter" expanded into a church; the papal residence was added later. He had also built another church at the "shrine of St. Paul" on another hill on the Ostian Way. But the papal advertisement of Rome as the location of the death of Peter and Paul is based on hearsay evidence. Constantine I donated the Lateran Palace of his second wife Fausta as the official residence for the pope—perhaps to redeem himself for having her executed. All this was done to cement the fusion of church and state, with the pope being the cornerstone. The Vatican and the pope became the small counterparts to the empire and the emperor.

An architectural symbol of the symbiosis of church and state was the "basilica" (from the Greek *basileios*, "king"). It was the Christian imitation of the ancient Roman courthouse: a rectangular hall divided into three sections by two rows of columns, and an "apse"—"a large semicircular or polygonal recess, with a domed roof, typically at the eastern end, and usually containing the altar."[43] Such a style affected the character of worship, making it look royal. There was a throne for the bishop with benches on either side for clergy. The "altar" (from the Latin *altus*, "high") was a block of marble, or a solid table made of another attractive material, with remains of saints or martyrs placed under it. Worshipers assembled in front of the altar, distanced from the clergy in the altar space. Besides the basilica, two other buildings appeared: the baptistery, with sufficient water for immersion (later just a font for sprinkling); and a chapel built over the tomb or relics of a martyr or a saint. In the West, the rounded arches were replaced by pointed ones; the floor was often constructed in the form of a cross. In the East, the altar was hidden by a massive solid screen, adorned with icons or other depictions of saints; the screen opened after the priest had completed the Eucharistic "mystery" ready for worshipers in the sacred elements of bread and wine. In the West, there was the "chancel" (from the Latin *chancelli*, "crossbars"), the space of the altar for the clergy, and the "nave" (from the Latin *navis*, "ship") for the laity. A pulpit (from the Latin *pulpitum*, "scaffold") was located between the chancel and the nave.

42. NOAD. Later, it was also be conferred by the pope on an archbishop.
43. "Basilica," in NOAD.

Christendumb

The images of a ship and a scaffold lend themselves to the judgment, given the ups and downs of worship performances, that some preachers hung themselves with bad sermons on the "scaffold," and worshippers rocked like anxious passengers in the "ship" below. Moreover, they either stood or sat in seats they brought along. Pews were introduced later. Eastern Orthodox churches do not have pews. Side altars also became popular as the sites for special prayers to saints represented by statues and paintings.

It is an irony of history that a church replaced Nero's circus—"the show must go on!" Pope and emperor were a powerful team that recalls a satirical proverb coined by the Roman politician and philosopher Seneca (5 BCE–65 CE), "One hand washes the other." The pope ruled over the souls and the emperor over the bodies. The earthly church became known as the "church militant," led in the struggle against evil by both rulers, and becoming the "church triumphant" in the end.

Since the fourth century the pope presided over a hierarchy of offices (reserved only for men), resembling military order beginning at childhood. It began with the position of a "reader," an older child who could become an "acolyte" (from the Greek *akolutos*, "follower"), an assistant to the priest in worship. The next steps, sub-deacon" and "deacon," led to the priesthood at the age of thirty (since 1215 the age of twenty-five). After ten years a priest could become "bishop." But this time-line was often shortened by special privileges and patronages. Some men moved quickly from adult baptism to the episcopacy, quite often by lobbying, indeed by bribing a pope. By the fifth century, the Roman bishops, the "popes," were completely in charge of everything in the city. The pope did all the baptisms, usually at the vigil on the night before Easter. He alone celebrated the Eucharist on Sunday and, after the celebration, had the consecrated element of bread and wine distributed by acolytes to the parishes.

Papal power rested on the historical judgment that the bishop of Rome was the successor of Peter who had founded the church by a mandate of Christ (Matt 16:18). But the biblical proof-text is not foolproof. The word "church" (*ekklesia* in Greek), "gathering") means local congregation because no organized groups of churches existed. Interpreters of the text are divided: some contend that Jesus meant by "rock" the confession of Peter that Jesus was the Messiah and Son of God; others argue that Jesus was referring to the person of Peter. The notion of "hierarchy" (from the Greek *hierarkos*, "sacred" and *arche*, "beginning") is linked to a heavenly order of angels. It is also applied to the secular succession of blue blood royalty, often red-hot with ambition for power. Roman emperors pronounced themselves "gods" and required veneration of their statues with incense offering. There is also a pragmatic reason for hierarchical action in cases of emergency, exemplified by the sequence of action in a medical emergency, say a heart attack, when the treatment moves without hesitation from providing oxygen to heart surgery, beginning with a paramedic, to surgery by a cardiologist. Defenders of the apostolic succession of the papacy claimed that it is the earthly parallel to the angelic hierarchy in "heaven." In the fifth century, a list of popes appeared in a collection of papal biographies, beginning with Peter, the *Book of Popes* (*Liber Pontificales*), filled with a mixture of fact and fiction. Satirical journalists maintain that hearsay is known to become a fact if a story is repeated for a long time. This insight is anchored in a saying attributed to William James (1842–1910), the father of modern psychology, "There is nothing so absurd that, if you repeat it often enough, people will believe it."

Tied to papal power was "Canon Law" with its rules and regulations for all members of the church, enforced by secular authority. Moreover, the papal office became a financial power house through endowments, government subsidies, and private donations. This was a far cry from the injunction of Jesus not to worship Mammon (Matt 6:24). Some popes tried to create a better image of their office by devising a system mandating a fourfold use of money: running an Episcopal office; providing a salary for priests; repairing church buildings, especially lighting; and helping the poor. But the abuse of money persisted.

The transfer of political power from Rome to Constantinople after the conquest of Rome by Germanic tribes made the Roman bishop the most visible political authority figure. He used the brief revival of western imperial power through Justinian I (527–565) to cement his reputation by appealing to the alleged unbroken Petrine apostolic succession. Justinian did embody a "caesaropapism," so dubbed by historians, to define the fusion of church and state. Christianity became the state religion. But it was known best as "Roman Catholicism" led by the pope in Rome.

The trajectory of papal authority led to the problematic dogma of "infallibility," promulgated at the First Vatican Council in 1870. The convoluted wording is without equal.

The Roman Pontiff, when he speaks *ex cathedra*—that is, when in the exercise of his office as pastor and teacher of all Christians he defines, by virtue of his supreme apostolic authority, a doctrine of faith or morals to be held by the whole church—is by reason of the divine assistance promised to him in blessed Peter, possessed of that infallibility with which the divine redeemer wished his church to be endowed in defining doctrines of faith and morals and, consequently, that such definitions by the Roman Pontiff are irreformable of their own nature and not by reason of the church's consent.[44]

Three unique claims are made in the dogma: 1) *ex cathedra* decisions are divine through the promise of Jesus to Peter to be the "rock" of the church (Matt 16:18); 2) they encompass doctrinal teaching and ethical conduct; and 3) they represent an authority that cannot be questioned by the church. The pope is elected by a majority vote of cardinals; but his *ex cathedra* decisions cannot be challenged by a vote because in this special role as the head of the church and its unequaled teacher, he represents God rather than the church. In this sense, the penultimate has become the ultimate, time has become eternal, and one no longer sees "in a mirror dimly" (1 Cor 13:12). If "original sin" is the desire "to be like God" (Gen 3:5), the infallible pope is the most original of all sinners in a world waiting for the end-time.

Papal infallibility was challenged by an action of the Sixth Ecumenical Council of Constantinople in 681, which condemned Pope Honorius I (625–638) for teaching the old Trinitarian heresy, "Monotheletism"—the view that Christ had only one will (*monos thelema* in Greek), combining his human and divine natures. Consequently, "the case of Honorius" became "proof" that a pope cannot be "infallible" because of a heretical link in the chain of the succession from Peter to the bishops of Rome. That is why a number of bishops and their dioceses walked away from papal Roman Catholicism and founded the "Old Catholic Church" in 1889, consisting of about 200,000 members in various parts of Europe. They created ties with the Church of England (Anglicans), which originated with Henry VIII (1491–1547) and Elizabeth I (1533–1603), who was excommunicated by Pope Pius V in 1570 as a "heretic." "Old Catholics" became quite active in ecumenical relations.

Rome prevailed by hook and by crook. A bizarre sample of such papal behavior is the condemnation and trial of Pope Formosus (891–896) in effigy by his successor Stephen VI, who accused him of perjury and other crimes. He had the cadaver of Formosus dug up, taken to a council, later dubbed "cadaver council," "propped upon a throne in full pontifical vestments," and conducted a trial. After the conviction, "three fingers of his right hand [by which he swore oaths and gave blessings] were cut off and

---

44. "Infallibility" in NCE.

his body was thrown into the Tiber River." Some time later, a monk recovered the body, and he was reburied with honors by a later pope.[45] This is one example how Peter, the "rock" of the apostolic chain, turned into sand—a fraudulent tradition created by political greed. "When in Rome, do as the Romans do"—grab power, advertise it as the center of the world, and find a strong ally to enforce the alleged global authority. Pope and emperor became the "new" Romans claiming to continue the glorious pagan tradition of the ancient Roman emperors who claimed to be divine and demanded to be venerated in a special cult. They were strange bed-fellows. For they stayed together only if their union yielded political advantages for each of them. There was not much love lost between them, and, like porcupines, they kept a safe distance between them. The proverbial caveat comes to mind: "How do porcupines make love? Very carefully."

A Fuzzy Fusion

Although Constantine's fusion of church and state put the church on the map of the world it was never without cracks because of human frailty. Historians call the fusion "Caesaropapism." The fusion was modeled best by the powerful emperor Justinian I (483–565) who established an empire with Christianity as the only religion defined by Roman bishops. The "Justinian Code" codified a summary of ancient Roman laws used to establish a Christian state. The denial of the Trinity and a second baptism resulted in the death penalty. The architectural symbol of the empire was the patriarchal cathedral in Constantinople, the Hagia (or Sancta) Sophia, meaning "holy wisdom." Justinian is said to have gone into raptures at its inauguration in 537 (it is now a museum). But exceptions prove the rule. Members of the imperial court and rich families still adhered to non-Christian philosophical views, exemplified by lively gatherings around an attractive pagan mind, Lady Hypathia (from the Greek *hupate*, feminine adjective of "highest") in Alexandria, Egypt. She became known as the first female scientist, a mathematician advocating empirical knowledge over against mysticism and speculation; she was murdered by a Christian mob in 415. Common people also still sought entertainment in pagan festivals with their emphasis on the "pleasures of the flesh." The emperor had limitless legal power. Pope and bishops provided the appropriate Christian ideology, summarized in

---

45. "Formosus" in Richard P. McBrien, *Lives of the Pope*. Such tales usually combine fact and fiction.

rules for Christian citizenship. Clergy had special privileges, manifested in higher income and gifts of land. Like Constantine, Justinian enforced "orthodoxy" through the Fifth Ecumenical Council at Constantinople in 553 and had the anti-Trinitarian "Monophysites" condemned. But they, too, like members of the court and common folk, did not adjust. They moved to Egypt where they established the "Coptic" (meaning "Egyptian" in Arabic) Church, also called "Jacobite" (from the leader Jacob Baradai). The church still exists.

Another monophysite church survived in Ethiopia (North Africa, on the Red Sea). It was shaped by Judaism and an admiration for the Ethiopian eunuch who was converted by the apostle Philip (Acts 8:26–40) and for King Solomon and the Queen of Sheba. But the flourishing church wilted away when the famous Marib dam broke in the sixth century and destroyed the irrigation for a wealthy agricultural society; the dam was never rebuilt. Eventually, Ethiopians became part of Eastern Orthodoxy and of other Christian communions, especially Lutherans (about six million today).

Syrian Christians became ardent missionaries through their business in Central Asia, especially India. Tradition has it that the apostle Thomas (who had doubts about the resurrection of Jesus, John 20:24–25) created the Indian "Mar Thoma Church" which had good relations with non-Christians. It is part of the tangled web of the history of Christianity that they still harbored some monophysite ideas and were persecuted by Western Roman Catholics in the sixteenth century and reduced to a tiny minority.

In the West, the fusion of church and state remained popular because it showed worldly success. Pope Gregory I (590–604), the son of a Roman senator, lobbied the invading Germanic nations to convert, especially the Lombards in Italy and the Goths and Franks in the north. He sent missionaries to England motivated by an apocryphal story: when he saw attractive young children in a slave market in Rome, he was told that they were *Angli* from England and he called them "angels," the mythical basis for "Anglo-Saxons" (Saxons appeared in England in the fifth century). Gregory sent a team of Benedictine missionaries to the British isles for a successful conversion of the Celts, with centers in Canterbury and York. The legendary St. Patrick established a church in Ireland, followed by Columba (c. 521–597) who created a monastic community on the Scottish island of Iona, Scotland. Another monk, Boniface (680–754), became the "apostle to the Germans," traveling with twelve companions to the continent, praised by pope and emperor for the successful Christian invasion of the heartland of Germanic culture. A dramatic event established his fame: in Hesse where he challenged the power of the popular deity Thor who was worshiped under a large oak tree. Boniface cut it down with an axe without being cut down himself by an expected thunderstorm as the punishment for blaspheming Thor. A chapel supplanted the holy oak tree, and in 744 a monastery in Fulda became a center for Christian life.

Just after Pope Gregory had cemented the fusion of church and state, it was threatened by the rise of Islam. Its founder, Mohammed of Mecca (c. 570–632), advocated teachings that took quickly hold of people in Arabia. He thought of himself as the last of Semitic prophets from Abraham to Jesus. He claimed that Jewish and Christian traditions had to be purified and transformed into one and only religion God had in mind. Mohammed was born in Mecca and had his first revelations as a successful merchant. His immediate family sided with him, but he was not successful in persuading people in Medina to follow him. In 622, the beginning of the Muslim calendar, he mediated a civil war and removed the idols from the ancient Arabic shrine, a square stone called "Kaaba" (Arabic for "square house"); it became the holy shrine of Islam. Pilgrims had to visit it every year. Mohammed began to establish a Muslim state which, like the Christian empire in the west, fused secular and spiritual powers. When Mohammed died, most of Arabia had become Muslim. "Caliphs" ("successors" in Arabic) became the leaders of the new world religion. "Islam" means literally "submission to God," and believers are known as "Muslims" or "Moslems." The religion was uniform in language since no translation of the Koran was permitted.

The Koran ("recitation" in Arabic) contains Mohammed's revelations written down by his disciples. Then there is the "Sunna" ("path" in Arabic), an oral tradition of specific ways of life mandated by the prophet and written down in a collection; it provides the core of a legal system. Finally, there is the "ijma" or unanimous consensus achieved with the guidance of learned men; there are no priests. All Muslims must adhere to "five pillars of faith": 1) a profession faith in God, "Allah" ("god" in Arabic) and in Mohammed as the last and greatest of God's prophets; 2) ritual prayer, preferably in a mosque; 3) almsgiving of one fourth of a man's annual revenue; 4) fasting, especially at "Ramadan" (meaning "be hot"—during a hot month, but the Muslim lunar calendar "cools" the date by advancing the time eleven days earlier each year); there is to be complete abstinence from pork and intoxicating beverages; and 5) a pilgrimage to Mecca once in a life time. Some Islamic writers added a sixth obligation, "holy war" ("jihad") against idol-worshiping pagans to force their conversion, although most Muslims would resist such a way of proselytizing. But Jews and Christians were tolerated as monotheists. Jews were met with courtesy even during the terrible Christian crusades, climaxing with the murder of Muslims and Jews in Jerusalem—an impressive lesson from non-Christians to Christians regarding the love of enemies (Matt 5:44). After 700, Muslims controlled most of the Mediterranean coastlines and islands, cutting most relations between the Christian East and West. They also had begun to move to Spain.

Islam had become a powerful religious competition, labeled "Antichrist" by the church. Ancient Judaism, the breeding ground of Christianity was only an imagined threat to the church because Jews did not engage in a mission to convert people to their faith. But a Christian mission was accompanied by a vicious anti-Semitism that condemned Jews for denying Christ as the "Messiah" as the mediator of a salvation without any competition. This anti-Semitism was intensified by Christian polemics against a Jewish rabbinical commentary on Mosaic law after the dawn of Christianity known as the "Talmud," a "fence around the Torah." It made no claims to provide the only way to salvation as Islam did. But Christians viewed the Talmud as an attack on the uniqueness of Christianity and used it for centuries to denounce Judaism as the worst enemy of Christianity. Christian anti-Semitism topped any other hatred of the Jews for centuries and contributed in large measure to a hatred that led to the Jewish holocaust of the regime of Adolf Hitler (1941–1945).[46]

Mohammed and the pope had become the two opponents who struggled for superiority in the name of the same God. Both engaged in "holy war." Muslim rule separated Eastern and Western Christians for centuries. When Muslim armies were forced to withdraw from Vienna in 1529, Muslim rule stayed in southwestern Europe and in the Middle East. The Turks bequeathed on Vienna the culinary pleasures of the croissant and Turkish coffee, served in coffee houses—an enjoyable substitute for the smells and taste of the jihad. But Christian crusades against Islam, combined with a vicious, enduring Christian anti-Semitism, undermined the highest Christian mandate of loving God and the neighbor (Matt 22:37–40).

---

46. The Talmud appeared after 200 CE with a deep veneration of Mosaic Law and of the sayings of renowned rabbis as a source of endurance under persecution. But Rome condemned the Talmud a few decades after its appearance. Adin Steinsaltz, *The Essential Talmud*, 80.

Mission Impossible?

The fusion of church and state was also threatened by infighting among the New Germanic converts. The Frankish kings developed their own political structure with the king as highest authority, but without sharing it with Rome. So the king had exactly what the pope had demanded: absolute authority without any outside interference. He only tolerated territorial churches, governed by bishops and imperial synods. A royal edict of 614 declared that papal power could only be exercised with the king's approval—contrary to the papal refusal to be subject to a secular authority. But the church in the West succeeded to expand its influence. Some "heretical" Arian churches began to accept Roman Catholicism in the sixth century, and almost all Germanic territories followed suit by 800, led by the clever diplomatic pope, Gregory I, who once again exercised the unique papal power.

In the waves of political decline, the rise of Benedictine monasticism kept the fusion intact. Benedict (c. 480–c. 547) was a native Italian who founded the famous monastery Monte Cassino with the Benedictine Rule. His sister, Scholastica, was a nun nearby and worked with him. The Rule called for a large community of men in a monastery loyal to the ecclesiastical establishment identified with Rome. In contrast to earlier forms of monasticism in the east, Benedictine discipline was moderate, not ascetic, and geared to farming based on Italian peasant life. Chastity and obedience were secured through a vow of stability, that is, staying in the monastery for life to avoid heterosexual pleasure. The monks were open to the world through hospitality and charity; they also ran a school intended to educate children for a monastic life. In France, Benedictines made their own popular brandy, Benedictine Liqueur, usually consumed after a good meal reflecting joyful moderation. One of the brothers, Dom Pierre Perignon (c. 1638–1715), is said to have produced the famous French champagne through a secondary fermentation, and he was the first to press grapes in a way that produces white wine. In 1965, Pope Paul VI proclaimed Benedict the patron saint of Europe (at the dedication of a new monastery Monte Cassino, replacing the one destroyed in World War II). Generations of Benedictine monks stamped Western culture with their skills in agriculture, copying of ancient manuscripts, and recording the past.

The first seven centuries had produced a Christian church identified by the biblical canon, a "Rule of Faith" or "Creeds" (Apostles', Nicene, Athanasian), and the Episcopal office.[47] Pope and Emperor understood

---

47. The "Apostles' Creed" was not composed by the twelve apostles, assumed by

themselves to be the divinely destined guardians of a fusion of church and state. But cultural differences between east and west cracked the fusion. The devil is in details, in this case in cultural differences. Two church fathers of the second century illustrate these differences in their culture-bound theology: Origen in the east and Tertullian in the West.

Origen summarized his dogma of the Trinity in the Greek formulation "one being" (*ousia*, "that in which everything else is grounded") and "three entities" (*hypostases*, "standing under the 'being'"). One could say more flippantly "one being with three natures." Origen wanted to avoid speaking of three "gods," or of "one god" with three emanations. Yet his logical attempt to describe the Trinity is hampered in Platonic Greek philosophy which presupposes a mysterious relationship between "nature" (*physis*) and what is "behind" (*meta*) it, the "metaphysical." But even the most sophisticated metaphysics does not do justice to the logical paradox of the "word" become "flesh" (John 3:14).

Tertullian summarized his dogma of the Trinity in the Latin formulation "One substance, three persons." In Latin culture, "substance" is a legal term, meaning a "person of substance," a wealthy, powerful human being, "a man of substance."

Metaphysical notions are excluded. Otherwise, one would have to translate the Greek "metaphysical" into "supernatural" (from the Latin "above nature" (*super naturam*). What is "behind" in Greek is "above" in Latin. Eventually, Tertullian's formulation was adopted in the West because it avoided the rationalist logical dilemma of eastern formulations. He avoided any explanation of the Trinity based on the Johannine notion of Jesus being the divine "word" ("logos"). The Sixth Ecumenical Council at Constantinople in 680/81 again established the Trinitarian orthodoxy by condemning "Monotheletism" (the Christological doctrine of "one will").

By the end of the seventh century, differences between east and west had become quite obvious. "Going to church" in the east, one stood (no pews) and saw an altar with closed, wing-shaped doors. Behind it, the priest consecrated the elements of bread and wine and, when he had finished, the doors opened for Communion—a strict separation of clergy and laity based on the notion that only priests had access to the divine mysteries. In the east, mystery and mysticism dominated. Greek orthodox doctrine used the notion of "divinization" (*theosis* in Greek) implying a divine penetration

---

hearsay, but was a brief summary of faith composed in Rome and used in baptisms since c. 400. Its final version appeared in the West and in the eighth century.

of the human being foreshadowing eternal life. Worship already opens the heavenly door, symbolized by the opening of the altar door for the reception of Eucharistic bread and wine. The eastern mystical way of Christian life has been summarized by the Egyptian bishop Athanasius who, inspired by Ireneaus, declared that Christ, the Son of God "has made man that we might be made God."[48]

Western Latin Christianity stressed penance as the proper attitude in a world filled with evil, sin, and death. That is why a mandated auricular confession preceded Holy Communion. In the east, the church created an atmosphere of spiritual union with creation and its recreation through Christ, "experienced" in part at Holy Communion. The Eastern tradition was summarized by the last of the great fathers of the eastern church, John of Damascus (c. 675–749) in "The Orthodox Faith," the third part of his major work "*The Fount of* Wisdom" (preceded by a critical description of "philosophy" and "heresy"). The church consists of local sacramental communities headed by a bishop. The difference with the west is also indicated in the way the Christ event is depicted at the top of church steeples: in Greek Orthodox churches Christ is "Pantocrator" (from the Greek *krateo panta*, "ruling over everything")—holding a globe. In Roman Catholic churches, it is the cross, indicating sacrifice and suffering.

Given the diverse aspects of Christianity in its first seven centuries, marked by simple faith, sophisticated theology, and political power plays, Jesus' mandate for mission looks like the TV series *Mission Impossible*. At its worst, it was marred by folly, fear, and failure. At its best, it can be compared to an air force mission in World War II, with pilots trying to find their target, hampered by thick clouds, heavy anti-aircraft fire, and enemy dog-fighters. But some always made it—disclosing the mystery and the cost of discipleship.

---

48. "On the Incarnation," 54 in the *Nicene and Post-Nicene Fathers*, 1, 65.

2

Edifice Complex
700–1400 CE

> You are no longer strangers and aliens, but you are citizens with the saints and also members of the household of God, built upon the foundation of the apostles and the prophets, with Christ Jesus himself as the cornerstone. In him the whole structure is joined together and grows into a holy temple in the Lord; in whom you also are built together spiritually into a dwelling place for God.
>
> —EPHESIANS 2:19–22

AN EAST-WEST WALL

LIKE THE "OEDIPUS COMPLEX" in Freudian psychoanalysis,[1] a Christian "edifice complex"[2] began to dominate in Christianity after seven centuries. Structures of doctrines were to edify believers to demonstrate the wonders

---

1. NOAD: "The complex of emotions aroused in a young child, typically around the age of four, by an uncontrollable desire for the parent of the opposite sex and a wish to exclude the parent of the same sex." Greek mythology tells the tragic story of Oedipus who unwittingly kills his father, the king of Thebes, and married his mother. In a fit of madness, he cut out his own eyes, and his mother hanged herself.

2. Word-play on the Internet: "The tendency of politicians to have large buildings and stadiums built as a concrete reminder of their legacy." It could be said that the tragedy of an abusive sexuality in the "Oedipus complex" is matched by the tragedy of an abusive humility in the "edifice complex" of Christianity.

of the Christian faith. They corresponded to the architecture of "cathedrals" and, when labeled "ex cathedra" declarations from the seat of the bishop of Rome, the pope, would be viewed as "infallible." Worship and education were the principal means of edification, trying to rule the hearts and minds in the church, its priesthood, religious orders, and the laity. Such edification created the earthly "church militant" on the way of becoming the heavenly "church triumphant." Greek Orthodoxy, the "Greek rite," in the East and Roman Catholicism, the "Latin rite" in the West, gradually used edification to build a wall of separation which, unlike the infamous Berlin Wall in the 1960s, was erected by both sides in order to preserve a mutually exclusive "orthodoxy."

The complex of theological edifices in the first seven Christian centuries were constructed with the help of ancient Greek philosophy and science. When Greek and Roman cultures became interwoven, aspects of mystery religions were added, revealing a secret knowledge summarized as "Gnosticism" (from the Greek *gnosis*, "knowledge"). It usually teaches about a dualistic world, defined by the struggle between good and evil, darkness and light, the material and the spiritual, sin and redemption through colorful rituals linked to the sun, the moon, and the stars. Some of the mysteries were absorbed by later philosophical movements linked to Plato and Aristotle. They, in turn, accepted a standard view of the world provided by the second-century Greek astrologer and geographer Ptolemy: the earth as the center, with the sun, the moon, and the stars in its orbit. His geocentric view dominated until the sixteenth century when Nicholas Copernicus proved that the sun was the center. Aristotle (384–322 BCE) filled the holes of knowledge provided by Socrates, Plato, and other minds; creating a philosophical framework for the understanding of nature and super-nature—that which is within and above earthly existence.

East and West soon differed in their views regarding the truth of perceived reality. A case in point is a major controversy in the eighth century over the use of Christian art, especially pictures. Church members began to focus on icons depicting Jesus, Mary, and honored deceased "saints." Soon word spread that some icons had miraculous powers of healing. Believers in such miracles became known as "iconodules" (from the Greek *eikon doulos*, "a slave of icons"). They were opposed by rigorous Bible readers who invoked the Second Commandment of the Decalogue, which prohibits the making and worship of an "idol" (Deut 5:8). In 726, Emperor Leo III, who hailed from Asia Minor, enforced the commandment and prohibited

Edifice Complex

the use of images, a move known as "iconoclasm" (from the Greek *eikonoklastes*, "image breaker").[3] They were especially offended by icons of Christ. But in the West, icons were favored and supported by the bishop of Rome. After all, icon worship only increased loyalty to the church. In 787, Empress Irene, widowed and mother of an infant successor, revealed that she was an ardent icon worshiper. She persuaded, or ordered, the patriarch of Constantinople, to follow suit, and in 787 she convened the Seventh Ecumenical Council in Nicaea to agree. Then she had iconoclasm condemned. The council distinguished between "worship" and "veneration" of icons. The former, invocation for help and salvation, was prohibited; the latter, just honoring them as exemplary Christians, was allowed—a very subtle, confusing distinction. The decision may have influenced artists who created icons without showing the real features (as in a photograph), reflecting a two-dimensional heavenly spirituality rather than a three-dimensional earthly reality. Rumor has it that bishops censured artists and believers when the nose of an icon seemed to be so real that it tempted touching as a means to experience supernatural power. When iconoclasts gained power again, Empress Theodora, ruling for her infant son, summoned a council in 842, re-establishing the use of icons. So widows and mothers played the decisive roles in the controversy.

East-west relations deteriorated further in 800 when Pope Leo III crowned the most powerful convert of the "barbarian invasions" (dubbed by historians "the migration of peoples," *Völkerwanderung* in German), the Frankish king Charles I, as emperor during the Christmas Mass at St. Peter's in Rome using the title "Holy Roman Emperor." The king had come to Rome to protect the pope from attacks by the Roman nobility who disliked the papal competition for royal glory. The act of coronation attributed glory to both emperor and pope. The worshiping crowd hailed the new emperor as "the most pious Augustus" (from the Latin *augustus*, "venerable"), the title of the extinct heathen Roman emperors. People loved to see the glory of Rome preserved as "Christian." The title inferred that Charles inherited the power of ancient Rome, linked to the pope as the supreme authority for all Christians. Now the tradition of the fusion of church and state was further strengthened. An emotional crowd played into the hands of the pope, identifying him with the glory of pagan Rome. Soon, this new power of the pope was "proven" by a series of sensational forgeries similar to the

---

3. According to NOAD, "Iconoclasm" also refers to "the action of attacking or assertively rejecting cherished beliefs and institutions of established values and practices."

"Donation of Constantine." The forgeries use an impressive pseudonym pointing to the famous Spanish scholar Isidore of Seville (c. 360–435). But its author was Isidore Mercator, an otherwise unknown scholar who put together "letters" and "decretals" of popes in legalese. Preserved as *The Decretals of Pseudo-Isidore*, they contain a *Book of Popes*, a history of the "apostolic succession" from Peter to Leo IIII. The forgery was accepted as genuine literature for eight centuries, until 1628 when the Protestant Reformed (Calvinist) historian David Blondel (1591–1655) unmasked it. Even the most ardent defenders of papal apostolic succession agreed with Blondel since he also demonstrated that the only female pope Johanna (855–857), known from anti-papal hearsay since the thirteenth century and made popular by Protestants in the sixteenth and seventeenth centuries, was a fabricated legend.[4] The crudest part of the Isidorean forgery were letters attributed to the bishops of Rome and their mandate that they are free from any lay control.

Emperor Charles I (768–814), also known as "Charlemagne" (French for "Charles the Great") intensified the distance from the east by cementing the wall with a Germanic culture through educational reforms, beginning with an elitist Palace School in Aachen, Germany, headed by the British scholar and bishop Alcuin (735–804). He became Charlemagne's trusted advisor, tutored his children, and established schools throughout the empire. He created an image of the emperor as the divinely chosen leader to create a better world. But nothing could be further from the truth: Charles's eldest son rebelled against him; he sired a number of illegitimate children while married; and his only surviving son, Louis, could not prevent political corruption and cultural decay. The remaining northern tribes fought each other, ignoring the rule of the Frankish emperors.

The case of Photius is a telling example of political machination and manipulation in the tug-of-war between East and West. It is a situation-tragedy albeit with comic features. In 858, Photius was appointed patriarch of Constantinople by the Byzantine emperor Michael who had deposed Ignatius, a sympathizer of Rome. Photius, a layman, was awarded all required priestly offices within six days even though it normally took years to acquire them. The deposed Ignatius persuaded Pope Nicholas I to condemn Photius for having been improperly ordained, and Ignatius was again made

---

4. Scholars guess that she may have been a well-educated young woman from Mainz, Germany, and was said to have appeared in men's clothes representing Pope John Anglicus. "Popess Joan" in NCE.

patriarch. Photius, in turn, deposed Ignatius, convoked his own council in 867, and condemned the papal mission to Bulgaria where Eastern Orthodoxy had established a strong foot-hold. Shortly, thereafter, an ambitious member of the Byzantine court, Basil, assassinated Emperor Michael, seized the throne, forced Photius to resign, and reinstated Ignatius. When Pope Nicholas I died, his successor, Hadrian II, excommunicated Photius, hoping for better relations with the East. But Patriarch Ignatius viewed the papal action as an interference in the internal affairs of the Byzantine government. Moreover, to show his disdain for Rome, he successfully sought reconciliation with Photius—echoing the sailor's wisdom, "Any port in a storm." After all, "Love your enemy," if it helps defeat a more dangerous one! So the two Easterners united against the pope in the West. Photius did not last long as patriarch. Another eastern ruler, Leo VI, hated him and exiled him to a monastery where he died in 891. The case of Photius demonstrates the fortunes of ecclesiastical cultural wars and the vicissitudes of Christian history.

New theological material was added to the wall in the West from the work of Boethius (c. 480–524) who had translated Aristotle's works on logic from Greek into Latin, thus transmitting the philosophical structure for later, medieval, theology. It rests on the foundational Aristotelian principle that worldly reality is constituted by self-sufficient "substances" that are perceived in "forms" (*accidentes* in Latin). This earthly, physical reality is linked to a metaphysical world, like an inverted pyramid: "physical" categories move from the bottom to the top, the "prime mover" or "God" who, like a linchpin, connects with the invisible, meta-physical "world"—a convenient exercise of thinking that looks like a rational "proof."[5] Boethius created a spa for popular metaphysical gymnastics, keeping the church as "the body of Christ" lean and mean. Theologians and bureaucrats became control freaks, trying to create institutional uniformity, marked by uniformed officials. But Boethius became victim of Western Roman Catholic power politics which suspected him of treasonable correspondence with Greek Orthodox leaders in Constantinople. Before his execution, he consoled himself by writing a treatise on the liberating power of philosophy, *Consolation of Philosophy*. It became a medieval bestseller.

---

5. One can "prove" the existence of God, for example, by moving from the bottom of the pyramid to its top, from the many to the one, assuming that one can always think of something higher than one thought of before, and in the end there is only "one," the highest "being."

Christendumb

But matters got worse. Popes used the quarrels between Frankish kings to strengthen their power after 800. Papal power, unchecked by secular leaders, led to a cultural decline, especially in Italy. It produced a radical decay of culture in Rome. From 896 until 962 there was a "pornocracy."[6] Rich Roman families feuded with each other for power. They "elected" twenty popes in sixty-seven years using them as political toys. At one time, the widow of a senator controlled Rome, and the pope, using her sex appeal. She married three more times to stay on top. Hearsay made her teenage daughter the concubine of a pope; their illegitimate son became Pope John XII (the only "evidence" of a pope who was the son of a pope). The widow was finally defeated by her son, a product of her third marriage who continued her tyranny in his own way. The crowning of Emperor Otto I in 962 stopped the cultural decay in the West. He used his power in Germany for church reforms in Italy, especially in the church where the two most enduring prime ecclesiastical sins dominated: simony, the sale of offices for the highest bidders, and the violation of clerical celibacy. Otto used the power of the state to lift the church from its moral morass. Popes became servants of emperors who appointed them. In this sense, Germans told Italians what to do. This state of affairs is illustrated by the fact that Otto deposed the infamous pope John XII in 963 and made a layman pope, Leo VIII (963–965).

Pope Leo IX (1049–1054) tried to oppose such a political intrusion by having himself elected through the clergy and people of Rome, playing the role of a penitent reformer. Since popularity is not reliable, and to avoid increasing criticism, he created a fail-safe election method: he used the title "cardinal" (from the Latin *cardo*, "door-hinge"), given to a group of renowned clergy in Rome in the sixth century, then also to specially elected bishops outside of Rome, and constituted them as a "senate," as it were, to elect a pope from their midst. But it took some time until 1271, to make the group of cardinals a "conclave" (from the Latin *con clavis*, "a locked room") which elected one of its members as pope—the only elected office on the Roman Catholic Church. When the restless Christian Normans launched one of their military ventures from France ("Normandy") to Italy, Pope Leo IX fought them with his own army but was defeated in 1053 and kept in

---

6. From the Greek *porneia*, "harlotry," and *krateo*, to rule"—"the rule of harlots." The Roman Catholic historian Robert Baronius (1538–1607) used this term to describe this period; drawing on its facts and fiction. Some historians call it "dark age" (from the Latin *saeculum obscurorum*), limited to the city of Rome, though sometimes applied to the "Middle Ages."

custody. He died one year later, but not before condemning the patriarch of Constantinople for refusing papal jurisdiction. The incident also reveals the confusion of ecclesiastical and secular power: popes as "generals" of armies when the spiritual weapon of excommunication did not work.

The Benedictines assisted in the work of reform in the west by creating many new monasteries, guided by the one in Cluny, France. They also had been successful missionaries in the north, led by Ansgar who created an archbishopric in Hamburg in 831 and successfully evangelized Denmark and Sweden; he was known as "the apostle to Scandinavia." After the Holy Roman Empire in the West recovered with Emperor Otto the Great in 962, he renewed the old promise to protect the papacy just as Charlemagne had done in 800.

In 1054, the tug-of-war between East and West ended in a schism. A papal delegation appeared in Constantinople, strutted to its religious center, the Hagia Sofia church, and solemnly deposited a "bull" of excommunication (from the Latin *bulla*, "bubble," or "seal") addressed to Patriarch Michael Celarius. Shortly thereafter, Celarius countered with his own bull against Pope Leo X. The schism between Eastern Orthodoxy and Roman Catholicism was sealed. Now the wall between East and West had become a permanent symbol of mutual condemnation.

Greek customs were eliminated in the West, especially the part of the Eastern rite of Holy Communion with the officiating priest hidden behind the altar. Eastern patriarchs reciprocated by prohibiting western Latin customs, such as flaunting the priestly power of the Mass in the miracle of "transubstantiating" Christ into bread and wine. The East made fasting a requirement: on the eve before Sunday; in the first week Lent the consumption of fatty food (milk, butter, and cheese) was prohibited. National churches were established, led by patriarchs, especially in the mission fields of the Balkan (Bulgaria), in Eastern Europe (Moravia, now the Czech Republic), and in Russia. Mystical and ascetic tendencies hampered church relations in the East since bishops or "metropolitans," led by patriarchs, did not cooperate as well as did bishops in the West where the pope embodied and exercised supreme power. The enduring key issue between East and West was the Western version of the Nicene Creed with its insertion that the Holy Spirit proceeds from the "Father" *and the Son* (*filioque* in Latin).[7] News of the Western innovations made the patriarch of Constantinople remove the name of the pope from the diptychs at the altar (used like a book with two hinges listing leaders of the church). Calls for reunion ceased.

7. Above, 37.

Christendumb

The infamous Christian crusades intensified the hostility between Rome and Constantinople. After the first crusade in 1095, the Latin crusaders not only murdered Muslims but also Byzantine Christians. A "children's crusade," said to involve about 30,000, ended in death, slavery, and other terrors. In 1204, crusaders sacked Constantinople, an event bewailed in a dramatic description by a contemporary Greek historian[8]—one of the dumbest and most blasphemous events in the history of Christianity! The Catholic crusaders stole most of its religious treasures in the famous cathedral, the Hagia Sophia, even destroying the altar in order to sell its pieces. They showed up later, with other pieces, in France and Italy. Precious items, such as pieces of the cross from the crucifixion of Jesus and other relics earned much money in Rome and other Roman Catholic centers. The crusaders were merciless terrorist, killing babies, raping nuns, and burning books. Moreover, the literary treasure of the city, more books than inhabitants, was destroyed or stolen—the literary treasure of the ancient world.

The powers of church and state in the East deteriorated while in the West papal and imperial rulers strengthened their rule. Christians became a tiny minority in the East, but endured in a civilized co-existence with Islam. In 1274, an Ecumenical Council in Lyons, France, made a feeble attempt for a reunion. But the attempt was motivated by a political power play rather than by a desire for Christian unity. Charles of Anjou, conqueror and king of Sicily, brother of King Louis IX of France, had ambitions to become Byzantine emperor through a crusade. The threatened Byzantine emperor, Michael VIII, offered to unite Greek Orthodoxy with Rome if the pope would oppose the invasion of Charles of Anjou. A Greek Orthodox envoy to the council even agreed to accept the controversial Western addition to the Creed of Nicaea, the "filioque" (the Holy Spirit proceeds also from the Son). But other Orthodox leaders rejected any union with Rome. Moreover, Charles of Anjou had to struggle with a revolt in Sicily, the "Sicilian Vesper" of 1282;[9] the union deal was off. Other minor attempts towards a

---

8. Nicetas Choniates (c. 1155–1215), *History* (*Historia*) of the Roman empire from 1118-1207). I used a translation of the segment on the "sack" by D. C. Munro, *Translations and Reprints from the Original Sources of European History*, Series 1, Vol. 3:1, 15–16.

9. So named because the revolt began during the "Vespers" (Evening Prayers, from the Latin *vesper*, "evening") during Lent on March 30. The French had occupied Sicily in 1130, lost control in the revolt, and the island became occupied by other powers, among them Germans under Emperor Fredrick (1122–90), the first emperor known as "Holy Roman Emperor," also named "Barbarossa" (from the Italian *barba* rossa, "red beard"). Revered in Germany for his glory, he became the subject of a legend that said he did not die but was asleep in a cave in Berchtesgaden, Bavaria, where he would rise to lead a new

union were made until the fifteenth century when Constantinople was captured by the Muslim Turks in 1453, ending all Christian influence. Kemal Atatürk, who served as president of the republic of Turkey (1923-1938), introduced religious liberty to make Turkey a modern secular state.

After Eastern Orthodoxy had a successful "Slavic mission" in Eastern Europe, Russia competed with Rome and Constantinople. Moscow became "the third Rome." Russian Orthodox leaders patted themselves on the back as the preservers of Orthodoxy since, in their judgment, Rome and Constantinople had messed up Christianity with relentless power plays, heresies, and a decay of morals. Russian Orthodox churchmen spread the notion that God had sent pagans, the Germanic tribes, to punish unfaithful Christians in the West, and enemies of Christianity, Muslims, to punish them in the East.

But the abusive fusion of church and state also appeared in Russia when Ivan the Terrible (1547-1584) became the first "Czar" (from the Latin *Caesar*) and proclaimed himself "successor of the Roman emperors" and protector of the church—a spitting image of Charlemagne. "Caesaropapism" had become "Ceasaropatriarchism" when the Czar made the patriarch in Moscow the head of the church. Now megalomania raised its ugly head also in the East. One patriarch called himself "The Great Sovereign," another, an ideological liturgist, mandated that the sign of the cross be made with three fingers raised, not two, as had been the custom; he may have honored the Trinity in this manner. Opponents of such liturgical changes split from the church and became known as "old ritualists" or "old believers"; they were persecuted and many were burned at the stake. Some of them believed that persecution signaled the end of the world. Others looked at the Greek Orthodox Church as a replacement of the Russian Orthodox Church. In 1721, Czar Peter the Great responded by abolishing the office of patriarch in favor of a "Holy Synod"; it consisted of bishops controlled by the Czar. Such action caused the underground "old believers" to view the Czar as the Antichrist. Some even wanted a "priest-less" church opposed to the Czarist state.

Empress Catherine II (1762-1796) reacted with anger to these issues and declared all monastic property possessions of the state. This measure made Russia a fertile field of sects. Many turned to mysticism, some to Free

---

glorious Germany. In the 1930s, Adolf Hitler built his personal retreat in Berchtesgaden, fancying himself to be Barbarossa (even though his small mustache was a degrading substitute for the imperial beard that was to keep growing through the centuries).

Masonry. Fanatics were known as "Flagellants," "Spirit Wrestlers," "Milk Drinkers." Some linked up with mystical dualists who, like the ancient Gnostics, shunned the physical world as evil. In the seventh century, the "Paulicians" (named after the apostle Paul) adhered to a dualism of matter and spirit. They survived on the Balkan as "Bogomiles" (named after a priest) until the thirteenth century. They rejected major traditional Christian teachings, such as the Trinity and sacraments, advocating an ascetic life style excluding marriage. At the end of the eighteenth century, a group practiced self-castration, the "Scopts" as a mark of radical abstention (based on Matt 19:12)—trying to be a holy cut above others! Russian Orthodox spirituality survived through centers like Optino, a famous hermitage ("dwelling of a hermit"), which attracted pilgrims, like the renowned Russian writers Nikolai Gogol (1809–1852), Fyodor Dostojevsky (1821–1881), and Count Leo Tolstoy (1828–1910). The Russian Communist Revolution of 1917/18 ended the Czarist fusion of church and state, indeed defined "religion" as an "opiate of the people." But deep-rooted Orthodox Christianity prevailed. During the dictatorship of Joseph Stalin (1879–1953) the Orthodox Church cooperated with him in the life and death struggle against the forces of Adolf Hitler during World War II. After 1945, an unsteady peaceful coexistence revealed that Stalin neither praised nor persecuted the church; and Orthodox Christians did not openly oppose their agnostic government. Alliances between church and state weakened, indeed disappeared.

Some Eastern Orthodox churches accepted a union with the Roman Catholic Church. They are known as "uniate" churches, and they adhere to papal authority without any significant changes in their spirituality. Traditional worship and cultural customs stay in place. "Uniate" churches appeared in Romania in 1712, in Armenia in 1748, and in Bulgaria in 1839.

In 1948, Orthodox churches became members of the World Council of Churches and participated in efforts towards a global visible unity of churches. The Roman Catholic Church is not a member of the world body. But Pope John XXIII opened his church to ecumenical dialogue in the Second Vatican Council (1962–1965), and he advocated new negotiations with Greek Orthodoxy. In 1965 an opening was created in the wall of separation: Pope Paul VI and Patriarch Athenagoras I cancelled the mutual excommunication of 1054. But this decision did not create any agreements. It was a sign of repentance that could have created a hole in the wall for ecumenical feelers. But such feelers were not extended by either side, probably because Roman Catholicism claims to represent the only "true" church. Consequently, Rome views the achievement of Christian unity as a return to Roman Catholicism. Such a view is disappointing in the light of the plurality of churches in addition to Greek Orthodox ones. Today, 300 million Greek Orthodox Christians are represented by an Ecumenical Patriarch, Bartholomew I, with tiny, humble, and isolated headquarters in Istanbul, Turkey, where ninety-nine percent of the population is Muslim.

Popes continued to win in their power games. Most Germanic territories relinquished their "Arian" (non-Trinitarian) Christianity and adhered to the Roman orthodox faith. The success of the popes was symbolized by artists in pictures of St. Peter carrying the keys of the door to heaven and opening it for departed souls. The British monk Columbanus (d. 615) is credited for advocating a "veneration of St. Peter as the gatekeeper of heaven." Such advertisement for the papacy only increased the separation of East and West. Only the Eastern practice of individual auricular confession was approved in the west. It originated as a monastic custom when the abbot ordered his monks to confess secret sins every evening to one of the brothers. Soon lay people were asked to do the same; private confession became a mandate in 1215 as a prerequisite to first Holy Communion at age seven. The popular belief in the immortality of the soul also created the custom of "Masses for the dead" and the image of purification in a "purgatory" between death and resurrection.[10] It echoed Germanic pagan notions of a cult of the dead, assisting the living.

What irked Greek Orthodox patriarchs the most was the increase in papal political power through its relation to the newly converted Christian emperors, beginning with Charlemagne in 800. Greek Orthodoxy had originally acknowledged a God-willed union of church and state. But the schismatic wall between East and West and the power of Muslim rulers forced the shift from a fusion of church and state to a formation of independent "autocephalous" (from the Greek autos, "self," and *kephale*, "head") national churches, headed by an Ecumenical Patriarch, chosen by bishops as "first among equals." What constitutes unity is the divinization of believers through the mysteries of worship, not uniformity in doctrine and politics. This doctrine of "theosis" (from the Greek *theos*, "God," and *usia*, "being")

---

10. "Purgatory" (from the Latin *purgare*, "cleansing") is a place where souls expiate remaining sins before going to heaven. Church fathers use 1 Cor 3:14–15 as a proof text (being saved through fire), and the church adopted the Jewish notion of a "hell" (*Sheol* in Hebrew) where God "kills and brings to life," 1 Sam 2:6). Dogmatic definition in 1274. "Purgatory" in NCE.

teaches participation in the divine nature (based on 2 Peter 1:4 "you become participants of the divine nature"). Moreover, the power of mystery cautioned Greek Orthodox theologians to aim for doctrinal unity in ecumenical dialogues that have become popular since World War II, especially with the Roman Catholic Church which defined unity as obedience to the authority of the papal office. Moreover, to Orthodox eyes, unity is anchored in the celebration of Christ's presence, beginning with meditation and climaxing in the Eucharist. Institutionalized ecumenism looked like a market for negotiating doctrines, trading some for others until a compromise is achieved. Such a quest for unity revived memories of old contentions about "explanations" of the Trinity certified by councils.

Skyscrapers, Bunkers, and Sandboxes

On the western side of the wall, there was business as usual. Popes continued to enhance their power. It can be compared to the building of skyscrapers rising from small foundations and scraping the clouds in the sky. Saint Peter's Cathedral in Rome is the prime example, "the mother of all churches," an erection begun by Emperor Constantine in the fourth century. It was significantly expanded in 1509 at the height of papal power and completed in 1614 with a capacity of sixty thousand worshipers. The church is filled with tombs of popes and kings as well as with famous art, like the *Pieta* of Michelangelo Buonarroti. The cathedral is a symbol of Roman Catholicism as the only legitimate link to heaven.

The papal doctrinal ideology was fortified in bunkers staffed with minds who guarded the ecclesiastical system, dubbed "the medieval synthesis," with sophisticated notions designed to overcome any heresy. Most of these minds belonged to monks whose physical and spiritual skills were hard to match. But nothing is perfect. Occasionally, skyscraping minds produced notions that created embarrassing situations, indeed shook the foundations. There also were simple minds who, like playful children in a sandbox, generated a fragile spirituality that enjoyed God in a child-like faith.

The pope was guided by the Roman "Curia" (from the Latin *curia*, "meeting place"), the papal court with its various departments of government usually headed by a cardinal. An ornate papal headdress symbolized the increased power, a bejeweled Tiara, with one crown, expanded to three by 1314. It was an expression of princely secular power. The Episcopal "miter" (from the Greek *mitra*, "headband," worn by women in ancient Greece, a turban in Arabia) was added when the pope presided at the liturgy. Pope Gregory VII (1073–1085) viewed the Tiara as the symbol signaling the declaration that the pope was "the supreme ruler of the world." He compared the relationship between church and state to the one between the sun and the moon, the state being the moon receiving its light from the papacy. He fought his enemies with the sword, quoting the prophetic curse in Jeremiah 48:10, "accursed is the one who keeps back the sword from bloodshed." Gregory used it as a proof-text for his merciless crusades.

It is one of the many ironies of church history that Gregory's most dangerous opponent was Emperor Henry IV (1050–1106), also king of Germany. He resurrected the old tradition of his predecessor Otto I (912–973), namely, the right of "lay investiture"—the appointment of bishops as "prince bishops" entitled to govern their dioceses and even defend them with military force. When Henry IV appointed bishops in Italy, among them the powerful archbishop of Milano, Gregory threatened the emperor with excommunication, claiming that only the pope could appoint bishops. This was not an empty gesture because a papal ban was a mandate for all subjects to cancel their allegiance to their banned ruler. In 1076, the two sides engaged in a power play: the pope excommunicated the emperor and the emperor had his bishops in Germany depose the pope. The power play and its conclusion resembled the tragic and/or comic irony of a Shakespearian drama. When Henry learned that many German princes sided with the pope, he, his wife, and a servant fled to the Canossa Castle in the foothills of Tuscany, Italy, the fortified residence of a family friend, Countess Mathilda. It so happened that Gregory was also a guest there while traveling to Germany. Mathilda may have arranged the simultaneous visits, anticipating the rare entertainment of a clash between the two most powerful men of the century. In any case, Henry schemed for a removal of the papal ban. So he played the role of an ordinary Christian, doing penance before a priest and asking for absolution from punishment. First, Gregory refused. Henry put on ragged clothes and was said to have stood for three days (January 25–28, 1077) in ice and snow outside the castle asking for forgiveness. Gregory conceded that he had to do his priestly duty and withdraw the punishment of excommunication. One can only speculate what the deposed emperor confessed to the pope. The rest of the story revealed that not much changed.

German princes were appalled by the Canossa incident which they viewed as a humiliation of secular authority. Pride and prejudice continued the power play. The princes no longer trusted Henry and elected a rival who threw Germany into a civil war because Henry refused to resign. He defeated his rival and regained supremacy. So Gregory excommunicated him again, and Henry had bishops elect a rival pope, Clement III. The two popes stayed in office for two decades. (1080–1100). Henry stormed the city of Rome in 1083, and Gregory fled to Salerno, a harbor on the west coast, where he died. According to a tradition of preserving the final words of famous people, he, like other big guns, blamed others for his demise. The words also reflect the sit-com of his life and career: "I loved justice and hated iniquity. Therefore I die in exile."[11]

The issue of lay investiture was settled in favor of the popes. In 1122, the Concordat of Worms agreed on a compromise: the pope invests bishops with "spiritual power" as heads of their dioceses, symbolized by a ring (kissed by the subjects in an audience) and the staff (the sign of shepherding); and the king or emperor invests bishops with secular power (if they owned territories), symbolized by a scepter (from the Greek *skeptron*, "something to lean on," a "staff"). But this secular investiture existed only on paper and could only be realized after the conquest of a "prince bishop." Popes no longer descended from their main corporate office on top of their skyscraper, as Pope Gregory VII did, for close combat with an emperor. They issued their orders with little, if any resistance. Moreover, they were supported and defended by monastic orders which became the bunkers where the Roman Catholic tradition was fortified in an ascetic style of life.

One such bunker was constructed in 1084 by Bruno, a French teacher and administrator who founded an order in La Grande Chartreuse, near Grenoble. He vowed that the order would never need reform—in contrast to the moral decline of Christian life in and outside its monastic confines. Bruno and a dozen disciples abandoned much of the well-known French cuisine. They fasted, French style, of course: eating no meat and drinking watered wine; on Sundays they indulged in eggs and cheese. Only limited conversation was allowed and sleeping in hairy shirts was the order of the night. Lay brothers were drafted to live in houses next to the monastery to provide the few physical needs of the "Carthusians" (named after the town Chartreuse). The monks did manual labor and copied books. Their meditation was highlighted by the funeral liturgy, the "Night Offices for the Dead," from midnight to about 3:00 p.m. After some time, women joined the order, but in very limited numbers. The Carthusians are known still today as the strictest Roman Catholic order.

11. "Gregory VII" in NCE.

In 1098, the Benedictine abbot Stephan Harding founded another strict order, "Cistercian," named after the French city of Citeaux meaning "stagnant cisterns" (near Dijon) guided by a tough discipline absent in the Rule of Benedict. It could be said that the new order gave up the mild Benedictine Liqueur and switched to the pungent Dijon Mustard. The Cistercian Rule bound monasteries together under the supervision of a "chapter of abbots" who gathered annually to enforce a strict life, with simple worship, without any ornamentation and without any outside visitors. The monasteries were located in deserted places, often at the bottom of a valley while other monasteries could be seen on a hill or mountain. Monks continued the Benedictine work of farming, cattle-raising, and wine-making. But they also cleared forests, drained swamps, produced wool and a variety of new fruit in their gardens. They wore white garments (not well suited for the Cistercian labor with dirty soil). Next to each monastery was a nunnery headed by an abbess. Both communities were strictly separated. A nun could only receive a man who was a priest administering last rites when she was dying, and for her funeral. Cistercians also created an Institute for Lay Brothers who were subject to the Rule but were not allowed to have any leadership functions; they came from the lower social class and did the hard labor. Bernard of Clairvaux (1080–1153) was the first abbot and most renowned member, known for his diverse talents. His savvy settled divisive quarrels in favor of ecclesiastical unity; his French preaching attracted large crowds (who loved him even when they did not know French), and he inspired generations with his mystical devotion to Christ as a baby and especially as crucified in paintings. They were later identified with the "catchword" *Ecce Homo* (Latin for "Behold [see] the [tortured] man), the words of Pontius Pilate when he exhibited Jesus with a crown of thorns, asking to have nothing to do with him (John 19:5).[12] It was a parapsychic, indeed necrophilic, spirituality marked by focusing on the crucified body-parts. The rationale for such a focus was the notion that a link to the body of Jesus at his crucifixion was the means to unite the soul of believers with the resurrected Christ who had become their polygamous "bridegroom." The spiritual experience was depicted in the erotic language of the biblical Song of Songs, Bernard's favorite biblical book. Such a spirituality was a far cry from the cool, rational theological reflections based on the mind, not the body, if one uses the model of Aristotle. Yet this discrepancy did not

---

12. The scene of Pilate and Jesus inspired many painters, above all the Dutch painter Rembrandt in 1634.

prevent the church from canonizing Bernard a saint who, by tradition, is an ideal to be imitated, indeed invoked for help.[13] Since the monks trained large dogs to find and save victims of mountain climbing and of avalanches, the St. Bernard dog made St. Bernard immortal in a secular way. To this extent, he, like the Dominican "dogs of the Lord," was a special breed. Bernard also praised the Templars as the order that combined spiritual and military power to save souls from the avalanches of heresy and paganism. Such advertisement made the Templars very popular. In the twelfth century, nuns imitated Bernard by an intensive devotion to the "heart of Jesus," depicted as pierced (by a Roman soldier at the crucifixion in John 19:34). Small paintings showed a bleeding open heart with other wounds, and nuns would become virtually ecstatic in their concentration on the picture. A similar practice was the devotion of Jesuits to pictures of the heart of Mary in the sixteenth century—erotic symptoms among men and women living in enforced celibacy?

In 1120, the desire to do things right produced another new monastic order known as the "Premonstratensian Canons" (from the Greek *kanon*, "rule" and the French town of Premontre), that is, priests who served in a diocese. It was founded by a friend of Bernard, Norbert of Xanten, who became archbishop of Magdeburg, Germany, where the Premonstratensians trained to work among the Wends (a Slavic tribe).

But the new ambitious religious orders did not criticize one of the worst collective sins of the church, the "crusades" against the Muslims in Palestine (1096–1270). "Hospital orders" came into being, dedicated to care for the victims of the crusades, beginning in Jerusalem in 1099. They consisted of groups of pilgrims from various countries. Members did not live in monasteries but took the three vows of poverty, chastity, and obedience. Again, the ever-present sins of pride and prejudice struck. Some members were knights who rejected hospital duty in favor of fighting the Muslim "infidels." They functioned as a military organization and took an additional oath to defend the church. The most famous group appeared

---

13. "Canonization" is a complex Roman Catholic "ruling" (from the Greek *kanon*, "rule"). First, there is "beatification," allowing a general veneration. Then, the life of a saint is investigated for heroic deeds; finally, the pope "canonizes" a dead saint after at least two miracles are attributed to him before being honored in worship and invoked for assistance as a member of the heavenly saints being with Christ and Mary, the foremost saint. In the New Testament, all members of the church are called "saints" (Rom 1:7, "God's beloved in Rome, who are called saints"). Canonized saints exist since c. 1000. "Beatification and Canonization" in NCE.

Edifice Complex

in 1119, known as "Templars" (from the Latin *milites templi*, "temple soldiers") because their group of eight French noblemen was permitted to live on the temple mount in Jerusalem to protect pilgrims. They were also known as "the poor fellow-soldiers of Christ," depicted by a horse with two riders symbolizing poverty. Each knight had to give all possessions to the order. They wore a white robe with a red cross and were commandeered by a "Grand Master" for life. In 1129, the papacy acknowledged the Templars as an order of the church. Their story is filled with drama and mystery. They quickly moved from poverty to riches through the acquisition of real estate and, according to legend, through the sale and exhibits of archeological treasures. Rumors circulated that among the collected treasures the Templars possessed the "holy grail," that is, the chalice Jesus used at the Last Supper. In any event, they threw the oath of poverty to the wind and eventually became the richest organization in Christendom, especially through banking, managing much of the church's finances in Paris, France, where they had established their own temple. But a power struggle between King Philip IV, "the Fair" of France and Pope Boniface VIII over the right of taxation of the clergy almost eradicated the Templars. The king used trumped-up charges, such as heresy, fornication, and black magic, as reasons for "treason." But the real reason for persecution was the confiscation of the Templar wealth. Mass arrests occurred on Friday 13, 1307—creating one of several legends of superstition regarding the number thirteen, combined with other legends about them. The Inquisition of the church hunted them down, and Pope Clement IV dissolved the order in 1312. Some Templars survived in Scotland and went underground as Free Masons in Germany in the eighteenth century.[14]

A German branch was founded as the "Teutonic Order" (from the Latin *teuton*, indo-European for "people")[15] in 1199 in northern Germany.

---

14. Free Masons were said to have been founded by fourteenth-century stonemasons who communicated with each other through secret signs. Businessmen founded a Grand Lodge in London in 1717. They accepted the philosophy of "Deism" in the European Enlightenment with its affirmation of an anti-Trinitarian God without a Christ through "natural reason," advocated by the philosopher David Hume (1711–1776). Members quickly spread to the continent and to the United States. In Italy Free Masons established a Roman Catholic Lodge in 1860 in Turin. Pope Leo XIII condemned them in 1884. Secret "illumination" became part of Free Masonry. They can be linked to ancient Christian Gnosticism. Above, 35.

15. "Indo-European," or "indo-German" is a three-thousand-year-old language, combining cultures ranging from India to Europe. A "Teutonic" tribe has been traced to the fourth century in Jutland, a peninsula now stretching from northern Germany to Denmark.

It consisted of knights, priests, and laymen. Emperor Frederick II gave them a northern German territory near the Baltic Sea known as "Prussia." They wore a black robe with a white cross and became Lutheran in the sixteenth century; they survived as a charity organization doing work in hospitals and in schools.

The "crusades" exhibit a dangerous combination of the arrogance of papal power, anti-Semitism, and mob mentality. Pope Urban II called for crusades because he saw himself as the commander of "St. Peter's Militia" (*militia sancti Petri* in Latin), ignoring the warning of Jesus during his arrest when a disciple used a sword to cut off the ear of a member of the arresting unit of the high priest (Matt 26:52: "all who take the sword shall perish by the sword"). The prophesy was fulfilled when Ottoman Turks stopped the crusades by wiping out about one hundred thousand crusaders in 1396 at the battle of Nicopolis in Bulgaria.

The logical pyramid of Aristotle became the foundation for the most popular theological skyscrapers. By the twelfth century, Muslim scholars had translated Aristotle into Arabic, and now Christian intellectuals hurried to translate the great Greek mind into Latin. They began to talk about a logic of Christianity, and soon argumentative tomes began to appear, the foundational structures of medieval ecclesiastical skyscrapers and, at times, bunkers. Most tomes originated and were manufactured at the new Christian intellectual center, the University of Paris, the Sorbonne (named after its founder Robert de Sorbon, c. 1257); these tomes became the mental edifices which, like the sky-line of modern cities dominated the mind of the "Middle Ages."[16] Its scholastic spirit became known through the sound-bite "faith seeking understanding," as Anselm of Canterbury (1033–1109) put it. A native of Italy, Anselm became a Benedictine abbot in France and an archbishop of Canterbury, known as a stark defender of the papacy. Anselm tried to "prove" that thinking of a God as a "rational" concept, demonstrates that God exists, is a "reality." Using the Aristotelian pyramid and Plato's supernatural world of ideas, one moves from the "many" at the bottom to the "one" at the top—God being "the prime mover." Then, another pyramid continues, upside down, revealing the supernatural world of the soul in

---

16. A traditional designation of European history from c. 500–1453, between the fall of the ancient Roman empire and the conquest of Constantinople by the Turks, marked by the emergence of separate kingdoms, the growth of trade, of urban life, and of the power of the Latin church in the West. The Middle Ages were followed by a revival of art in the Renaissance, linked to a critical philosophical movement, Humanism, in the fifteenth century—the beginning of modern times.

the company of God. Anselm also tried his syllogistic hand on a "theory of satisfaction," explaining why and how sinful human beings must be saved by God: sin against God must be satisfied; sinful human creatures cannot earn their salvation; so God saves them by becoming incarnate in Jesus.

The rabies of theologians (like the disease of mental confusion in animals, transmissible through saliva to humans), first evident in the controversies about the Trinity defined at the First Ecumenical Council of Nicaea in 325, once again infected the church. "Realists" argued on the basis of Aristotle that rational concentration on a single "thing" (*res* in Latin) leads to "universal" insights—"universal truths are in general things": (*universalia in rebus*). "Nominalists" contended that universal truths cannot be known but only "named" as abstractions of the human mind; they exist not in but "after the things" *(post res* in Latin). Centuries later, the German philosopher and principal voice of the European Enlightenment, Immanuel Kant (1724–1804), made mince-meat of both groups by drawing attention away from timeless Aristotelian logic to time and space.[17] This move encounters the relativity of human existence as a penultimate interim between birth and death. Such a context no longer permits any "proof" of a meta-physical reality, be it God or anything else.

One theologian foreshadowed Kant: the notorious French theologian, Peter Abelard (1079–1142), a fierce debater known for his scandalous love affair with a student, Heloise and his castration arranged by her uncle. Questioning the work of his predecessors, he built a bunker from where he attacked virtually everything. His weapon of choice was a literary diatribe titled *Yes and No [Sic et Non]*. He also wrote an autobiography, *The Story of My Misfortunes*. Abelard argued that any knowledge is grounded in "Nominalism—the doctrine that universals in general or general ideas are mere names without any corresponding reality, and that only particular objects exist; properties, numbers, and sets are thought of as merely features of the way of considering the things that exist."[18]

But most medieval theologians remained bewitched by Aristotle, disclosing their habit of imagining philosophy as the "handmaiden of theology" when, in reality, it was a slave used like a fist against opponents. The fusion of faith and reason created a hierarchy of truths, skyscrapers of logistics in support of the political ones built by the papal church. Churchmen in Rome added materials made of a mixture of laws, fortified with the

17. Below, 150.
18. NOAD.

ban of excommunication. Since 1200, they promoted higher education for Christian life at "universities." They were not schools for general "universal" knowledge, as they are today, but corporations of teachers and students for the purpose of developing vocations as the basis for an orderly, intelligent Christian life in the world. Eventually four areas of higher graduate education emerged: theology, law, medicine, and science. The pre-requisite of graduate education in the university was a mastery of "seven liberal arts": three fields (*trivium* in Latin) of basic communication—grammar, rhetoric, and dialectic; and four (*quadrivium* in Latin) basic skills—arithmetic, geometry, astronomy, and music. Examinations required debates with professors, based on assigned written topics and oral debates of them. Graduates received Master and Bachelor degrees (the latter being the equivalent of a modern doctor's degree).

The theological curriculum was based on a textbook by the Italian bishop and scholar Peter Lombard (c. 1100–1160), *Four Books of Sentences*. "Sentences" designated a set of propositions, "theses" that had to be studied as methodological guidelines for specific topics. He taught at Notre Dame and was bishop of Paris. The textbook summarizes four basic theological topics treated by theologians in the previous fifty years: 1) God; 2) creatures; 3) incarnation and redemption; 4) sacraments and last things. Lombard also listed the seven sacraments of Roman Catholicism: baptism, confirmation, penance, ordination, Eucharist, marriage, and final unction. Mastery of the *Sentences* was awarded with the degree of "Sententiary" (*sententiarius* in Latin). Lombard taught theologians to strive for a balance between "natural" and "supernatural" truths," the God-willed intent of a harmony between "creation" (stained by sin) and "re-creation" (achieved by faith in Christ). The two largest begging orders, "mendicant" (from the Latin *mendicare*, "begging") friars, supplied the theological brainpower for theological skyscrapers, the Franciscans and the Dominicans.

The Franciscans, founded in Italy by Francis of Assisi (1181–1228), called themselves the "order of the minor brethren" (*ordo fratrum minorum* in Latin, abbreviated as O. F. M.). Francis, the son of a rich Italian clothier, converted to radical poverty, based on Matt 10:9–10 (the sending of the apostles without any personal possessions). February 24, 1208 is celebrated as "the day of St. Francis' marriage to poverty." Francis was a peculiar person, indeed an odd-ball, growing up playing in a spiritual sand-box: he changed places with a beggar at St. Peter's in Rome; he embraced a leper (equivalent to kissing an HIV patient today), he heard Christ speaking to him from a painting, he became a hermit, he used money from begging for church repairs, and he received the "stigmata" (from the Greek *stigma*, "a mark made by a pointed instrument")—"marks corresponding to those left on Jesus' body by the Crucifixion, said to have been impressed by divine favor on the bodies of St. Francis and others."[19] Francis's proverbial love of nature is attested in his love for animals and his popular "Canticle to the Sun." Francis also attracted a wealthy young heiress, Clare, persuaded her to give up her possessions, cut her hair, and took her to a retreat. Following his example, throngs of homeless followers begged in the streets of rapidly developing cities, and by 1253 the church approved an order of "Franciscans" with nuns called "Poor Ladies."

The zeal for poverty was also exhibited by a group of lay people in Italy, led by a French merchant, Peter Waldo in 1170. He sold his possessions as a protest against the riches in the church. His followers were known as "Waldenses." They had a child-like faith in their own sand-box. But since they criticized the pope for not being poor like Jesus, Pope Innocent III condemned them as heretics—obviously in defense of the status quo which was a far cry from the biblical ideal of the simple life, rejecting "Mammon" (Matt 6:24). So it was a matter of "Mammonites" versus "Waldenses," a very uneven match. The latter built their own secret bunker, as it were, in the French Alps where they established their own simple church. Pope Innocent III launched a crusade against them in 1209. But the "Waldenses" survived and became "forerunners of the Protestant Reformation"; they maintain a small but thriving Seminary a stone's throw from the Vatican in Rome— a small, but sharp, thorn in the flesh of the Vatican. They and the Franciscans represent an oxymoron in the annals of history: whereas the Waldenses were persecuted for their call to poverty, the Franciscans were praised for it. Moreover, simple ideals often spawn radical movements. Some Italian Franciscans joined a radical Cistercian, Joachim of Flora, who predicted the end of the world in 1260.[20] The "Fraticelli," as they were called (Latin for "little brothers"), shared the fate of the Waldenses.

The Dominicans, named after the Spaniard Dominic (1170–1221), became an "order of preachers" (*ordo fratrum praedicatorum* in Latin, abbreviated as O. P.) who wanted to communicate teachings to believers who doubted or violated Roman Catholic doctrine. They were nicknamed "dogs of the Lord" (*Domii canes*, a Latin a pun of their name)—the crew

19. NOAD.
20. See above, 28.

in a bunker trained to snuff out and defeat suspicious visitors of the papal skyscraper. Dominic was the opposite of Francis: of noble birth, well educated, and a fierce crusader against the heretical "Cathari." The ambitious Pope Innocent III quickly granted the establishment of an order when Dominic had attracted sixteen followers. He adopted the Rule of St. Augustine followed by the "Augustinian Hermits." Dominicans focused on study, preaching, and mobility. The monastery served as a retreat center for finding ways to combat heresy and to convert pagans. Church and state used the Dominicans to preserve religious uniformity through inquiry and inquisition.[21] Dominicans also shaped academia, patterned after the world-renowned university of Paris. "Dominican Sisters," however, were limited to the education of girls to become good wives and mothers. Unlike in the real dog world, only males could be "the dogs of the Lord," on special assignment to guard the papal skyscrapers.

The Franciscans and the Dominicans created the most formidable bunkers and silos of doctrine for the medieval "scholastic theology." Like seasoned medical doctors, the best theologians were known by titles disclosing their specialties. The British Franciscan scholar Alexander of Hales (c. 1180–1245), known as "the unbreakable doctor" (*doctor irrefragabilis* in Latin), taught in Paris and published a massive textbook of theology. He is known for two influential doctrines. 1) The doctrine of "Concomitance": since Christ is in both bread and wine in the Eucharist, it is valid if only one element is offered (if you get the one it is as good as if you get both). In 1215, Rome used the doctrine to withhold the wine from the laity—presumably to avoid the danger of spilling. Only the priest drank the wine. 2) The doctrine of the "treasure of merits" (*thesauros* [Greek for "storage"] *meritorum* [Latin for "merits"]): the abundant merits, accumulated

---

21. The "Inquisition" was created in 1232 as a papal department to preserve the purity of doctrine and to eliminate heresy. "Inquisitors" were subject only to the pope and resembled the special police of modern dictators. They interpreted and enforced the laws of church and state. When in trouble, they had the right to absolve one another from excommunication. An Inquisition began in a suspicious region with a "proclamation of grace" (usually one month) calling for voluntary confession and repentance of heresy; the punishment was light (fasting, pilgrimages, or works of charity). Then, subjects would be apprehended and faced two witnesses whose identity was not revealed. Inquisitors were both prosecutors and judges. Subjects had no defenders and had to prove their innocence in interrogations. In 1252, Pope Innocent IV permitted torture. Sentences were pronounced in public as an "act of faith" (*auto-da-fe* in Portuguese), a public pledge of the attending crowd to support the Inquisition. Punishment consisted of excommunication, confiscation of property, exile, life imprisonment, and burning at the stake by the state as the church's executioner. "Inquisition" in NCE.

by Christ who was "without sin" (Heb 4:15) and paid on the cross "for the sins of the whole world" (1 John 2:2), have created a "treasure," increased by the merits of canonized saints. The whole treasure was given to the church to grant forgiveness of sins through "indulgences—the extra-sacramental remission of the temporal punishment of sins granted by the church in the exercise of the power of the keys (given to Peter and his successors, Matt 16:19) through the application of the superabundant merits of Christ and of the saints."[22] The doctrine was converted into an eternal decree through a papal bull by Pope Clement VI in 1343. One of Alexander's students was the Italian Franciscan Bonaventure (1221–1274), known as the "seraphic doctor" (*doctor seraphicus*) because students thought of a hierarchy of angels when they studied his amazing arrangement of topics that exuded an attractive mysticism. The German Dominican Albert the Great (*Albertus magnus*, (1193–1280), known as "the doctor of universal knowledge" (*doctor universalis*), researched the relation of theology to natural science.

Pope Innocent III (1198–1216), one of the most powerful CEOs in Rome, cemented scholastic theology into church doctrine and practice. He did so by repeating the claim of superiority over secular rulers with an emphasis on the Petrine "apostolic succession" as a succession of ancient Greek and Roman power to the German emperor Charlemagne. Consequently, any election of an emperor must be approved by the pope. Innocent practiced what he preached. In 1212, he excommunicated King John of England for refusing to appoint Stephen Langton as archbishop of Canterbury; and he ordered the French king to invade England to punish John. John surrendered England to the pope who returned it to him as a fief. Hence John was known as "King John without a land." In 1213, Innocent lifted the ban of excommunication. This application of papal superpower had interesting consequences. British barons used the weakness of their king to gain individual rights in the famous Magna Carta of 1215 which sowed the seed for a constitutional government. The pope's ban of it remained a gesture without any effect.

At age thirty-seven, Innocent III celebrated his papal superpower at the Fourth Lateran Council of 1215. In three weeks he instituted seventy-nine arbitrary canons or decrees without any opposition from four hundred bishops, nine-hundred abbots and priors, envoys from almost every European country; and two thousand other participants. Innocent also ordered another cruel crusade to the Holy Land; it turned out to be an

---

22. "Indulgence" in NCE.

unsuccessful attempt to put Greek Orthodoxy under papal control. The Fourth Lateran Council established enduring features of Christian life in the West: the papacy is divinely willed; obligatory auricular confession of sins before first communion at age seven (motivating parents to tell kids what to confess), followed by annual Confession to a priest; the Eucharistic doctrine of "transubstantiation";[23] ordination of celibate males at age twenty-five resulting in a unique "indelible" sacramental disposition that not even the church can remove (*character indelebilis* in Latin). Moreover, Innocent prohibited the formation of new monastic orders because he feared that too much diversity threatened uniformity guarded by the pope. But the prohibition existed only on paper and monastic orders continued to flourish. The Council also decreed that Jews and Moslems must be known in public: Jews had to wear a yellow patch, or a cone-shaped special hat in some regions; Moslems had to wear a blue patch. Rumor increased that the pope was the Antichrist. When Pope Gregory IX accused Emperor Frederick II of disobedience, the emperor made the accusation "Antichrist" official and besieged Rome in 1241. Gregory excommunicated Frederick, then died in the midst of the quarrel. A successor lasted a few months, but there was no pope for the next two years—another broken chain n the apostolic succession of Roman bishops.

The struggle between church and state created one of the greatest disasters in Roman Catholicism: the "Babylonian captivity of the papacy," as the satirical Italian philosopher Francis Petrarch (1304–1374) called it (analogous to the captivity of the people of Israel, 585–536 BCE). Between 1309 and 1377, seven popes transferred their residence to Avignon, France, where they lived with great pomp and circumstance. But their only legacy was the production of a popular wine, "Chateaneuf-du-pape" ("the castle of the pope"). From 1377 to 1415 two popes ruled the church, one in Avignon and the other in Rome, excommunicating each other. They were threatened by a third pope, elected by a council of bishops in Pisa, Italy. Another council, held in Constance, Germany (1414–1415), finally ended the schism by

---

23. Grounded in Aristotelian philosophy, the doctrine uses the distinction between "substance" (*substantia*) and "form" (*accidens*). Example: I am "substantially" a human being and "accidentally" a person with specific biological characteristics (short, tall, male, etc.). The resurrected Christ is the "substance" present in physical "accidents" of bread and wine. When the priest intones the "Words of Institution" ("This is my body . . ."), the elements of bread and wine become the substance of Christ. But the "accidents" (his historical "form" of flesh and blood) remain absent—there is no "transaccidentation."

removing the third pope, John XXIII[24] and electing Martin V as the one and only pope. The papal skyscraper in Rome began to crumble.

The papal schism was caused by the age-old idolatry of "mammon," namely, the accumulation of wealth through taxation of the clergy and the monasteries by the state. Pope Boniface VIII (1294–1303) declared in a bull that only the pope can do it. Secular rulers would be excommunicated if they continued their taxation. The papacy had become the richest power in Europe, with an elaborate bureaucracy and armed forces; the ceremonial "Swiss Guards" are a symbolic remnant of the papal army.[25] Secular rulers lobbied to get their share of riches. France took the lead in the struggle with Rome. King Philip IV, known as "the Fair," was supported by all classes of French citizens when he refused to oblige the pope. Boniface VIII retorted with a harsh bull in 1302, titled *Unam Sanctam* (the first two words were used as its title). It made obedience to the pope a matter of salvation: "For every human creature it is necessary for salvation to be subject to the authority of the Roman Pontiff."[26] The claim was backed by a casual biblical reference to "two swords" (Luke 22:38) as proof-text that the pope controls "secular" and "spiritual" authority. Frederick had a military commando arrest the pope a year later. Weak and demoralized, Boniface VIII died shortly thereafter. Under the political thumb of French kings; his successors moved to Avignon.

The city of Rome had become the playground of ambitious local politicians, and Philip seemed to be the only protector of the pope who happened to be a former French archbishop, Clement V. He moved to Avignon in 1309. It was Philip who ordered the pope to condemn the Templars in France because of their financial power.[27] When Pope John XXII (1316–1334) banned King Louis of Bavaria because he had not sought papal approval, German and Italian nobles stuck to the king who had himself anointed in Rome by a counter-pope, Nicholas V. In the midst of this scandalous turmoil, one sane voice was heard. The president of the University of Paris, Marsilius of Padua, published a revolutionary treatise in 1324 titled "Defender of the Peace" (*defensor pacis* in Latin). It called

---

24. This pope is not listed in the official succession of popes. The true John XXIII served from 1958–1963.

25. Until the sixteenth century, many Swiss men made a living as mercenaries in foreign armies. A small unit of about two hundred contracted to be the bodyguard of the pope and a ceremonial police of the Vatican.

26. "Unam Sanctam" in NCE.

27. Below, 81.

for an end of independent papal power. Peace could only become a reality, Marsilius contended, when church and state are controlled by the citizens of a country and its laws. Needless to say, such a reactionary proposal, foreshadowing modern democracy, made Marsilius the target of papal wrath. But the new emperor, Louis of Bavaria, protected him, indeed made him an imperial ambassador in Rome! Moreover, the Franciscans also supported the emperor because the pope had criticized them for taking poverty too seriously and thus become estranged from their rich church.

Frustrated by the continual struggles between emperors and popes, German princes negotiated a new way of electing the Holy Roman Emperor. In a "Golden Bull" of 1356 ("golden" because it was sealed with gold rather than wax—also used by "bully" popes). Emperor Charles IV was eager to approve the new regulations. Three ecclesiastical rulers (the archbishops of Mainz, Trier, and Cologne) and four secular princes (the king of Bohemia, the duke of Saxony, the margrave of Brandenburg, and the count of Palatinate) were designated as "electors." The regulations nixed once and for all papal demands to approve an emperor—a tradition begun by chance with the papal coronation of Charlemagne in 800. But the power of the Golden Bull ended after the Thirty Years' War in 1648.

Popular complaints and politics called for the return of the pope to Rome. Two "holy" women agitated for it, Birgitta (1303–1373), a former Swedish princess who founded her own order, and Catherine of Siena, (1347–1380), an Italian Dominican; they both became canonized "saints." So Pope Gregory XI returned to Rome in 1378, but died in the same year. The College of Cardinals could not agree on one name and elected two popes, Urban VI (1378–1389) who stayed in Rome, and Clement VII (1378–1394) who returned to Avignon. The "Babylonian captivity" of the popes in France had become a papal schism. Its history, and the attempts to end it, read like a comedy of errors, albeit with tragic moments. Both popes had their following: Rome was supported by Germany, central and northern Italy, part of the Balkan and England. Avignon claimed France, Sardinia, Sicily, Naples, and the Hapsburg territories (now Austria, Hungary, and Spain). Internal turmoil, violence, and mutual excommunications became the order of the day. Investigative commissions echoed the popular question, "Will the real pope stand up?" No one has ever decided which of the two popes were genuine, infallible successors of Peter. Individuals, tracts, and public assemblies called for "a reform of the church from top to bottom" (literally "in head and in members"). Theologians, lawyers, and politicians tried hard to cure the dreadful spiritual disease of a schismatic papacy.

The two best-known reformers were the priest-professors John Wycliffe (c. 1325–1384) and John Hus (c. 1369–1415),[28] the former a scholar at Oxford University, the latter a disciple of Wycliffe at Prague University in Bohemia (now Czech Republic). Exchange students from both countries followed the call for reform resulting in an international movement, indeed a revolution ending in bloodshed. Wycliffe advocated the abolishment of the papacy and a return to the Bible as the highest authority, "the law of God." His argumentation led him to a denunciation of the entire hierarchical-sacramental system which was led by the pope as the Antichrist, marked by financial greed and the drive for secular power. Instead, the church should exhibit a genuine spirituality marked by poverty and true love of neighbor. He was blamed for an uprising of peasants in 1381, a slave revolt, since peasants were totally subject to the nobility and had no civil rights. He also was blamed for the rise of "Lollards" (from the Dutch *lollen*, "to mumble"), a popular resistance movement. Wycliffe's publications were burned; he withdrew from the lime-light to a small parish. But Rome did not rest and punished him as a heretic after his death.[29]

Latin Christianity in the West, Roman Catholicism, had become stuck in the morass of church-state relations begun with the anointing of Charlemagne by Pope Leo III in 800. Greek Orthodoxy in the East experienced a brief threat through the "Mongols," (perhaps from the Mongolian *mong*, "brave"), a people settled in Mongolia, a sparsely settled desert empire between Russian Siberia in the north and China a in the south. Papal efforts to convert the Mongols by baptizing their emperor failed In 1208, the legendary emperor Genghis Kahn (died in 1227) invaded Eastern Europe, devastated Russia, Poland, and Hungary. But Mongol law tolerated other religions and did not persecute Christian missionaries (who were intolerant!). Moreover, popes, not patriarchs, were the better diplomats and negotiated the establishment of archbishopric in Peking in 1307. But most of the Mongols became Moslems.

---

28. Below, 122.
29. Below, 122.

Christendumb

Silos of Doctrine

The chief doctrines of Roman Catholicism were developed through the theological argumentations among and between renowned Franciscan and Dominican theologians who were faithful and, at times, critical servants of the church. The results of their work were stored in archives, libraries, and in Canon Law which were like "silos" (from Spanish, via Latin from Greek *siros*, "cornpit"): "a tower or pit on a farm used to store grain; an underground chamber in which a guided missile is kept ready for firing."[30] The double image of storage for food and sophisticated weapons for survival is quite fitting: doctrines became food rations and weapons as protection against heresy. Three theologians constructed systems of doctrine which, maintained in the silos of schools and libraries, could be used by future generations. 1) The Italian Dominican Thomas Aquinas (1225–1274), labeled the "angelic," "common", and "universal doctor" (*doctor angelicus, communis, universalis*); 2) the Franciscan Duns Scotus (c. 1265–1308), known as the "subtle doctor" (*doctor subtilis*); and 3) the Franciscan student of Scotus, William of Occam (1280–1349) whom students celebrated as "venerable initiator" (*venerabilis inceptor*) because of his call for a more "modern" way of thinking. Thomas became the most influential of the three. His work was critically evaluated by the other two whose doctrinal systems represented a challenging mix of doctrine for future generations of theologians.

Thomas Aquinas, a student of the German Dominican "Albert the Great," is a fascinating example of contradictory characteristics. Celebrated as the greatest theologian of the Middle Ages, his system, called "Thomism," was declared eternally valid by the pope in 1879—nine years after the dogma of papal infallibility, the penthouse of the doctrinal skyscraper in Rome. Thomas was born in the castle of his noble parents near Aquino in Southern Italy. His parents sent him at age five to the Benedictine abbey in Monte Cassino (halfway between Naples and Rome) where he was schooled under the supervision of his uncle, the abbot, until he was fourteen. Then he matriculated at the University of Naples for undergraduate studies in the Seven Liberal Arts. Fat and slow, he was nicknamed "dumb ox." But he shone as a student, especially in disputations. At age nineteen, he joined the Dominican Order. His parents had tried to dissuade him with a prostitute, by having his brothers kidnap him and return him to his parents, and by

30. NOAD.

promising him the archbishopric in Naples. But Thomas stuck to his guns in the Dominican bunker. In 1252, he returned to Paris for an extraordinary career as a teacher, scholar, and theologian, with teaching stints in Rome, advising the pope and his cardinals, and at Dominican schools in his final years in Naples, his alma mater. Two years before his death he was said to have had a vision that his works were insignificant, like "straw." When the pope sent him to the Council of Lyons, France, in 1274 to participate in negotiations for unity with Greek Orthodoxy, he fell from the donkey he was riding (perhaps because of his weight) and struck his head on a fallen tree. Cistercian monks nursed him for several days. They were radical Benedictines, the order he refused to join. Moreover, he is said to have died while commenting on the Song of Songs, the most erotic biblical text—a sign of secular pleasure before imminent death?

Thomas' literary production is mind-boggling. It consists of 1) biblical commentaries on Old Testament books and on Matthew, John, and the letters of Paul; 2) commentaries on the principal works of Aristotle; 3) a commentary on Peter Lombard's *Sentences*; 4) a systematic theology in the form of a handbook (*Compendium*), of polemics against outsiders (*Summa contra Gentiles*); as a summation of theology for insiders (*Summa theologiae*); and specific disputations and questions (*Quaestiones disputate* and *Quaestiones quodlibetales*). These works provided the theological foundation of the "medieval synthesis"—a Christian uniform view of the world. The *Summa Theologica* became the textbook for the education of the clergy.

According to Thomas, "theology," "God-talk," is a scientific discourse and a "sacred doctrine" based on "analogy" (*analogia* in Latin, from the Greek *analogos*, "proportionate")—"a comparison between two things, typically on the basis of their structure and for the purpose of explanation or clarification."[31] Analogy is the instrument of the theological gymnastics that made Thomas the champion among medieval theologians and the most revered member in Rome's Hall of Fame for theologians. Accordingly, one can speak of the infinite God only in "comparison" with the finite nature and human nature. Physical motion, for example, leads to the logical conclusion that there is a first mover; consequences of human actions lead to the logical conclusion that effects point to a final cause; and human ability to love and to be good leads to the notion of God as perfect love and goodness. But these divine faculties are beyond human description because human thought and speech are finite and cannot describe anything infinite. God's

---

31. NOAD.

"god-ness," as it were, is beyond human description. But human knowledge of "reality," that which "is" (*esse* in Latin), is always part of the knowledge of God, the creator of reality; such knowledge is "essential." That is why human knowledge is ultimately "the beatific vision of God" (from the Latin *beatificus*, "blessed"). A preliminary, finite, embryonic feature of this vision is provided by faith in Jesus Christ who promised to make it real when he returns at the end of time. The promise reveals a God of love. "Scripture" (the Bible) and "tradition" (the "teaching authority" [*magisterium*] of the church consisting of a council of bishops chaired by the pope), preserve the promise of salvation; theology guards and nurtures the promise through a dialectic of faith and reason.

God revealed the ultimate purpose of humanity first in the "law" (the Decalogue and "natural" law anchored in conscience), then in the "gospel" as the "good news" of salvation through Christ who restores human nature from the contamination of sin. It is a work of "satisfaction" and creates four basic "virtues": prudence, temperance, justice, and fortitude; they are linked to the three supernatural virtues of faith, hope, and love. The virtues are "conditions" that make it possible to become stronger on the path of salvation—like an athlete becomes stronger in mastering the law of gravity. The church offers training, as it were, through its sacraments which disclose Christ as the master trainer of Christian life.

Thomas's "system" looks better than it actually is. Not everything is well presented and connected. Moreover, Thomas died before he completed the famous *Summa Theologica* (it stops at the sacrament of penance, and a student elaborated the rest of the topics). Other medieval scholastic theologians were more interested in his treatment of specific questions (*Questiones*) than in the summation of theology (*Summa*). Some disciples wrote "corrections" of his thought, often quarreling about it. Thomas is not the very best theologian, even though it was said that he was to theology what Aristotle was to philosophy—the very best. Thomas was not. Three years after his death, the bishop of Paris condemned a list of 219 propositions of Thomas dealing with the absolute power of God. The bishop claimed that Thomas had violated the church's doctrine of God's absolute power and linked it too closely with Aristotle's logic. Absolute divine power, contended the bishop, is beyond any rational description. Another offensive teaching was Thomas' denial of the "immaculate conception" of Mary, albeit with a casuistic formulation: she conceived in sin but was not "stained" by the original sin of Adam and Eve. Other theologians have said the same. Franciscans celebrated Mary's "immaculate conception" since 1263, and Pope Pius IX declared it an "infallible" dogma in 1854—part of a liturgy became an "infallible dogma"! The declaration discloses the difference with Thomas: Mary was freed from original sin "in the first instant of conception."[32] Nevertheless, Thomas was canonized a saint fifty years after his death. His theology continued to be praised as the most orthodox. In 1923, Pope Pius XI issued the solemn declaration that Thomas's teaching is the church's teaching. The "dumb ox" of Naples became the bright watchdog of Roman Catholicism. Benevolent hindsight won the day.

Since 1880 Thomas is the patron of Catholic education in general. He also is praised for his clear rejection of heresy and its annihilation by inquisition and capital punishment, even though he could be declared a heretic for his rejection of the immaculate conception of Mary—if he had been around after 1854 when that doctrine was promulgated. The English writer G. K. Chesterton (1874–1936), a humorous and often satirical convert from Anglicanism to Roman Catholicism, commented on a legend claiming that Thomas levitated. While in that condition, "the Blessed Virgin Mary appeared to him comforting him with the welcome news that he would never be a bishop."[33]

The theological system of Thomas is based on the twelve "principles" (according to his counting) of the Apostles' Creed. It is driven by the notion that there is a God whose very essence is love. Whatever went wrong through the mystery of sin is corrected and turned back to the original relationship of love between God and human creatures. An immortal soul provides a sense for what is divine and supernatural. There is a natural inner "illumination," strengthened by the infusion of grace into the soul. The experience of grace is the beginning of eternal life when the beatific vision becomes reality. Grace becomes "material," as it were, through sacramental "infusion." The seven sacraments are designed to keep believers going from cradle to grave towards the final "beatific vision." Since the sacraments are only available through the church, there is no salvation outside the church—a notion affirmed since the third century.[34] Death is the punishment for sin as well as the entrance to eternal life. The cooperation between human nature and divine grace, natural inner illumination though the soul, combined with the reception of sacraments, provided Roman Catholicism

---

32. "Immaculate Conception" in NCE.
33. G. K. Chesterton, "Essay on St. Thomas," *The Spectator* (February 27, 1932) n.p.
34. First by Cyprian of Carthage. Above, 42.

with the notion that believers can participate in the process of salvation by penance and "good works." That is why "penance" became the most important of the seven sacraments in the Middle Ages. It motivated sinners to appease God for sins defined and forgiven by the church through "confession, absolution, and satisfaction," and, more often than not, the "satisfaction" consisted of sums of money given to the church.

Duns Scotus (from "Scotsman") became a Franciscan at an early age and, during the four decades of his life, produced the most sagacious summary of doctrine in a voluminous commentary on *The Sentences* of Lombard, the textbook for the general study of theology. The commentary and other works present an alternative—or, like modern missiles, an advanced stage of their former power—to Thomism, made popular by Scotus while he was teaching at the renowned universities of Oxford, Paris, and Cologne where he died. Scotus limited the authority of Aristotle in theology by granting only the logical assumption of the existence of God through an analogy of motion (from many motions to one prime mover) and effect (from many effects to one cause). But the God as the "Father" of Jesus Christ is only known by an act of will leading to faith. In the context of modern anthropology, the distinction between "thinking" and "willing" is quite artificial because a human "decision" cannot be traced to either "reason" or "will." Scotus and other Franciscan theologians used the distinction to show that "faith" in salvation through Christ is not the result of a logical operation. It is something we call "conversion" today, the move towards a totally new attitude affecting all of life. The notion of a "free will" had already been the subject of a hot debate in the fifth century between Augustine and Pelagius. The Pelagian doctrine of a "free will" was rejected and survived in some minds as "Semi-Pelagianism"—the view that faith is the result of a human decision which is also "predestined" by God.[35]

The "system" of Scotus is annoyingly "subtle—so delicate or precise as to be difficult to analyze or describe."[36] It is anchored in the notion that God wills what is good, especially for the human creatures who had abused their freedom by refusing to obey God in the original "paradise" (Genesis 3). But this "sin" was neither "original" nor "inherited" and did not result in the loss of the freedom of the will. Mary, the mother of Jesus, remained a virgin and conceived—a consequence of her "free will" not to lose her virginity through Joseph and to obey God as the "Father" of Jesus.

35. Above, 39–40.
36. NOAD.

Edifice Complex

What happened to the God-given sexuality? The ecclesiastical addiction to virginity, especially in the case of Mary, dishonors the joy of sexual union of Adam and Eve who "knew" each other and "produced a man with the help of the Lord" (Gen 4:1). Joseph must have been thoroughly puzzled! Roman Catholicism "solved" the puzzle by making him a saint.[37]

Scotus and his disciples stressed "faith" as a decision for Christ, infused by sacramental grace which enables believers to "satisfy" God with their works of love. Scotus rejected any "theory of satisfaction," pioneered by Anselm. Instead he created the popular medieval Roman Catholic doctrinal platform of salvation: it is offered by the story of Jesus as the Son of God and savior of humankind (the "gospel" as "good news"); by a free decision for Christ, combined with the reception of the seven sacraments in the church; and by the will of God, expressed as love, a divine approval of the human decision to be re-united with God forever. This kind of theology remains popular and is exhibited in the enduring call, medieval and modern ("evangelical"), "Accept Jesus Christ as your Savior and you will have eternal life."

William of Occam, a Franciscan student of Scotus, was trained at Oxford and taught at the University of Paris. But his revolutionary views prevented him from being awarded a chair. The Thomist chancellor of the university ordered an investigation because of "suspicion of heresy" disclosed in Occam's major work, a commentary on the *Sentences* of Peter Lombard, the textbook of theology. Agreement with the book was the condition for a tenured position in a university. Occam was accused of denying sixty-nine assertions of "orthodox" teaching, and he was summoned to appear before a papal court in Avignon, France, in 1324. Pope John XXII appointed a commission to investigate the accusations—an irony of history because the legitimate location for the defense of orthodoxy was Rome; but political ambitions had made popes vassals of the French king. The investigation lasted three years. But, like a hung jury, the commission could not agree on a verdict. Occam used the delay of a decision to seek support. He found it in the head of the Franciscan order, the Minister-General Michael, who was involved in a conflict with the pope over the Franciscan

---

37. Shortly after the dogma of Mary's immaculate conception, Pius IX proclaimed Joseph a "patron saint" assisting the faithful in their struggle against doubt and hesitation, as well as the a model of a "happy death" since he died in the arms of Jesus and Mary. Moreover, he also assisted in the fight against Communism. Subtly becomes simple! The veneration of Joseph began c. 800, with a feast day on March 19. Since 1989 "Josephology" is a part of theology.

oath of poverty. John XXII, a conservative Dominican, had ordered the Franciscans to modify their radical oath of poverty by accepting gifts. Michael asked William of Occam to evaluate the papal order. The evaluation proved that the pope had contradicted previous papal decisions. John XXII responded by ordering the Franciscans to elect another Minister-General (popes could install only bishops not heads of religious orders). Fearing persecution, Michael, William, and two other Franciscan friars secretly boarded a ship on the river Rhone and sailed to Germany for protection by Emperor Louis of Bavaria, a major player in the political intrigues of the day, opposing the pope. William was given asylum in Munich where he continued his work. When Emperor Louis died in 1347, William reaffirmed his loyalty to the papacy. He died of the Black Death two years later amidst rumors that he signed a form of recantation.

Occam provided a radical alternative to Thomist theology by denying the validity of Aristotelian logical reasoning, be it "proofs" for the existence of God or any other ways of bridging the gulf between faith and reason. Metaphysics is sheer speculation. Philosophy cannot be the handmaiden of theology. Any supernatural knowledge is the result of an act of will to accept what God reveals through the church. The real is not in the rational. "God" and other "universals" are only assumed "names." That is why William and his disciples were called "nominalists" and "fideists" (from their emphasis on "faith", *fides* in Latin), the former indicating philosophical skepticism, the latter stressing the authority of divine revelation through the church. The removal of metaphysical "universals" from proper theology was called "Occam's razor—the principle that in explaining a thing no more assumptions should be made than are necessary."[38] It can also be viewed as a reference to his sharp, critical mind. His "new way" or "modernism" discloses a peculiar "orthodoxy": true Christian faith relies solely on the revelation of an omnipotent God to the community of his Son, Jesus Christ, in the world, the "church" as the "the body of Christ." Occam foreshadowed the eighteenth-century European Enlightenment which, in its philosophical "stars" like David Hume (1711–1776) in England and Immanuel Kant (1724–1804) in Germany, ended the "medieval synthesis" of faith and reason, isolating its brainchild, Thomism, in a silo used by antiquated Roman Catholics. On the other hand, Occam combined his critique of traditional medieval theology with an uncritical acceptance of the doctrines of the Roman Catholic Church as the only recipient of the revelation of salvation by

38. NOAD.

Edifice Complex

the arbitrary will of an omnipotent God. If Occam had lived a miraculously long time, he, in his uncritical acceptance of the church, would have had to become a Thomist since the church adopted Thomas Aquinas as its master-theologian whom Occam opposed. Death and time saved Occam from a dreadful decision.

A French Franciscan contemporary of Occam, Nicholas of Lyra (c. 1270–c. 1340), added a shed, as it were, to the silos of doctrine, storing instructions of how to interpret the Bible as the source of church doctrine. The instructions became the standard of biblical exegesis. Lyra adopted the Jewish, rabbinical method which stressed the simple "literal" sense of the Bible. Medieval theologians worked with three other "senses:" the "moral" (what to do), the "spiritual" (where to aim), and the "allegorical" (what to believe). A popular example of this fourfold sense of the Bible was the word "water": literally, it means physical element; morally, it is an emotion like weeping sorrow; spiritually, it is eternal happiness; and allegorically, it can mean almost anything, with a preference for baptism. Thomas Aquinas preferred allegories in order to substantiate his theological imagination with biblical texts. Accordingly, Genesis 1:3 ("Let there be light") means an act of creation, revealing the light of Christ illuminating believers on their way to heavenly glory. Lyra did detailed work on the Hebrew and Greek texts of the Bible, covering it in its entirety in eighty-five volumes; the literal sense prevailed.

The storage of doctrine was accompanied by a mystical movement led by three German Dominican mystics, "Master" John Eckhart (c. 1260–1327), Henry Suso (c.1295-1366), and John Tauler (c.1300-1361). They provided a balance between the dominant "scientific" theology and a "practical" spirituality. Eckhart was the scholar among them, teaching at the universities of Paris and Cologne. His work offers a critique of the medieval theological textbooks, the *Sentences* of Peter Lombard and the *Summation* of Thomas Acquinas. But his most influential publications are sermons and a book on "consolation" in German. The principal issue is his description of the "birth of God in the soul." It happens when one contemplates to "empty" oneself from any material, creaturely desire and lets God touch the divine "spark" (*Fünklein* in German) in the soul. This mysterious touch generates an eternal unity with God, visible in the love of neighbor by doing "good works." Since he saw more power in mystical experience rather than in the sacramental system, the church accused Eckhart of heresy; he died during the hearing and was excommunicated two years later—another reminder that the church "sticks at nothing" (literally "stepping over corpses," *über Leichen gehen* in German). Suso exhibited his mysticism in a radical, repugnant ascetic style of life. But in his later life he became an attractive preacher and author of a best-seller, *The Little Book of Eternal Wisdom*. Tauler was the most influential preacher of his time, calling for repentance in the face of hard times caused by the Black Death, an earthquake in 1356, and the quarrels between pope and emperor. A book entitled *German Theology* (*Theologia Germanica*) made him famous because the renowned reformer Martin Luther edited it with much praise in 1516 as a work of Tauler. But the book is the work of an anonymous author.

Greek Orthodox monks created peculiar mystical views at a monastery on Mount Athos in Greece. They were called "Hesychasts" (from the Greek *hesychia*, "stillness," "silence") because they fell in a trance while repeating a brief, traditional "Jesus Prayer": "Lord Jesus Christ, have mercy on me!" The praying was coordinated with breathing. One monk reported that he performed the prayer 12,000 times in one day, each time while inhaling and exhaling, resulting in a feeling of warmth and a vision of light.[39] Opponents viewed such behavior as egotistic and spread the news that monks also used concentration on the navel, nicknaming the practitioners "navel-gazers." The group caused a lengthy quarrel in the church about the legitimacy of mystical visions (1341–1351). But the prevalence of mysticism in Greek Orthodoxy moved church authorities on the Balkan and in Russia to sanction Hesychasm as a legitimate form of Eastern spirituality.

The silos of doctrine in the West provided the various ingredients for a defense of the "medieval synthesis." With Aristotle and beyond him, theologians stored the ingredients for the spiritual nourishment offered by the church. One particular doctrine created "neuralgia"—intensive intermittent pain along the course of a nerve, especially the head and the face" (not to mention the stomach)[40]—of "the body of Christ," the church. It was the teaching about the "treasure of spiritual merits" (*thesaurus* [from the Greek *thesaurus*, "storage"] *meritorum*, "of merits" its in Latin)—a minor part of the theology of Alexander of Hales.[41] The doctrine was used to amplify the

---

39. The "Jesus Prayer" is part of a popular writing from the Greek Orthodox monastery at Mount Athos, titled "The Love of Beauty" (*Philokalia* in Greek). The mystical experience is also described as "Tabor Light" from the story of the transfiguration of Jesus on a mountain, thought of as Mount Tabor (Mark 9:2–123). Details in Thomas Bremer, *Cross and Kremlin*.

40. NOAD.

41. Below, 88.

Sacrament of Penance (called today "Sacrament of Reconciliation") which developed from a simple practice to complex regulations in legalese resembling "casuistry—the use of clever but unsound reasoning, especially in relation to moral questions, sophistry; the resolving of moral problems by the application of theoretical rules for particular instances."[42]

Among the first Christians, sins were forgiven in baptism, and spiritual discipline was maintained by the congregation through pastoral visitation (Matt 18:16-20). But when adult baptism declined in favor of infant baptism, questions arose regarding the forgiveness of post-baptismal sins. A second baptism was rejected because it was viewed as a heresy to be punished by death since the sixth century—presumably because baptism was a once and for all initiation into the church. Moreover, the power to forgive sins was understood to be a mandate given to the church by Jesus, with special reference to the apostle Peter (Matt 16:17-19). Already in the second century, a "second penance" after baptism was granted in public worship. But very quickly the monastic practice of a private, indeed secret, confession to a priest was introduced, foreshadowing the omnipresent temptation of consumerism—to attract individual believers to consume healthy, organic spiritual food in the comfort of personal, private consultation. But the attraction was also mixed with fear of punishment for specific "venial" or "minor" sins and "cardinal" or "deadly" sins. The latter were specified in the sixth century as "enemies" of "virtues." A list of seven deadly sins threatened seven virtues: "Lust" (*luxuria*) vs. chastity, "gluttony" (*gula*) vs. abstinence, "greed" (*avaritia*) vs. generosity, "sloth" (*acedia*) vs. diligence, "wrath" (*ira*) vs. patience, "envy" (*invidia*) vs. kindness, and "pride" (*superbia*) vs. humility. The Italian poet Dante Alighieri (1265-1321) popularized these sins in his famous work *The Divine* Comedy, as an entertaining guide to hell. The Sacrament of Penance was enacted in three steps: confession, absolution, and satisfaction. Since 1215, going to confession was an annual requirement. Penitents had to go to the priest in the "confessional" (an enclosed stall with room for one person and the priest behind a screen) to list and repent of their sins, then receive absolution, and they were ordered to do "good works" (analogous to a verdict in court accompanied by a mandate for "community-service" or similar activities). Volunteers for a holy cause, like a crusade to the Holy Land, or a pilgrimage to a holy place with relics, were granted an indulgence without private confession. It did not take long to view the various ways of doing penance in the same manner

42. NOAD.

as psychiatry today—ways of reducing, indeed curing anxiety, or lowering the numerous fear factors in a medieval culture humming with physical and psychological dangers, ranging from natural disasters to depression through superstition. The church issued instruction manuals for priests designed to urge believers to go to confession. The manuals prescribed "contrition" (from the Latin *contrition*, "breaking something"), defined as "a sorrow of the souls and a hatred of sin committed, with a firm purpose of not sinning in the future." Then there is "attrition" (from the Latin *attero*, "to wear away by rubbing"). Such softening of resistance to penance was clinched with the threat of going to hell, or a location between heaven and hell called "purgatory—a place or state of suffering inhabited by the souls of sinners who are expiating their sins before going to heaven."[43]

All these casuistic ways of doing penance were grounded in the doctrine of "the treasure of the church": it consists of the abundant merits accumulated by Christ who was "without sin" (Heb 4:15) and paid on the cross "for the sins of the whole world" (1 John 2:2). This "treasure" was increased by the merits of canonized saints who, like Christ, also earned more merits than they needed, and all of these merits were given to the church. Penance, like financial investments, created "credits" (from the Latin *credere*, "to believe") for clients who "believe" to improve their lives through investments. Similarly, the church grants forgiveness of sins, "indulgences" [from the Latin *indulgere*, "to be forbearing"]—the extra-sacramental remission of the temporal punishment due, in God's justice, to sin that has been forgiven, which remission is granted by the church in the exercise of the power of the keys given to Peter and his successors (Matt 16:19) through the application of the superabundant merits of Christ and of the saints."[44] Pope Clement VI converted this doctrine into a papal bull in 1343.

It was decided that baptism atones for "original" and "inherited sin" of Adam and Eve, and going to confession, the Sacrament of Penance, atoned for all other sins. In short: the church as "the body of Christ" on earth was given the profits created by Christ to issue "credit" to sinners who owe more than they could afford to appease God for their sins. Their visit to the confessional assessed how much of the "treasure of merits" they needed to avoid divine punishment. This practice of penance assumes that God is, above all, a judge who demands punishment for sins defined by the church. Medieval Roman Catholicism developed a complex system of sin

---

43. "Contrition, Attrition" in NCE.
44. "Indulgence" in NCE.

Edifice Complex

and salvation. Fear of punishment in purgatory and in the final judgment after the end of this world increased fear of death and delivered believers into the hands of the sellers of indulgences, mostly enthusiastic monks engaged in the trade by bishops. When fear virtually replaced faith and began to strangle hope for heavenly joy after death, the yearning for hope and joy finally burst into a religious revolution and caused the enduring schism in the sixteenth century, precipitated by Martin Luther.

Pay, Pray, and Obey

Christian life in the Middle Ages of the West was marked by a variety of features intended to create cultural uniformity known as "Christendom." Rituals and many other requirements kept brains washed for obedience to Roman Catholicism. But much of common piety still constituted a translation of pagan heritage into Christian features. Gods became saints, and general superstitions were maintained in new ways, Christianizing pagan festivals related to earth and sky, reflecting changes like seasons and awe about the sun, the moon, and the stars. Pagan temples became Christian churches.

The establishment of cities led to a greater influence of the regular clergy since bishops became distracted from their pastoral role through secular political ambitions which focused on territorial power; they became "prince bishops." Financial interests always dominated. Priests were paid by gifts of land and by fees for baptisms, weddings, funerals, and other services. Eventually, "indulgences" became a chief source of income; instead of going to confession one could buy an indulgence for the remission of sins—foreshadowing modern taxation through checks and credit cards rather than a personal appearance for transmitting money to the government. The papal bureaucracy accumulated the highest income with fees for bestowing offices, especially those of bishops and archbishops. In addition, Rome also collected part of the taxes for properties in the church at large. Communion was viewed as necessary for salvation. Already in the second century it was customary to take consecrated bread home and eat a portion every day as an antidote to sin, mirroring modern habits to take pills, "just in case." Lay people could only receive the bread. The priest drank from the chalice. after elevating the consecrated bread called "host' (from the Latin *hostia*, "victim," a reference to Christ) and reverencing it on his knees. Sermons were rare. Only mendicant orders preached (like the Franciscans who were known as the "order of preachers"). But every day there was some kind of worship service announced by bells, known since the eight century (first in France). The day was divided into a sequence of devotion consisting of prayers, "doing the hours." Parishioners were encouraged to demonstrate their faith by body-language when going to church: dipping their hands in the holy water of the baptismal-font at the entrance, combined with making the sign of the cross; lighting candles; kissing relics and pictures of saints; genuflecting when facing the main altar with its ornamented receptacle used for consecrated bread (host) and wine, called "tabernacle" (the "tent of the meeting" in Exod 25:31, 35–40, a complex description of the "ark of the covenant as the instrument of communication with God). Moreover, there was always a procession somewhere for spiritual entertainment, sometimes short pilgrimages. Churches were "smoked" with incense, a symbol of prayer (Ps 141:2, "Let my prayer be counted as incense") and, on hot days, a deodorant.

Pastoral contact was established through penance in the confessional, sitting on a bench behind a metal grid listening to the confession of sins by the parishioner on his/her knees—similar to a visit of a prisoner who is behind glass and is connected with the visitor through a telephone. The confessional provided secrecy and protection from the temptation of inappropriate contact, especially on the part of priests known for their desire to "know" women in a biblical sense (Gen 4:1, "The man [Adam] knew his wife Eve, and she conceived and bore Cain"). Another pastoral contact occurred in the wedding ceremony. Since the thirteenth century, weddings had to be announced in church, known as the "banns of marriage," and after the legal ceremony couples were blessed in the church. Gradually, priests were empowered to make the wedding legal in a brief ceremony at the entrance to the church. "Proof" of marriage was its sexual consummation, provided by the couple's testimony, or in the Germanic territories by eyewitnesses who saw the couple enter the wedding chamber. Such "proof" indicated that the divinely instituted contract to live together and have children was enacted (Gen 2:24, "they become one flesh"). In the fourteenth century, priests acted as representatives of the law and conducted the ceremony at the entrance of the church. After the fifteenth century, both the legal and sacramental validity of marriage became one ceremony, presided by the priest in the church.

Feast and saints days increased, topped by the Feast of Corpus Christi proposed in 1246 by a nun in Liege, Belgium, who had visions about Christ.

Since 1264, the feast is celebrated on the Thursday after Trinity Sunday (one week after Pentecost) by carrying the Eucharistic elements in a public procession—a physical vision, as it were, of Christ's presence. The cult of his mother, Mary, was equally significant since she was viewed as "the mother of God" (*theotokos* in Greek) and as an assistant in redemption (*redemptrix* in Latin)—"Just in case the Son is busy, go to His mother" some people were heard to say. Petitions were addressed to Mary in the context of the popular prayer known as "Ave Maria" (from *avere* in Latin, "greetings" from the angel announcing the birth of Christ in Luke 1:28), consisting of Mary's Song of Praise (Luke 1:46–55). A string of beads was sold to keep Marian devotions alive in nervous hands and anxious heads, the "rosary—a form of devotion in which five (or fifteen) decades [ten parts] of Hail Mary's are repeated, each decade preceded by an Our Father and followed by a Glory Be (the congregation said the rosary); a string of beads for keeping count in such a devotion, 55 or 165 in number; a book containing such a devotion, from the Latin *rosarium* 'rose garden.'"[45] Since the twelfth century the view prevailed that Mary was "assumed" to heaven after her death even though the formal dogma of her "assumption" was not promulgated before 1950. Strings of beads were, and still are, used in business deals to calm the nerves of Arabic businessmen, especially during negotiations for the price of important goods like a camel or a horse. Songs of chivalrous knights and noblemen became Marian songs. Sheer fantasy invented St. George, the killer of dragons, as protector of crusaders. Everything was blessed by the church be it babies or utensils for labor. The touch of Holy Water near the entrance of churches became spiritual fast food. In Greek Orthodoxy almost everything is blessed, be it a new home, a vehicle, an animal, or any other tool for living. The sign of the cross is made as often as one feels change. Mary and the saints were believed to help in all emergencies. In a life and death situation one could simply yell "Help St. Francis!" The call was like the modern "911," though not with an immediate guaranteed response. The medieval call became known as "spiritual ejaculation." A medieval best-seller was the tome *The Golden Legend*, also known as *Lives of the Saints* (c. 1275), by the Italian Dominican monk Jacob of Voragine. He offered a massive collection of stories about the miraculous work of saints. The most fictitious, yet popular, tale is told about St. Nicholas, who was a bishop in Myra (Asia Minor) and died in c. 353. He is honored on

---

45. "Rosary" in NOAD.

December 6 as the protector of sailors and merchants in Greek and Russian Orthodoxy. In Germanic regions and today he is known as "Santa Claus."[46]

Angels (from the Greek *angelos*, "messenger") were the divine mail-carriers, as it were, announcing significant events like the birth of Jesus (Luke 2:8–14). Medieval scholastic theologians portrayed them as bodiless but able to appear in one. They protect human souls and fight demons as illustrated in the defeat of a dragon by the arch-angel Michael and his colleagues (Rev 12:7–12). He was the favorite miracle-worker and "guardian angel." At a time when salvation was expensive, angels offered the best deal.

The "church year" was divided into seasons, beginning with "Advent" (from the Latin *advenire*, "to come") in the sixth century. This season lasted the period of four Sundays before Christmas on December 25 in the West since the third century, taking the place of the pagan Roman celebration of the winter solstice. In the East, it was called "epiphany" (from the Greek *epiphania*, "manifestation"), celebrated on January 6, as the appearance of God's revelation in Jesus. The festival began in Egypt in the second century, recalling the baptism of Jesus. In the West, Epiphany was linked to the visit of the "wise men" (Matt 2:1–12).

There was a controversy about the date of Easter, preceded by four weeks of penitential discipline (fasting and other activities). Before Lent, there was public revelry, climaxing in the final days before Ash Wednesday, known as "carnival" (from the Latin *carne vale*, "farewell to meat"). In Syria and Asia Minor, the Easter Day, the resurrection of Jesus, was the fourteenth day of the lunar month Nisan, assumed to be the date of the Jewish Passover, a spring celebration of the exodus from Egypt marked by the divine killing of every Egyptian firstborn and the "passing over" the death of Jewish children (Exod 12:12–13). Christians adopted this Jewish celebration as the date when Jesus became the "sacrificial lamb" (1 Cor 5:7). The Council of Nicaea (325) decreed that the proper day is the Sunday after the full moon following the spring equinox (between March 2 and April 25). But the controversy continued because of different calendars.

---

46. The "Santa" discloses fascinating details. As a baby he practiced fasting by drinking milk from his mother's breast only on Wednesday and Friday; he gave his first surprise gifts, money, to a nobleman who had become a pimp, using his daughters as prostitutes; he converted the pimp and his daughters back to decency; and after his burial holy oil and water flowed to the pilgrims who touched his marble coffin (sarcophagus). The figure of Bishop Nicholas appears on the eve of December 6, accompanied by a devil-like figure who frightens children into a confession of bad behavior; but they always end up with gifts.

Edifice Complex

The Julian calendar of Julius Caesar from 46 BCE assumed 365 days for one year and every fourth year 366 days. The Gregorian calendar of Pope Gregory XIII in 1582 made a ten day adjustment. Greek Orthodoxy did not adopt it. Easter was concluded with the "Holy Week," beginning on Palm Sunday since the fourth century, recalling Jesus's entry in Jerusalem (Mark 11:1–11, "palms" are "leafy branches" in verse 8). Thursday was the day recalling the last supper of the disciples with Jesus on the Jewish Day of Passover (called "Maundy" Thursday from the Latin *mandatum novum*, "new mandate" of foot-washing in John 13:34, "green Thursday" (*Gründonnerstag*], a reminder of the first green plants in the Spring in Germany since the sixteenth century). Foot-washing was a sign of hospitality (Luke 7:44) and mutual love. The Pope and bishops adopted the practice of washing the feet of twelve strangers—a sign of hypocritical humility, separating "pomp" from "circumstance." There was no Good Friday before the fourth century. In the East, there were Eucharistic services ending with a symbolic burial of Christ. In the West; it was a day of penance marked by fasting. In 1687, after an earthquake, a Peruvian Jesuit priest, Alonso Messia Bedoya, is said to have instituted a three-hour devotion from noon to 3 p.m. in Lima. The custom quickly spread and included in the event "the last seven words of Jesus on the cross" (the number is a selection from the four Gospels).[47] An Easter Vigil on Saturday was used for baptisms, ending with a Eucharist in the morning. Since the fourteenth century, "passion plays" were staged to depict the suffering and crucifixion of Jesus. They originated in western Europe and became popular in the Bavarian town of Oberammergau since 1634; they are performed by the towns-people every ten years.

Forty days after Easter, the ascension of Christ was celebrated (Acts 1:1–9) since the fourth century. Fifty days after Easter, there was the festival of Pentecost (from the Greek *pentecoste*, "fifty"), with a celebration of the birthday of the church through the gift of the Holy Spirit given to the apostles who founded a megachurch of three thousand (Acts 2:2, 41). The Sunday after Pentecost was devoted to the dogma of the Trinity. A peculiar

---

47. Their use for meditation and preaching can be traced to the sixteenth century. Preaching on them on Good Friday between noon and 3:00 p.m. became popular in American Protestant churches—the Marathon run of sermons! The sayings are 1) "Father, forgive them; for they do not know what they are doing (Luke 23:34). 2) "Truly I tell you, today you will be with me in Paradise" (Luke 23:43). 3) "Woman, here is your son" (John 19:26), 4) "My God, my God, why have you forsaken me?" (John 19:28). 6) "It is finished" (John 19:30). 7) "Father, into your hands I commend my spirit" (Luke 24:46).

feast day was All Saints' Day on November 1, begun in 609 with the consecration of the Pantheon (from the Greek *pan theoi*, "all gods") in Rome, converted to a Christian basilica to honor "saint Mary and all the martyrs." It was followed by All Souls' Day on November 2 as an opportunity to pray for the souls in purgatory.

There was some longing for a more internal, indeed mystical, piety over against the external spiritual busyness, removed from ecclesiastical business. A reform of the church from within, in the hearts of the faithful, seemed more attractive than external political and scholastic moves. So in the second half of the fourteenth century lay people organized a group known as "Friends of God," based on a reading of John 15:14 where Jesus tells his disciples, "You are my friends if you do what I command." The group had its center in Strasbourg, France and spread southeast along the Danube river. The group was joined by monks, nuns, and people of various social ranks. Members of the group were perturbed by the terrible papal schism and ecclesiastical corruption. Their chief voice was Rulman Merswin of Strasbourg who penned a popular analysis of the ecclesiastical corruption and the need for change, *The Book of Nine Rocks*. It compares life to climbing rocks, always held back by the devil, until one has a vision of arriving at the heavenly top. He alerted readers to the corruption of the church, easily identified as the rock of the abusive papacy derived from Peter (Matt 16:18). Simple faith seemed superstitious and was punished. One of the disciples of Merswin, Nicholas of Basel, was tried by the Inquisition and burned at the stake in Vienna in c. 1395.

Another group also sought reform through spiritual formation. They originated in Deventer, Holland, where a lay preacher, Gerhard Groote (1340–1384), and his followers had created a voluntary association, "The Brethren of the Common Life." They also became known as advocates of "A Modern Devotion" (*devotio moderna* in Latin). Following the tradition of the "imitation of Christ," they called for true catechetical education as a counterpart to rationalistic scholasticism. Very quickly they found numerous followers in France, Italy, and Spain.

Three women became role models for a mystical spirituality as the basis for reform. Hildegard of Bingen (1098–1179) in Germany, Bridget Birgitta (1303–1373) in Sweden, and Catherine of Siena (1347–1380) in Italy. Hildegard was the abbess of a Benedictine convent. At age thirty-three she had a vision about the "ways of God," expressed in music, poetry, and a formation for a healthy life. Despite some initial opposition from the church, people began to contact her for advice, among them kings and popes. She stayed above the political fray and did not violate any church teachings even though she sounded apocalyptic when speaking of the end of the world and the reform of the church through teaching and prayer. She is admired by modern advocates of a "new age" and by practitioners of a combination of medicine and "creation spirituality."

Birgitta of Sweden was a feminist mystic who taught a new reading of the incarnation of God in Christ, viewing the mother of Jesus, Mary, as a co-redeemer because she participated in her Son's suffering on the cross. Moreover, Birgitta saw in Mary the ideal of motherhood which includes sexual experience—in stark contrast to the long established ideals of virginity and celibacy. Married to a Swedish nobleman and mother of eight children, she moved to Rome in 1349, where she founded a new order, the "Bridgettines." Nuns, monks, priests, and lay brothers could join the order, though living in separate quarters, led by an abbess who represented Mary. The order quickly became very popular, given the decay of spirituality and of ecclesiastical institutions. Pope Urban V (1370) was "going with the flow" and approved the new order—an extraordinary event, considering Birgitta's unique, feminist spiritual discipline in the context of a "holy" male chauvinism. In this case, popularity does not breed contempt but success. In eight books of 700 heavenly visions Birgitta coordinated the popular motif of the "imitation of Christ" with an "imitation of Mary" symbolized in motherhood as part of the salvation in Christ. She called this view "the gospel of Mary."[48]

Catherine fasted and meditated from an early age and joined the Sisters of Penance at the age of sixteen. Soon she became known through her visions which she published as *Dialogues* (with God). She depicted her union with God in the soul as being like a fish in the sea and the sea being in the fish. She also pleaded for penance regarding the terrible situation of two popes, and, together with Birgitta, lobbied for a return of the pope of Avignon to Rome. All three women were canonized as saints.

Fear of punishment in an after-life kept people tied to the church with its many offers of salvation. The "dance of death" by actors playing a skeleton became popular since the fourteenth century. Noblemen wanted to be buried in monastic garb to hide their sinful lives of pleasure before the judgment throne of God "on the other side." Cities became crowded

---

48. There is also an apocryphal book with this title, but about Mary Magdalene, a loyal disciple of Jesus (Mark 15:40–41).

with ecclesiastical institutions. The German city of Cologne had c. 40,000 inhabitants in the fourteenth century, with nineteen parishes, more than a hundred chapels, twenty-two monasteries, and seventy-six nunneries. The doctrine of Mary's immaculate conception expanded the cult of Mary to include her mother Anna. Parts of dead saints, relics, were collected like stamps today and exhibited on All Saints' Day. The rush for pilgrimages reminds one of the modern use of drugs, taken to have a sense and taste of spiritual happiness. Favorite spiritual "highs" were trips to the tombs of Peter and Paul in Rome (without any hard evidence that they died there) and to Jerusalem. There were innumerable other quick ways to get a "high" with blessed body-parts.

A more positive piety is evidenced in the rare preaching in the vernacular by responsible parish priests. There was some responsible care for the sick and the poor in the face of the teaching that alms earn salvation. That is why beggars harassed worshippers at the entrance of churches to warn them that, if they would not give them money, they would be damned.

Ritual and ceremony were viewed as media of miracles. Almost everyone could tell a story about a miracle. Emotional religious exuberance became the soil for pious fraud. Visionaries fell into ecstasy, claiming to have cured the sick, and they created mass movements for specific causes like crusades against heretics and infidels. Witches and Jews became the preferred scapegoats for almost any disasters. Women were viewed as a major source of evil (perhaps because of Eve who seduced Adam to sin); they were employees of the devil. Witches were said to kill babies, eat human flesh, and frighten minds through astrological visions. When caught by the Inquisition, such women were interrogated with torture; if they cried they were pronounced guilty. Anti-Semitism blamed Jews for the "murder" of Christ and became anchored in the ridiculous myth about the crime of deicide which must be punished without mercy. It was assumed that the destruction of the temple in Jerusalem in 70 CE was a punishment for crimes against Christians who claimed that the divine promise of being the "people of God" had been transferred to Christianity, the "new Israel."

Fear was fed well by images about punishment in purgatory, in hell, and on the Judgment Day at the imminent end of the world. Churches exhibited relics of deceased saints, usually behind a glass wall under an altar so that worshipers could pray to a visible saint, assisted by touching a sculptured one. Remnants of saints were sold as tactile means of redemption, touching or kissing them. Parts of saints were concealed by knights in their armor. Peasants liked to buy drops of Christ's bloody sweat and drops of his mother's milk at local fairs. Frequently thieves stole relics from one church and sold them to another. Pilgrimages satisfied the longing for travel and adventure. Rome, Canterbury, and Compostella (Spain) became famous tourist attractions as spas for spiritual health. Only the most devoted traveled the long and hard road to the Holy Land. The Bubonic Plague or "Black Death"[49] from 1348–1350 created panic and an intensive fear of a miserable death. People tried to battle their fear of death with works of satisfaction, called "good works," such as fasting, almsgiving, enduring prayer, pilgrimages, new holy edifices, becoming monks or nuns, or even by self-flagellation as ways of penance, the bridge from the earthly church to eternal life. Christian medieval culture exhibited more fear than hope; heaven seemed to be reserved for ecclesiastical entrepreneurs. Sober minds spoke of "pious fraud."

Architecture, literature, paintings, and sculpture depicted medieval life as a painful struggle of life and death, ending in heaven or in hell. Cathedrals were skyscrapers in stone, built higher and higher, with sunlight radiating from many stained glass windows, reminding simple folk in their dark homes of heavenly glory. Going to church reminded simple minds of going to heaven. The architectural style was called "Gothic."[50] In addition, cathedrals were ornamented with numerous gargoyles—grotesque human or animal faces serving as waterspouts at the end of the roofs. Knights and troubadours composed secular love songs in the sea of religious music. The Italian literary icon, Dante Alighieri (1265–1321) managed to entertain readers with his view of hell as "divine comedy," dying in exile as a critic of the papacy. St. Francis inspired the painter Giotto and his students with illustrated legends about his life, using for the first time a naturalistic style with realistic human figures. Sculptures of saints and renowned rulers filled churches and public places. Salvation was available beyond the shadow of any doubt.

---

49. "Bubonic" (from the Greek *bubon*, "gland") and "black" because of the color of corpses. The plague killed almost half of the population in England in 1349 and almost a third on the continent. The disease originated in Central Asia and was imported to Europe by fleas on black rats. There was no cure.

50. From a Germanic tribe, the "Goths." The term was used centuries later, beginning in the sixteenth-century Italian Renaissance, to describe a barbaric style linked to the pagan Goths. Given the beauty of cathedrals and the decay of the church in the Renaissance, the proverbs apply: "Beauty is in the eye of the beholder," and the old Latin proverb, "One should not dispute tastes" (*de gustibus non est disputandum*).

Christendumb

"Indulgences" became the most convenient means to appease guilty consciences. Since the eleventh century priests began to speak about the forgiveness of sins for soldiers who had been killed in the infamous crusades against infidels. In the twelfth century such forgiveness was also granted to those who gave money to the church. The papacy in Rome controlled the custom by specifying a price for an indulgence, especially one for being exempted from punishment in purgatory. Believers received absolution from sins in the confessional and paid money for avoiding punishment in purgatory. Sometimes money was substituted for a personal appearance in the confessional. Purgatory and hell were no longer crowded.

Thirty-seven years of the papal schism (1378–1415) had eroded respect for the church, with one pope in Rome, another one in Avignon, and a third in Pisa Italy, occasionally condemning each other. Two or three popes cost more than one, living in pomp and circumstance, paid by the faithful in one way or another. Politics and commerce dominated in the church, and loud cries for reform were heard.

The seven sacraments were the core of religious control. 1) Baptism shortly after birth (original immersion soon became sprinkling) atoned for the "original" and "inherited" sin of Adam and Eve. In the ceremony of infant baptism parents and young godparents promised loyalty to the church (godparents substituting for parents because the lifespan was more limited than it is today). 2) Confirmation at age seven (the assumed age of discretion) strengthened baptism and was administered by a bishop with a mild box on the ear and followed by first communion at the Mass, a weekly requirement. 3) Penance focused on confession and absolution, an annual requirement, and ended with mandated deeds of satisfaction for rehabilitation (prescribed prayers, pilgrimages, or monetary indulgences—a quick and preferred way of "paying" for sins). In Greek Orthodoxy baptism, confirmation and first communion are administered together. 4) Eucharist or Lord's Supper could be celebrated only by the priest and lay people received the consecrated bread without the wine; there was an abounding of abuse to keep believers attracted to the church; masses were offered for the dead, often paid in advance by believers who wanted guarantees for avoiding hell and purgatory. 5) Ordination of men at age twenty-five by a bishop; it bestowed an "indelible character" on the soul, and even "unfrocking" could not erase it. To belong to the clergy was like being a spiritual "nobleman." It tempted pregnant mothers to dedicate a baby to the church as future priests, hoping the baby would be a boy. 6) Extreme Unction was administered at times of severe illness and/or imminent death. A priest anointed believers with holy oil, forgiving confessed sins, and commending believers to the grace of God. 7) Marriage between one man and one woman was the only sacrament enacted by the couple as a contract before God blessed by a priest (symbolized by wrapping the stole around joined hands). The sacramental nature was derived from Eph 5:31–32 ("two will become one flesh. This is a great mystery," the Greek *mysterion* was translated into the Latin *sacramentum*). The union allowed only "natural" birth control and prohibited divorce. But "annulments" were granted as evidence that the marriage was never intended. Whereas "good intention" lead to hell, "bad intentions" seem to lead out of it! Eventually, an "annulment" meant the same as a "divorce" (innumerable annulments are granted in an expense process based on Canon Law).[51]

In Greek Orthodoxy, sacraments are not depicted with scholastic language. Priests are allowed to marry, and there is not much focus on penance. Hope provided a mystical vision of a future life with Christ, putting much less emphasis on fear. Roman Catholicism also added "sacramentals," observances such as the use of holy water or the sign of the cross. God seemed to be everywhere. Participative devotion included praying the rosary, walking along the "stations of the cross" in a church, or doing a "novena" (from the Latin *novem*, "nine"), the name for nine consecutive days of worship and meditation.

Money ruled souls. Almost every aspect of spirituality had a price as the way to appease an angry God and avoid eternal punishment. Mendicant orders of monks begged for money in the streets, and popes were wheeling and dealing in their offices. The "treasure of the church" was Christ. But to receive forgiveness through him was very expensive. Magic, superstition, and belief in the devil competed with honest faith in forgiveness. Monetary gifts to the church provided some security but never guaranteed it—just as modern security systems never offer true relief from the fear of crime in a crowded city. The church used the biblical tradition about Satan (from the Hebrew for "accuser," the prosecuting attorney of God) and demonic powers to feed the fear of the faithful. Satan is the "ruler of the world" (2 Cor 4:4), the leader of "demons" (from the Greek *daimon*, "spirit"), and the "king of hell" (Rev 9:11). In the fourteenth century, "demonology"

---

51. Both the definition of marriage as a sacrament and its "annulment" or "impediments" is quite complex; there is an abundance of theological formulations mixed with legalese. "The Sacrament of Marriage" in NCE.

became popular when natural and political disasters dominated such as the "Black Death" and the papal schism. Fearful minds also imagined the imminent end of the world, accompanied by a Great Judgment. announced by Jesus (Matt 25:31–46). The church was like a mental hospital that offered a cure for spiritual disease grounded in fear. The rich and famous fared better, as they always do. But everyone had to pay, pray, and obey.

Nevertheless, a "new birth," a "renaissance," was on the horizon, exemplified by two very open minds, the French cleric and poet, Francis Petrarch (1304–1374) and the Italian writer Giovanni Boccacio (1313–1375). They cherished hope rather than fear in their enthusiasm for the beauty of the Greek-Roman past, the study of ancient literature, and a longing for immortality. Petrarch secularized medieval Christian love in a poetry of love for a woman, and Boccacio published satirical tales about the immoralities of the clergy, stressing honest, natural feelings as a substitute for a Christian morality burdened by guilt and anxiety.

The bad-ass of the Renaissance was the Swiss physician and occultist Paracelsus (1493–1541), dubbed "bombastic" (from the Greek *bombeo* "howling," and medieval Latin *bombax*, "silkworm")—"high-sounding language with little meaning, used to impress people, denoting raw cotton or absorbent cotton used as padding."[52] Arrogant, annoying, and egotistic, he nevertheless is acknowledged as a pioneer in medical chemistry and surgery.

---

52. NOAD.

3

Loose Ends
1400–2010 CE

> You yourselves know very well that the day of the Lord will come like a thief in the night. When they say, "There is peace and security," then sudden destruction will come upon them, as labor pains come upon a pregnant woman, and there will be no escape. But you, beloved, are not in the darkness, for that day to surprise you like a thief; for you are all children of light and children of the day ... But since we belong to the day, let us be sober, and put on the breastplate of faith and love, and for a helmet the hope of salvation. For God has destined us not for wrath but for obtaining salvation through our Lord Jesus Christ.
>
> —1 Thessalonians 5:2–5, 8–9

Retardation and Reveille

By the beginning of the fifteenth century, spiritual, socio-political, and economic retardation seemed unstoppable. Scholastic theology had made "faith" an infused intellectual "belief" which, like a pharmaceutical prescription, was to keep believers healthy enough to get through a brief earthly life to "heaven." This miserable trek from sin to salvation was grounded in papal abuses. The ecclesiastical hierarchy kept people in check by treating any violation of rules as abnormal behavior, a mental disease, as it were. Brains were washed in the Confessional and through other means of "pastoral care" to preserve uniformity. One is reminded of twentieth-century Soviet Russian dictators who kept citizens in check by sending dissidents to mental hospitals. There, they were slowly drugged to death—a death penalty hidden from the outside world. The medieval church, however, added the public burning of heretics at the stake to private obedience as a cruel warning to potential reformers. By the sixteenth century, the roles were radically reversed: The defenders of the status quo were viewed as mentally retarded, and reformers were "normal." They contended that the church, the "body of Christ" on earth, was in such dire shape that only revolutionary measures could restore spiritual health. Leaders of church and state, as well as common folk, began to call for reform in every corner of the medieval world. It was also a call for spiritual sanity.

The first two well-known reformers, John Wycliffe in Oxford and John Hus in Prague quickly experienced the tyranny of the status quo. Their well-argued opposition to the papacy as an illegitimate historical development was called heretical. Wycliffe's teaching was condemned in England and he survived in retirement at his local parish. John Hus was condemned by the Council of Constance (1414–1418). In 1415, he was burned at the stake. Wycliffe was given the same verdict posthumously. In 1427, Pope Martin V ordered to exhume Wycliffe's body from his tomb in St. Mary's Church in Lutterworth, England, to burn it at the stake, and to throw the ashes into the local Swift River. The disciples of Hus, called "Hussites," honored him as a martyr. When in 1419 a group of Hussites marched through the streets of Prague, someone threw a stone at them from a window on the upper floor of the Town Hall. The group of Hussites stormed the Town Hall and threw a judge, the mayor, and thirteen other officials out of the window, thus starting the infamous "Hussite wars" (1419–1436). The event became known as "the first Prague defenestration"; other such events are recorded.[1] The Hussites fought a murderous guerilla war against all their enemies. The center of the resistance was the Czech city of Tabor. The "Taborites" became the radical core of the Hussites who marked their military banner with a Eucharistic chalice; consequently, they were also called "Calixtines" (from the Latin *calix*, "chalice") and "Utraquists" (from the Latin *sub utrque specie*, Holy Communion "in both kinds," bread and wine, because Rome

---

1. Historians seem to be enamored by "Prague defenestrations." In 1618, a second defenestration started the Thirty Years' War; see below, 135–36. Other such events included the anti-Communist Czech Secretary of State who died in this manner in 1948 and, in 1997, the Poet Bohumil Hrabal who fell to his death while feeding birds.

prohibited the consumption of the consecrated wine by the laity). The Hussites were never defeated even though they were led by a blind general. But they succumbed to bloody clashes among themselves. In the eighteenth century they emerged from their underground positions and reorganized as a peaceful community, named "Moravian Brethren," and with the help of an Austrian Lutheran nobleman, Count Nicholas von Zinzendorf, they became known as "Moravian Brethren."[2]

The Council of Constance ended the terrible papal schism by forcing the two popes to resign—so much for being "eternally" elected! A new pope was chosen, Martin V (1417-1431). But the quarrel about reform continued, focusing on the issue whether a council or the pope should have the highest authority in the church. Another council dragged on the issue in Basel (1431-1491) with interruptions. But the delegates seemed to be addicted to favor the authority of the pope and, after a stormy session, elected another new pope, Eugen IV (1431-1447). He chaired council sessions in Florence, Italy, and he seemed to gain respect when he negotiated a "Decree of Unity" with the Greek Orthodox Church. But the Orthodox delegation used the Decree as a political trick to gain support in the West for military assistance in a struggle for survival against Muslim Turkish pressure. In return for help, the delegation promised to accept papal authority in Greek Orthodoxy if Rome would grant their custom of married priests; other doctrinal differences were glossed over. The agreement lasted for only forty-four years (1439-1453) because the Greek population totally opposed it. Moreover, many secular rulers once again sided with the pope as the leader of Christendom. After all, popes had established a union of church and state that had proven itself to preserve ambitious greed on both sides.

A reform by ecumenical councils seemed hopeless. Some theologians continued to pursue a mystical route of reform, such as the Frenchman Jean Charlier de Gerson who was active at the Council of Constance, advocating a compromise between reason and love centered in Christ. But his defense of councils as the highest authority made him a target of papal wrath. Popes continued to behave like secular princes, pursuing personal interests. Some popes became popular through their drive for pleasure in their pursuit of reviving interest in the arts and literature of ancient Greece and Rome. They reflect the French proverb about the drive for food: "a blind hen can sometimes find her corn." Historians call this papal interest, also shared

2. Below, 137-38.

by many intellectuals, "Renaissance" (from the Latin *renasci*, "born again") and "Humanism" (true knowledge of humanity through authentic literary sources). Such a rebirth of interests in pre-Christian times introduced a process of secularization in Europe, weakening, indeed side-lining, the power of the church. It is another irony of history that this process was begun as a hobby of popes who used their rich purses to sponsor the work of historians, philosophers, and artists. They founded the now famous Vatican Library with its fabulous collection of ancient texts. Rome and Florence were beautified with new churches, sculptures, and paintings such as the dome of St. Peter's Cathedral (begun in 1506), the (naked!) statue of the biblical David, and the immortal works of Leonardo da Vinci (1452–1519), Michelangelo Buonarotti (1475–14564), and Raffael Santi (1483–1520).

Pope Alexander VI (1492–1503) combined the "edifice complex" with a life of pleasure guided by tyranny and intrigue. He became known as the "infamous Borgia" (the name of his Spanish family). He fathered many children, among them the daughter Lucrecia, known for her bacchanalia (orgies) and the son Caesar who was made a cardinal before age twenty-five, then resigned to create his own territory in central Italy by force. He embodied the immoral "prince" depicted by the political philosopher Niccolo Machiavelli (1469–1527) in his book *The Prince* (1532) as a ruler who accepts no other laws than his own and enforces them without adhering to any moral laws. To be a "Machiavellian" means being "cunning, scheming, and unscrupulous, especially in politics or in advancing one's career."[3] Caesar Borgia did not last long in that ideology; he died in battle at the age of thirty-one.

A lone, odd, sensational reformer appeared in Florence, the Dominican priest Girolamo Savonarola (1452–1498). He incited masses in apocalyptic sermons predicting the end of the world with a punishment of the decadent Medici families and Pope Alexander VI. The radical retardation of culture and Savonarola's ascetic life style made it possible for him to become the new leader in Florence with a reveille, a call for reform. He succeeded to persuade the king of France, Charles VIII, to invade Italy and create a new city state in Florence; French kings had been enduring critics of the papacy. Now, Savonarola began to purify the "harlot church of Rome." Desperate in his struggle for survival, the pope offered the renegade priest a cardinal's hat, but in vain. Savonarola declared that only God could stop him. Envious of the success of the Dominicans, the Franciscans proposed

---

3. NOAD.

a cruel test of orthodoxy. One of them would challenge Savonarola to join him in a fire walk, and survival would be a divine sign of approval. But the Dominicans substituted another friar for Savonarola. The event moved from the sublime to the ridiculous: the flames spread through a city block; the Dominican chickened out, a thunderstorm killed the flames; and the Franciscans were declared the winners. Secular and church authorities condemned Savonarola and his companion as heretics. They were tortured, hanged, and burned; their ashes were scattered over the local river.

In the north, the "renaissance" of the fine arts began with a "master school" in Cologne, Germany, finding its zenith in Albrecht Dürer (1471–1528) whose paintings and engravings disclose imagination linked to sharp observation (in the famous depictions of "the praying hands" and "the rabbit"). Matthias Grünewald (c. 1460–1528) pointed the way to new painting with lively colors, exemplified in his large "Isenheim Altar Piece" (twelve panels, now in a Museum in Colmar).

"Humanists" matched the renewal of Greek and Roman architecture with the collection of ancient classical texts beyond the works of Plato and Aristotle used by theologians. Their treasure hunt made them learn Greek and Hebrew, the original languages of the Bible. The notorious Medici family in Florence also sponsored the treasure hunts. A philosopher and clergyman, Marsilio Fincino (1433–1499), translated Plato into Latin and founded the Platonic Academy to advocate a Christian renewal through liberal Greek thought. In the north, the German Humanist John Reuchlin (1455–1522) and the Dutch philosopher Desiderius (from the Latin *desiderium* "desire") Erasmus (1466–1536) pioneered Humanism. Reuchlin became the first Christian expert to read ancient Hebrew and its Jewish literature, especially the "Cabbala" (Hebrew for "tradition"), an extensive medieval mystical commentary on the Jewish religion with the assumption that there is a "Platonic" link between this world and the next. Reuchlin's love of Hebrew drew the wrath of the anti-Semitic status quo fundamentalists, the Dominicans in Cologne. They successfully lobbied the papacy to have Reuchlin condemned in 1520. But by that time the reform movement, led by Martin Luther and others, had revived enough common sense to make Reuchlin a hero rather than a villain, and he died as an admired Humanist. Spiritual sanity was making a come-back.

Erasmus of Rotterdam embodied the strong winds of change. Born out of wedlock, he went to a school of the "Brethren of the Common Life." He was ordained and served as a priest in a cathedral. Sent to the University of

Paris. He became one of its most renowned graduates, denouncing church abuses and becoming a top Humanist. Researching Christian roots, he Advocated their revival, simple Christian moral life based on the "philosophy of Christ." Its description in his *Enchiridion* (from the Greek *encheiridion*, "in the hands," a handbook) became a best-seller. In a treatise, *Praise of Folly*, Erasmus appeared as a sarcastic, satirical critic of the retarded medieval religious "barbaric" life. His view of Christ as a moral teacher is close to that of Thomas Jefferson (1743–1826), the third president of the United States, who edited the Bible by removing anything theological from it in his work *The Life and Morals of Jesus*, also known as "The Jefferson Bible." He linked it to an "enlightened" Unitarian Christianity. Erasmus also edited works of early church fathers and the Greek text of the New Testament. Although in sympathy with Luther's call for reform, he did not join the reform movement; in a literary feud, he rejected Luther's view of the "bondage" of the human will and asserted its "freedom."[4]

The reveille of Martin Luther (1483–1546) shook the foundations of Europe and created the second great Christian schism in addition to the one between East and West in 1054. It began with Luther as a reform movement against church abuses. But after Luther's condemnation by church and state in 1521, the movement spread and generated enormous cultural consequences, creating a new religious expression, known as "Protestantism." That may have been the reason why Luther has been listed as the third most significant figure in world history, after Christopher Columbus (1451–1506), a native of Italy who sailed for Spain, the discoverer of the "new world," America, and the U.S. inventor Thomas Edison (1847–1931), the mastermind of modern communication. Galileo Galilei (1564–1642) is listed as the fourth most famous figure, the defender of the heliocentric view of a round earth discovered by the Polish astronomer Nicholas Copernicus(1473–1543). Like Luther, he was condemned by the church. But, unlike Luther, he recanted his views, but published them in his retirement under house arrest. Time healed his reputation as a heretic. Twentieth-century popes praised Gallileo as a fearless hero of scientific research, and

---

4. The feud revived the issue of "free will," not affected by "original sin," and the "bondage of the will" (the title of Luther's view). It was first debated by Augustine and Pelagius in the fifth century. Augustine (and Luther, an Augustinian monk) viewed salvation as "predestined" by God's grace. Pelagius and Erasmus saw it as the result of a free decision. See above, pp. 39–40.

in 2008 the Vatican put a statue of Gallileo at one of its walls—one of the best examples of "Christendumb."[5]

At the beginning of the sixteenth century, Europe was ruled by three super-powers, Spain, France and England. Russia; Poland, Hungary; German territories also influenced power politics, with the House of Hapsburg gaining political momentum by political marriages, summed up in a Latin saying coined by satirical critics, "Others wage war, thou happy Austria marry" (*bella gerant alii, tu felix Austria nube*). As a result, Maximilian I (of the House of Hapsburg) became Holy Roman Emperor (1493–1519). In addition, the discovery of "the new world" by Columbus in 1492 created a new market in Europe with profitable imports; and the heliocentric view of the earth shattered the assumption of a flat world. John Gutenberg (c.1400–c. 68) invented a speedy way of printing.[6] Printed paper money, banks, and international trade made a few people very rich and many people poor. The medieval degrading of society through begging was now matched by usury grounded in virtually limitless rates of interest. The old way of "paying off" God for the sins invented by the church was now accompanied by heavy financial debts incurred for worldly pleasures that could never be satisfied.

The retardation of culture led to a growing interest, indeed enthusiasm, for new learning and a lust for the secular life. Penance for sins and fear of death were shelved in favor of a renaissance of learning and living. Luther began his reveille with the now famous *Ninety-Five Theses* posted at the Wittenberg Castle Church on October 31, 1517, on the eve of All Saints Day when anxious parishioners gawked at relics and prayed for help from dead saints. The *Theses* blasted the abusive traffic of indulgences, endorsed by the pope. They called for faith in Christ alone as the only way to be redeemed from sin; buying indulgences does not earn divine mercy. Luther separated faith from the fear of punishment for not doing enough "good works." He revived the assertion of the apostle Paul that faith "justifies" before God (Rom 3:28). In this way, Luther cut the "Gordian knot" of the

---

5. Legend has it that Galileo muttered after the recantation, "And yet it moves" (*Eppur si muove* in Spanish). The painter, Bartholome Esteban Murillo I (c. 1618–1682) painted Gallileo in a dungeon with the muttered phrase on the wall. "Martin Luther," Millennium Edition. *Life* (1997), 11–25.

6. Printing was invented in China c. 300, then improved from movable paper to movable wood type by 1000. First rare books appeared in Europe c. 1340. Gutenberg, a gold-smith by trade, invented a press, using wood and metal movable type (tin and copper). The result was the famous "Gutenberg Bible" of 1450, a large 42p-line Latin Bible.

confusing entanglement of the anxiety-ridden medieval piety.[7] Christians live "by faith alone" in the Christ who is to come to complete their liberation from sin, evil, and death.

His reform movement spread like wild-fire. By 1521, all of Germany stood behind Luther. A Vatican official sent a secret wire (diplomatic mail) telling the pope that nine-tenths of Germans raise the war-cry "Luther" while the other tenth yell "Death to the Roman Curia." Within four years Luther was condemned by church and state, but survived, protected by the prince of his territory, Frederick "the Wise" and other secular leaders. He also had the support of intellectuals who viewed a reformation of culture, beginning with religion, as the path to a new age without the triumphalism of the Catholic Church. Luther's reveille included the popular notion of an imminent end of the world. But, in contrast to medieval millenarians, he refused to speculate about a date for the Last Day. He was satisfied with the apostolic injunction that "the day of the Lord will come like a thief in he night" (1 Thess 5:2). Christian existence must always be end-oriented, "eschatological" (from the Greek *eschaton*, "end"). Such orientation makes faith "a living, daring confidence in God's grace, so sure and certain that the believer would stake his life on it a thousand times."[8] That is why he viewed such an orientation as an incentive to be bolder in faith. As he put it with his swell-known gallows humor evidenced in "table-talks:" "when we are brought to life on the last day we shall spit on ourselves and say, 'Fie on you for not having been bolder in believing on Christ, since the glory is so great!'"[9] Having survived fear of death in a thunderstorm as a twenty-one-year old law student, he had joined the tough Augustinian order, obeying his vow made to his family saint, St. Ann (the mother of the Virgin Mary). "Help, and if you do, I will become a monk"—she did and he did! Then, as a biblical expert and teacher at the new university in the small Saxon town of Wittenberg, he developed a reform program grounded in a "theology of the cross," stressing the experience of "temptation" (*Anfechtung* in Gerrnan, *tentatio* in Latin).[10] But since suffering, "the cross," points to

---

7. NOAD: "from the legend that Gordius, king of Gordium, tied an intricate knot and prophesied that whoever untied it would become the ruler of Asia. It was cut through with a sword by Alexander the Great" (356–323 BCE).

8. "Preface to the Epistle of St. Paul to the Romans," *Luther's Works*, 35:370.

9. "Table Talk" no. 203, *Luther's Works*, 53:27.

10. Luther used the term to indicate not only "temptation," but any painful experience: doubt, physical and mental illness, the wrath of God, or other discomforts. Above all, "Anfechtung" points to the crucifixion of Jesus who liberates his disciples from fear and death.

Christ who overcomes any "Anfechtung," the "theology of the cross" becomes a "theology of freedom" anchored in the Judeo-Christian mandate for unconditional faith in a gracious God. This faith stands and falls with commitment to Christ and love of neighbor as the best means to curb the self-righteousness of "original sin," the oldest human temptation, namely the desire to be "like God" (Gen 3:5). "A Christian lives not by himself, but in Christ and in his neighbor. Otherwise he is not a Christian."[11]

Luther was a monk, priest, professor, a wit, and a workaholic. His massive output consists of more than four hundred treatises (some of them are lengthy books) more than three thousand sermons, twenty-six hundred letters, and about five thousand "table talks" (recorded by students at numerous dinners with guests). At age forty-two he married a twenty-six-year-old apostate nun of noble stock, Catherine of Bora. Luther's boss, John Frederick "the Wise" of Saxony, who had founded the University of Wittenberg and had hired Luther, gave him the Augustinian monastery as a parsonage. There, the Luthers had six children in eight years, established a self-sufficient household run by "Sir Katie," as Luther addressed his wife in letters. Luther had no intention of leaving the Roman Catholic Church; he viewed his activity as leading a reform movement within the Roman Catholic Church. But Catholics nicknamed his reform movement "Lutheran." Reformers dubbed it "evangelical" (from the Greek *euangelion*, "gospel"). Luther's successful reform program used the norms of the Bible, the first four Ecumenical Councils, and the tradition of the first Christian centuries before the political establishment of papal power. Above all, Luther rejected the Roman Catholic teaching that "Scripture" and "tradition" are equally normative; that there is an "apostolic succession" from Peter to the Roman papacy; and that there is an ordination into an "indelible" priesthood. Lutherans rejected Canon Law in favor of an ethics of justice based on "love of neighbor." This meant that a secularization of morality governed new "Lutheran" territorial and national churches in central, northern, and southern Europe. The core of "secular" ethics was "justice," defined by "law"; "Christian" mandates no longer defined secular law.

Luther set the tone for "Protestantism."[12] He was a top scholar who combined research with a down-to-earth style of communication, most

---

11. "The Freedom of the Christian," *Luther's Works*, 31:371.

12. A designation derived from the official "Protestation" of six powerful German territorial rulers, led by Frederick of Saxony, against a prohibition of reforms at the Diet of Speyer, Germany, in 1529.

evident in his catechisms, preaching, pastoral counseling, and liturgical reforms, spiked with a wit unmatched in Christian history, well manifested in a gallows humor. "For one person I have done enough," he mused shortly before his death. "All that's left is to sink into my grave. I'm done for, except for tweaking the pope's nose now and then."[13]

He worked with a team, led by the Humanist and expert in biblical languages (Greek and Hebrew), Philip Melanchthon (1497–1560), a humanistic stage-name from the Greek translation of the German name "Blackearth" (*Schwarzerd, melan chtonos* in Greek). Melanchthon drafted the normative Lutheran document, the Augsburg Confession of 1530, and led the reform movement after Luther's death. Luther created a uniform German language[14] in his translation of the Bible (the Greek New Testament and the Hebrew Old Testament with help from others). Family life, especially marriage, education, and spirituality changed radically by being viewed as part of a secular, penultimate world of sin, evil, and death. Christian life on earth is to be grounded in hope for life in a "heavenly" kingdom of God ushered in by Christ's second coming.

Luther was able to defend his views in a public disputation with a Catholic theologian, John Eck, in Leipzig in 1519. It put him on the academic map as a radical theologian. But he unwillingly remained "medieval" in his recommendation that princes should become "emergency bishops" (*Notbischöfe*), replacing the 'heretical' Catholic bishops. They could do so on the basis of their baptism which makes them "common priests." Luther, however, did not view them as equal with their baptized subjects who were not noble, "blue blood." He demanded religious liberty for himself at the imperial Diet[15] of Worms in 1521 where he refused to recant with the now famous words: "I cannot and will not recant anything, since it is neither safe nor right to go against conscience. I cannot do otherwise, here I stand, may God help me. Amen."[16] He was able to speak this way at the diet because he

---

13. "Table Talk" no. 4465, *Luther's Works*, 54:343. See. Eric W. Gritsch, *The Wit of Martin Luther*.

14. German is part of an Indo-European language group. It begins with a Saxon version in the sixth century, is shaped by business and law into a common "office language" (*Kanzleisprache*) identified with the city of Meissen in the sixteenth century. Luther used this Saxon version and his recording (by notes) of how people spoke in the market place. He coined new words like "gutter" (*Dachrinne*, "running from the roof"). "High German" was significantly revised in 1966 and, after controversies, standardized in 2006.

15. NOAD: "a legislative assembly in certain countries."

16. *Luther's Works*, 32:13.

Loose Ends

was protected by the ruler of his homeland, the Saxon ruler Frederick "the Wise" who was one of the seven powerful "electors" designated to choose a successor after the death of an emperor.[17] But Luther did not grant freedom of conscience to Saxon peasants in 1525, when they requested his help in their quest for freedom from their enslavement by princes. He refused and praised the princes as obedient servants of God when they slaughtered the rebels in a "battle" in 1525. When Luther heard about the execution of the peasants' chaplain, Thomas Müntzer who had been a Lutheran, he praised the event as an act of God. Centuries later, Communist East Germany ignored the world-wide celebration of Luther's five-hundredth birthday in 1983 and honored Müntzer as a pioneer of liberation from oppression. Big men make big mistakes! Luther never asked for protection by the state but received it anyway. So he was able to die in bed.

During and after his death, imperial diets could not achieve religious uniformity. Political intrigues and a brief war between Lutheran and Catholic military leagues created an uneasy compromise. A peace treaty at Augsburg in 1555 legalized the division between Protestants and Catholics with the problematic decision of territorial liberty: "he who rules the region decides its religion" (*cuius regio, eius religio*). Dissenters had to go into exile. Territorial Lutheranism was tolerated.

Luther's "Reformation" spread. A converted priest, Ulrich Zwingli (1484-1531), successfully changed the city government of Zurich, Switzerland, into a "Reformed" community ruled by new religious laws prohibiting any pomp and circumstance, especially any artistic ornamentation of churches such as pictures and statues. But Zwingli was honored outside the large city church with a statue, holding a sword and a Bible. He died in a battle against Swiss Roman Catholics—the only time when Swiss citizens, known for their unusually democratic government, fought each other. A single theological item prevented unity between German Lutherans and "Zwinglians," namely, the interpretation of the Eucharist. Zwingli viewed it as a memorial of Christ's death, a "sign"; Luther defended the existing tradition that it is a sacrament, with Christ's mysterious "real presence."

In Geneva, the French part of Switzerland, the French lawyer and lay theologian John Calvin (1509-1564), created the most successful reform

---

17. Above, 92. When Emperor Maximilian I died in 1519, the vote of the electors for either Charles I of Spain or Francis I of France was tied, and Frederick cast the decisive vote for Charles who became Emperor Charles V—and owed Frederick political favors, including the fate of Luther, even though Frederick ("the Wise!") never favored Luther in public.

movement. "Calvinism" spread in western Europe fueled by the a tough spiritual discipline embodied in Calvin. Unlike Luther, he was humorless and puritanical, banning any entertainment for pleasure such as games, alcohol, and dancing. But Calvin shared the Humanist interest in history and religion. Besides biblical studies, he produced a widely used summary of Protestant theology, *Institutes of the Christian Religion*. In the *Ecclesiastical Ordinances* of 1541, inspired by King David in the Old Testament, he developed a plan for reform in Geneva, ruled by four offices: elders, teachers, preachers, and deacons. Elders supervised discipline, teachers taught the new doctrines, preachers led parishes, and deacons provided for worldly needs. A "consistory" of elders and pastors functioned as an ecclesiastical court chaired by Calvin. Called "the Venerable Company," they enforced the new rules; and became a Protestant version of the Catholic Canon Law. High society complained but did not revolt. Anti-Calvinist sentiment was expressed in the satirical remark "Before Calvin was in the city we drank good wine."[18] Calvin played his cards close to his chest; the public knew only that he was married and frequently ill.

Calvin tolerated no opposition, exemplified by imprisonment and even death penalties, with the sensational case of the Spanish physician Michael Servetus (1511–1553) who was a "Unitarian—a person, esp. a Christian, who asserts the unity of God and rejects the doctrine of the Trinity."[19] He called it an "error" because the Bible does not teach it. Calvin asked him to recant his "heresy." When Servetus refused, Calvin did the next worst thing and had "heretical" anti-Trinitarian writings of Servetus delivered to the Catholic Inquisition which condemned him to death by burning. He died with his book against the Trinity tied to his leg. Calvin is the only theologian who grounded his strict view of Christian life in a radical doctrine of "predestination—the divine foreordaining of all that will happen, esp. with regard to the salvation of some and not others."[20] God determined that "some are ordained to eternal life, others to eternal damnation."[21] Ever since, generations of Calvinists and others wonder "who's who" in Christian history. Zealots of ethics and sociology went so far as to suggest a love affair, as it were, between Protestant ethics and capitalism. They contended that economic success, evident in Calvinist frugality and wealth, is a sign of

18. Quoted in Bernard Cottret, *Calvin. A Biography*, 107.
19. NOAD.
20. NOAD.
21. *Institutes of the Christian Religion*, III, 21:5.

Loose Ends

God's favor, election to eternal life. This view was inspired by the tale about Job (42:10–17) whose repentance is rewarded with overwhelming economic happiness.[22] Some Calvinists rejected the teaching of predestination in favor of the human freedom to choose salvation by a "free will," advocated by the Humanist Erasmus.[23] They were led by the Dutch Reformed theologian Jacob Arminius (1560–1609) who was Erasmian. "Arminians" left the established Reformed Church which condemned "Arminianism" in 1619.

Protestant churches perpetuated the medieval Catholic stance of persecuting "heretics" although with less fire and brimstone. But Protestant unity again was made impossible by senseless quarrels about the interpretation of the Eucharist with reference to Christ's "real presence." Calvin and Calvinism believed in a "spiritual presence" of Christ when communicants are spiritually united with their Lord by faith in the Eucharistic meal. Lutherans asserted that Christ is "truly present" in the elements regardless of whether or not the officiant or the communicant have faith since the presence is unconditional; faith makes the presence beneficial but does not "prove" it. Non-believers "eat and drink judgment against themselves" (1 Cor 11:29). In 1540, Melanchthon had tried hard to reach a compromise with one word but failed. He altered the Lutheran interpretation by suggesting that Christ is present "with" (*cum* in Latin) bread and wine, omitting the words "in" and "under." But this change revived the medieval view of "consubstantiation" (*cum substantia* in Latin, "with the substance"), a theological opinion that was rejected in favor of "transubstantiation." The leading reformer in Strasbourg (on the west side of the Rhine river), Martin Bucer (1491–1551), also failed in careful, extended attempts to unite Protestants with the ambitious goal of regaining unity with Catholics. But the Eucharist remained a Protestant holy bone of contention until the twentieth century.[24]

Calvin, not Luther, was the most influential reformer. He provided clear, systematic rules for thought and life in the Reformation. Calvinists created a Reformed Church in Scotland in 1560. Dutch-speaking inhabitants of the northern Spanish provinces, "The Netherlands," successfully fought for independence in a bloody rebellion and founded a Dutch Protestant

---

22. So argued by the German Sociologist Max Weber (1864–1920) in *The Protestant Ethic and the Spirit of Capitalism*.

23. Below, 126.

24. Below, 190.

kingdom in 1581. In France, Calvinists were known as "Huguenots."[25] They fought a civil war against King Henry IV of France, ending in the Edict of Nantes in 1598, granting them religious liberty until 1685 when Catholicism again became the only religion. About a half-million Huguenots emigrated to various parts of the globe. Two small churches (Calvinist Reformed and Lutheran) survived in France.

In England, the idiosyncratic king Henry VIII (1509–1547) published a defense of the traditional seven sacraments against Luther in 1521 and was praised by the pope as a "defender of the faith" (*defensor fidei*). But ten years later he cut all political ties with the papacy because Rome would not agree to sanction a divorce. He seized all ecclesiastical property and declared himself the secular pope ("Supreme Head") of the Church of England. Henry's tenure is like a situation comedy with tragic ingredients: after his first two wives produced only daughters rather than a desired son, the king divorced the first wife, had the second one beheaded for alleged adultery, and married again resulting in the birth of a son, Edward, causing the death of his mother. Edward VI was too young and too weak to govern; a Privy (private) Council of noblemen did. The new archbishop of Canterbury, Thomas Cranmer, liked Lutheran theology, married the niece of a German Lutheran reformer, Andreas Osiander, and created a national church which survived an attempt by "bloody Mary," Queen Mary Tudor (1533–1558), the daughter of Henry's first wife, to make England Catholic again; her memory is kept alive by a strong cocktail, a "bloody Mary." Henry married two more times, executing the fifth "adulterous" wife, but being survived by the final, sixth one. Twice-widowed, cultured, and strong, she outlived Henry and married again! Elizabeth, the daughter of Henry's second wife, was the queen who ruled England with great skill (1558–1603) and laid the foundations for "Great Britain" closely tied to the established Protestant Church of England, also known as "Anglican" (the Latin root for "English").

In Scandinavia, kings declared their nations "Lutheran": Denmark (to which belonged Norway and Iceland) in 1536; Sweden in 1593; and in Finland through the reformer Michael Agricola (c. 1510–1557), sponsored by the Swedish crown.

---

25. A controversial designation, perhaps a French alteration of he Swiss German name for "comrades united by an oath" (*Eidgenosse*).

Territories in eastern Europe followed suit, led by Hungary; some Lutherans survived Catholic persecution in Spain, Italy, and the Hapsburg lands (Austria).

The fragmentation of the Reformation continued. "Protestant" dissenters left the mainline of the Reformation shaped by Luther, Zwingli, and Calvin. They have been labeled the "left wing" of the Reformation (with "mainliners" in the middle and Catholics on the "right") and/or "the radical Reformation" (from the Latin *radix*, "root") that tried to restitute Christian roots as the "golden age,"[26] the "early church" (identified as Christian life in the first three centuries). Dissenters contended that the "fall" from the "golden age" began with the adoption of Christianity by Constantine in 313. The "radical reformation" also has been likened to a landscape of mole-hills pointing to an underground spirituality. "Radical reformers" appeared first in Luther's hometown Wittenberg in 1521 while he was in exile for almost a year as "Knight George" (*Junker Jörg*) at the Wartburg Castle where his "boss" Frederick "the Wise" had hidden him from persecution. Luther called them "swarmers" (*Schwärmer* in German, analogous to wild swarms of bees). He secretly left his exile and quickly quenched the small riots of students and other restless folk from his bully pulpit. But he suffered from an allergy to "swarmers" for the rest of his life and let everyone know about it. "Swiss Brethren" formed a group in Zurich nicknamed "Anabaptists" (from the Greek *anabaptizein* "to baptize again"); they favored adult baptism. But when they re-baptized adults who had been baptized as infants, Zwingli ignored the trued and true Swiss democratic way of life and turned "Catholic": he enforced the sixth-century Justinian Code that demanded capital punishment without any trial for the "crime" of an unnecessary second baptism; it was part of medieval Canon Law.[27] It forced the "Brethren" to become refugees in 1527. In the same year, one of them, Felix Manz, was executed by drowning in Lake Zurich. But martyrdom never stopped Christian zeal. The Swiss Brethren survived, adopting

---

26. A designation used by ancient Greek and Roman poets to describe the "fall" from an ideal, idyllic, and perfect age of happiness to evil times. These poets depict the fall in three stages as the change from gold to silver, bronze, and iron. In the literature of the "radical Reformation" there are references to the change from a virgin (the first pure Christian community) to a prostitute (the established church after Constantine). Millenarians describe the change in terms of seven "ages" analogous to the seven days of creation or "dispensations," beginning with the sinless age of Adam and ending with the "kingdom": ushered in when Christ comes again.

27. First issued in the "Justinian Code." See above, 30-31.

a separatist style of life that focused on pacifism and spiritual formation for tough discipleship. In 1534, some Dutch Anabaptists broke rank and established their Biblicist version of "the kingdom of God" in Münster, Germany (on the Dutch border), instituting polygamy and executing dissenters as ungodly sinners. But a year later, Protestant and Catholic princes united to wipe them out. They put the executed bodies of Anabaptist leaders in cages and hung them from the steeple of the city church to rot; the cages are still there. The Protestant Reformation did not eliminate Catholic medieval ways of persecution. Remnants of Anabaptists were organized by a Dutch convert, Menno Simons (c. 1596–1561); they became known as "Mennonites," known for their pacifism as a sign of a total separation of church and state. Another radical group, the "Hutterites," named after an Austrian hatter, Jacob Hutter (German for "hatter") who was martyred in 1536, rejected private property (based on Acts 2:44, "they had all things in common") and established "communes of farming brethren" (*Bruderhof* in German) in various parts of Europe, Latin, and North America. They created the first kindergartens, or "day-care centers" and good schools. Some dissenters became mystics. Others rejected the dogma of the Trinity (since they found no hard evidence of it in the Bible) and became known as "anti-Trinitarians" or "Unitarians." They were led by two Italian Unitarians, the brothers Laelius and Faustus Sozzini who fled to Racov, Poland, where the local prince had granted asylum to "Polish Brethren," an apocalyptic group looking for a "new Jerusalem." They also denied the Trinity and became "Socinians," organized as the "Minor Reformed Church" in Poland. Faustus Sozzini's "Racovian Catechism" of 1605 became their doctrinal platform.

Lutherans quarreled among themselves about the legacy of Luther. Some followed Melanchthon, the "Philippists" (using his first name Philip), others remained staunchly "Luther-an," the "Gnesio-Lutherans" (from the Greek *gnesios*, "authentic"). Compromises laid the doctrinal foundation for Lutheran churches in *The Book of Concord* of 1570. But the debates continued. The faculty at Wittenberg University defended an "orthodoxy" based on an "infallible" Bible as the source for living by "faith alone" (*sola fide* in Latin). The logic of Aristotle was used to "prove" the link between immanent and transcendent life. Immanent life was seen as prescribed by the Bible which, as the "Word of God," was eternal. Lutheran "orthodoxiasts" taught that God as Holy Spirit God in the Bible reveals everything as true without error; the authors of the Bible are "the secretaries of the Holy Spirit" taking its dictation. Luther would turn over in his grave if he heard the most renowned "orthodox" theologian in Wittenberg, Abraham Calov (1612–1686), declare that one must believe the Bible even if the human mind cannot assent. To Luther, the Bible was not identical with the "Word of God"; The Letter of James "is flatly against St. Paul and all the rest of Scripture."[28] Today, the American Lutheran Church-Missouri Synod is still governed by this doctrine of biblical inerrancy.[29]

Calvinist Reformed churches presented their "orthodoxy" in the *Heidelberg Catechism* of 1563. The Church of England did so in *The Book of Common Prayer* of 1549 (with later revisions) and in *Thirty-Nine Articles of Religion* in 1571. Roman Catholicism streamlined its anti-Protestant stance with some institutional reforms and a summation of teachings elaborated by the Council of Trent, Italy (1545–1563). The Council was dominated by a new, ultra-conservative cadre of priest-theologians known as "Jesuits," members of the "Society of Jesus" (S. J.). Their Spanish founder, Ignatius of Loyola (1491–1556), a romantic knight involved in military ventures, transferred his military discipline to "Spiritual Exercises" (the title of a catechism) after a cannonball had fractured his left leg. Unable to offer himself to a lady in romantic love, he switched his allegiance to "Lady Mary" and her Son Jesus, represented on earth by the papacy in Rome. He studied for his ordination and, as priest, he went with several, other like-minded clergymen in 1534 to Montmartre in Paris, a location for lovers who vow to get married. The group offered their lives to Pope Paul III who approved their Jesuit order, with Ignatius as its first "general." The order amended the traditional third vow of obedience (besides poverty and celibacy) to unconditional obedience to the pope, dubbed "cadaver obedience," slavish submission. This special discipline made Jesuits the best-trained and most effective "special commando" of Roman Catholicism. They headed a militant "counter reformation" based on the teachings of Trent, especially its "Index of Prohibited Books" of 1564, a measure designed to keep brains washed. Ever since, bishops controlled the publication of books, banning suspicious ones and authorizing permitted ones with the label "Nihil Obstat" (Latin for "nothing hinders"). A mixture of facts and fiction depicted Jesuits as shrewd proselytizers who live by the moral rule that "the end justifies the means," also known as "Consequentialism—the doctrine that the morality of an action is to be judged solely by its consequences."[30] The

---

28. *Luther's Works*, 35:396.
29. Below, 169.
30. NOAD.

Italian Jesuit Robert Bellarmine (1542–1621) became the most renowned enemy of Protestants with polemics outlined in his three-volumes, *On Controversies* (*De Controversiis* in Latin). He was canonized a saint in 1930. In retrospect, it can be said that Calvin and Calvinism dominated in the promotion of the Protestant Reformation, and Ignatius and the Jesuits were the most zealous defenders of Roman Catholicism.

Catholic-Protestant tensions led to the devastating Thirty Years' War. It began when Protestants threw two Hapsburg officials and a secretary out of a window; they survived by landing on a pile of manure.[31] The war involved almost all nations on the European continent. The Protestants were saved by the Lutheran Swedish king Gustavus Adolphus who died in the decisive battle in 1631. The peace of Westphalia was negotiated in 1648 in the city of Münster where the cages of Anabaptist martyrs on a church steeple could still be seen. The peace granted freedom of religion only to Lutherans, the Calvinist Reformed, and the Anglicans. "Anabaptists," now a nickname for other Protestants, had to go underground to survive. Catholic and Protestant "orthodoxy" ruled. A popular Lutheran opponent of "orthodoxy" depicted the history of Christianity as a struggle between "true" and "false" teaching; contending that critical hindsight warrants the conclusion that heretics preserved what is truly Christian better than their persecutors claiming "orthodoxy." The "heretics," of course, are Lutherans because they viewed the Bible and the time of the first generations of Christians as highest authorities.[32] Other opponents called for a reform of piety, stressing community and commitment. Dubbed "Pietism," the movement was influenced by the best-selling work of the Lutheran pastor John Arndt, *True Christianity* (1610) who proposed stages of a mystical development revealed in a "sanctified" life with "the sweet taste of grace."

After the Thirty Years' War, in 1675, a Lutheran pastor in Frankfurt am Main, Philip Jacob Spener (1635–1705), generated the "Pietist" reform movement in a manifesto titled "Pious Desires" (*pia desideria in Latin*). It dramatized the social ills brought about by the devastating war in Germany, and it offered six proposals for reform: 1) Bible meditation on the Word of God in small groups; 2) A revival of the common priesthood of all believers; 3) a move from rational knowledge to practice; 4) avoiding unnecessary

---

31. Historians call this event the "second defenestration of Prague" after the first one in 1419. Below, 122.

32. Gottfried Arnold, *Impartial History of the Church and Heretics* (*Unparteiische Kirchen-und Ketzergeschichte*).

theological controversies; 5) a reform of training for the ordained ministry; and 6) simple, edifying preaching. These proposals foreshadow popular Protestant "pious" features: Bible study in small groups, pastoral care with good preaching, an anti-intellectual, anti-liturgical and anticlerical stance, theological education in "seminaries" (from the Latin *seminarium*, "seedbed") and an emphasis on "practical Christianity." Spener formed small groups for discussion (women were excluded but could listen in an adjoining room). The Pietist small group became known as "a little church in the big church" (*ecclesiola in ecclesia*). Spener's program was expanded into a "foundation" in Halle by a vivacious nobleman, pastor, and theologian, August Hermann Francke (1663–1727), an odd character who liked to wear colorful wigs, loved raising money for his projects, and established typical Pietist institutions such as Bible societies, schools, orphanages, hospitals, and missionary institutes to train people for service at home and abroad. He began with an orphanage for the victims of the war, motivated by an intensive "penitential struggle": (*Busskampf* in German), an emotional conversion experience. He liked to hear a good conversion story as the basis for faithful witness. Penitential piety and joyful love of neighbor shaped Francke's personality; it also reflected the distinct culture of his time, the age of "baroque" (from the Italian *barroco* designating a pearl of irregular shape)—"a style of European architecture, music, and art characterized by ornate detail."[33] The Prussian king, Fredrick William I (1688–1740), liked Francke and supported his Halle programs. But such close contact with the Prussian royalty was a two-edged relationship: it created a public school system based on Francke's ideas; but it also seduced him to bless a military academy for the training of "Christian" soldiers through a manual titled "The Pious Soldier, that is, a Thorough Instruction for the True, Blessed and Christian Men of War." A bizarre incident pinpoints Francke's dilemma: in 1714, a celebration of confirmation in a village church was rudely interrupted by royal Prussian recruiters who kidnapped the male candidates for confirmation just when they stepped to the altar for Holy Communion— a shocking case of Protestant church-state relations!

The sentimental aspect of Pietism was embodied in Count Nicholas von Zinzendorf (1700–1760), a refugee from the Catholic Hapsburg territory, Austria, with family ties to northern Germany where he became a gentleman farmer. In 1722, he invited Czech Hussites, known as "Moravian Brethren" (*Unitas Fratrum* in Latin, "the unity of the brethren") to settle

33. NOAD.

on a piece of land they would call "Herrnhut" (German for "protected by the Lord"). There, the Brethren farmed and developed a carpentry business. The community became a center of mission which, like a beehive, produced sweet, spiritual honey for global distribution. Only a highly disciplined organization is able to achieve such a goal. The Brethren were divided into "choirs" (because they liked to sing),[34] and "bands" of married and unmarried members, children and youth—always guided by worship and catechetical instruction. Members of the community who were unable to join the meetings for reasons of health or old age were guided at home by daily written Bible meditations called "watchwords" (*Losungen* in German, "lots.")[35] The Moravian mission began with Eskimos in the north and with natives in the West Indies in the south. But odd characteristics hampered the mission: a child-like, indeed childish, spirituality mixed with the image of "faith" as "being in love": with Jesus (often expressed in erotic language), and silly interest groups like the "order of little fools" (based on 1 Cor 4:10, "we are fools for the sake of Christ"). Zinzendorf himself cherished his "intimacy with the Savior" and addressed Jesus as "little lamb" in a trinity with "papa" (God) and "Mama" (the Holy Spirit). Somehow he managed to keep the Moravians attached to Lutheranism, perhaps because of their successful missions sponsored by colonialist German and Scandinavian governments. Migration to North America made Pietism an enduring feature of Lutheranism. Halle in Germany trained Lutheran pastors for work in America. One graduate, Samuel Simon Schmucker, established a seminary (1826) And a college (1832) in Gettysburg, PA, with an unsuccessful attempt to create an "American Lutheranism," without its European confessional base. This base was preserved by Henry Melchior Muhlenberg who organized a "Pennsylvania ministerium" in 1748. A small committee of clergy and laypeople, it became the infant structure of the Lutheran denomination in North America. When the European controversy about Christ's presence in the Eucharist raised its ugly head in a meeting between Lutheran and (Calvinist) Reformed immigrants, Muhlenberg satisfied them with a

---

34. In 1898, he Moravians established the first US choir in Bethlehem, PA for the performance of the oratories of Johann Sebastian Bach, an annual event.

35. The annual "watchword" collection began in 1727 and appeared in small booklets in 1731. The daily "watchword" consists of an Old Testament verse chosen from 1200 Old Testament verses selected by lot (thumbing through the texts), with "doctrinal" New Testament verses as a commentary. A prayer and a stanza from a hymn completed this daily spiritual exercise. The "Watchwords" are used globally in many languages by millions of Christians.

laconic interpretation: "It was the Lord who spake it; He took the bread and brake it; And what the Word did make it, That I believe and take it."[36] But familiar, odd views appeared here and there. American Pietism spawned Millenarians and other apocalyptic factions predicting the imminent end of the world. But they never attracted a large following.

The Protestant Reformation was meant to be a reform movement within the Roman Catholic Church, not a separation from it, a schism. But Rome condemned the reform movement and refused to engage in any constructive dialogue with Protestants. Such a dialogue, however, would have been difficult to organize, given the fragmentation of Protestantism with its numerous groups and their varieties in faith and morals. So Christian unity remained a "pipe-dream—an unattainable or fanciful hope or scheme . . . referring to a dream or referring to a dream experienced when smoking an opium pipe."[37] It is a note-worthy coincidence that the founder of atheistic Communism, Karl Marx, branded "religion" as a pipe-dream in his frequently quoted sound-bite, "Religion is the opium of the people"[38] But it was the "opium" of ambition, with its fantasy of dominating the world that plagued ecclesiastical and political princes. Ecumenists and Communists could co-exist in peace if leaders of church and state sobered up and would forswear their bad habit of self-righteousness.

Catholics noted with arrogant satisfaction that the reason for the various Protestant schisms was a lack of hierarchical leadership which would not permit fragmentation, leaving decisions about faith and morals in the hands of bishops and the pope. So the Protestant way of involving all members of the church in making decisions became a new heresy labeled "subjectivism—the doctrine that knowledge is merely subjective and that there is no external or objective truth."[39] Jesuits mixed their sophisticated polemics with a propaganda of popular superstitions, such as the cult of the "heart of Jesus" and of "the heart of Mary," based on alleged visions by nuns and children. Seventeenth-century baroque art, architecture, and music promoted emotional expression, ranging from serene to grotesque. The Dutch painter Peter Paul Rubens, the Italian architect Lorenzo Bernini

36. Quoted in E. Clifford Nelson (ed.), *The Lutherans in America*, 70.

37. NOAD.

38. In the "Introduction" of his "Critique of Hegel's Philosophy of Right," 1. Marx advocated the elimination of private property in favor of an economy run by a Socialist government grounded in the authority of the working-class, the "proletariat" (from the Latin *proles*, "offspring" fathered by a member of the lower class).

39. NOAD.

(1598–1680) and the composer Johann Sebastian Bach (1685–1750) represent the great variety of such expressions. A group of French Cistercian monks, led by Cornelius Jansen, threatened the papal and Jesuit drive for uniformity. Jansen had published a book, *Augustine*, in 1640 questioning the validity of the "father" of Catholic theology, Thomas Aquinas, who did not share Augustine's view of sin and grace, favored by Luther and other Protestant theologians. The "Jansenists" also represented the liberal French "Gallicanism" (from *Gaul*, the old designation of France). It became customary to identify "Gallicanism" with liberal Catholic views and "Ultramontanism" (from the Latin *ultra mons*, "beyond the mountains") as the conservative, papal view in Italy. The most radical "Gallican" was the philosopher Blaise Pascal (1623–1662) who advocated a Christianity without papal control. Rome, of course, rejected Jansenism and, when it continued to simmer in the pot of time, it was declared a heresy by a papal bull in 1713.

In England, the enforcement of Anglicanism as the state religion spawned another set of "radical reformers" or dissenters. Influenced by the continental Reformation, intellectuals at Cambridge University, and migrants from the continent questioned the notions of Anglican vestments, bishops, and women as heads of state. The movement was named "Puritan—a member of a group of English Protestants who regarded the Reformation of the Church of England under Elizabeth as incomplete and sought to simplify and regulate forms of worship."[40] Non-Episcopal ecclesiastical polity models were thrown into the controversy, mainly "Presbyterian" (the rule of elders), "Congregationalist" (the rule of independent parishes) and "Baptists" (governed by the "Congregationalist" model). Millenarians expected the end of all institutions, and theocratic Calvinists dreamed of a "Holy Commonwealth" governed by "covenants" grounded in the Bible. Baptists fled to Holland and adopted the custom of adult baptism from the Mennonites.

Puritans dominated, extending their influence to New England (Massachusetts) in North America. Their zeal is criticized in the satirical adage, "The Puritans first fell on their knees, and then on all the aborigines."[41] In 1642, Scottish dissenters accomplished a parliamentary rejection of the episcopacy and the king in favor of a Calvinist "Presbyterian" authority

---

40. NOAD.

41. Quoted in Eric W. Gritsch, *Toxic Spirituality: Four Enduring Temptations of Christian Faith*, 109.

modeled after Calvin's church structure in Geneva. The British sense for "fair play" managed a compromise at a synod in Westminster. Presbyterians and Episcopalians tolerated each other based on "The Westminster Confession" of 1646. But "fair play" also produced religious groups beyond Presbyterians, namely, Episcopalians, Congregationalists, and Baptists (rooted in Swiss and Dutch Anabaptism). All of them migrated to "New England." But Calvinistic Puritans did not tolerate Baptists because of their belief that one becomes a Christian through voluntary conversion, not through divine election. One group was not tolerated at all, the pacifist "Quakers," because they rejected patriotic, national self-defense. Known as "Society of Friends," they were disciples of George Fox (1624–1691) a mystic who believed that an "inner light" of the soul enables believers to experience an illumination of life manifested in love for all people as "friends." Quakers assembled for worship in silence until the Holy Spirit moved hearts (leading to "quaking") to go into the world to help the neighbor in need.

Fair play became a political game of wild cards when a member of the British landed aristocracy, Oliver Cromwell (1599–1658) organized an army of psalm-singing Puritans who routed the royalists and ended the monarchy with the dethroning of King Charles I in 1649. People could not fathom an England without royalty! But Cromwell behaved like a king, using the title "Lord Protector" as head of a "Parliament of Saints" begun in 1653. Surprisingly, the Puritan Cromwell became a "protector" of religious liberty. But the time without a king ended with his death, and the monarchy was revived by King Charles II in 1660. He tried to replace Puritanism and Anglicanism with Roman Catholicism but could not move the parliament to do so. To keep the crown, he affirmed Anglicanism yet remained Catholic in his heart. His brother occupied the throne as James II, openly advocating a return to Roman Catholicism. That was the last straw in the political power plays. The parliament asked the Dutch Prince William of Orange, husband of Mary, daughter of King Charles I, to take over the reigns and preserve Anglicanism. In 1688, he and Mary "invaded" England in "a glorious bloodless revolution" (there was minimal fighting when Dutch ships landed). One year later, the new king, William III (1689–1702) persuaded parliament to issue the famous "Act of Toleration" of 1689, granting religious liberty to all groups except Catholics and Unitarians. The Church of England prevailed.

Protestantism, Roman Catholicism, and Eastern Orthodoxy continued on their separate paths. Greek and Russian Orthodoxy became increasingly isolated due to their spiritual and geographic isolation. Religious groups, who were not tolerated, began to migrate to America which was the continent with the richest potential for religious liberty after its discovery by the Catholic (native Italian) Spanish explorer Christopher Columbus in 1492 and with the principle of religious freedom in the First Amendment of 1791 to the U.S. Constitution.

Mazy Means and Ways

Christianity became entangled in a maze of minds and movements in the "Age of Enlightenment" that dominated the eighteenth century. It was an age that liberated people from their dependence on the church through a philosophy of "natural reason" with a process of "secularization." The scientific discoveries in the previous century paved the way for new insights into the reality and meaning of human life: the rotation of the earth around the sun, together with other planets; the encounter with life in other continents; pre-Christian life, especially Greek and Roman, through Humanistic studies. Enlightened minds learned that centuries of Christianity had made unnecessary secrets out of the reality of human history. A joyful enthusiasm supplanted the superstitious fear generated by medieval Christendom. The light seen at the end of the dark tunnel of ecclesiastical faith and morals became a floodlight revealing a new world. The dates of edicts of toleration are political sign-posts of enlightenment: 1689 in England; 1781 in Austria, the bastion of Catholic Hapsburg rule; 1791 in the United States, and 1793 in France where a liberal "Gallicanism" opposed the conservative "ultramontane" Italian loyalty to the popes.

The European Enlightenment was virtually the opposite of the "medieval synthesis." Just as medieval theologians confidently used human reason to "prove" a divine, metaphysical realm so enlightened minds used reason with the same confidence to "prove" that medieval theology created a fiction. Christian faith and morals were reinterpreted. The Enlightenment began in the Netherlands (Holland), home of the renowned Humanist Erasmus and the first country to win a war of liberation against Catholic tyranny in Spain. From there, a maze of new philosophical world views extended throughout Europe. The mathematician Rene Descartes (1596–1650), a native of France, pioneered philosophical reflections summarized in the slogan "I am thinking, therefore I exist" (*cogito ergo sum*).[42] The slogan reflects a sense of human freedom no longer impeded by evil as "original sin." The human mind is free to judge what is good and evil. The Dutch Jewish thinker Baruch Spinoza (1632–1677) thought of God as "substance," dwelling even in inorganic matter, without any special revelation as taught in the Judelo-Christian tradition. Consequently, "religion" can only be "Pantheism—a doctrine that identifies God with the universe, or regards the universe as a manifestation of God."[43]

French philosophers offered various "enlightened" views. The Protestant Pierre Bayle (1647–1705) composed the first historical dictionary, listing Christian beliefs but criticizing them in annotations, especially faith in miracles. Encyclopedias mushroomed. The enfant terrible of the age of enlightenment was Francois-Marie Arouet with the pen-name Voltaire (1694–1778): a noble loud-mouth, satirist, and prolific writer of tracts, poems, and about twenty-thousand letters to virtually anyone of fame. He was known for the repeated sound-bite against the Catholic Church, "Erase the infamy!" (*ecrasez l'infame*). Blacklisted by the government and imprisoned some time, he fled to England, then stayed briefly with an even more powerful loud-mouth, Emperor Frederick William the Great of Prussia who had an arrogant opinion about everything and enforced it often with his proverbial Prussian officialdom. Voltaire died in France, believing in the god of "Deism—belief in the existence of a supreme being, specifically a creator who does not intervene in the universe."[44] Voltaire could have created the sarcastic deistic anecdote about the "Creator," God: when he once was bothered by a fly on his nose he could not intervene in its life and remove it; for he could not interfere in the process of creation which must run its predestined course; it can neither be interrupted nor stopped! "Conservative" Deists added a particular notion of God dubbed "Theism"—belief in one god as creator of the universe, intervening in it and sustaining a personal relation to his creatures."[45] The more cheerful mind among the flock of critics was Jean Jacque Rousseau (1712–1778) He rejected the view that human nature is sinful. Good, warm emotions, not cool, objective reason govern life. The heart must tame the negative power of reason. Rousseau

---

42. In par. 7 of *Principles of Philosophy* in vol. 1 of *The Philosophical Writings of Rene Descartes*, 195.
43. NOAD.
44. NOAD.
45. NOAD.

advocated his view not in philosophical treatises but in novels, such as *Julie, the New Heloise*. A romantic love of nature should shape human nature—an admirable point of view as long as one is not bitten by a mosquito or a poisonous snake. The mathematician August Comte (1798–1857) went beyond Deism and Theism by contending that they represent only preliminary 'theological" and "meta-physical" stages of historical development. A third culminating final stage is a "scientific" one; it discloses the laws or relationships of phenomena. Comte called it "Positivism"—that "every rationally justifiable assertion can be scientifically verified or is capable of logical or mathematical proof."[46] Comte predicted that this kind of thinking would create a universal socio-political order and "religious" morality not grounded in a belief in God but in humanity. Some cynical minds proposed that all "enlightenment" consists of physical comfort and sensual pleasure defined as "materialism—a tendency to consider material possessions and physical comfort as more important than spiritual values."[47]

In England, the globe-trotting philosopher Herbert of Cherbury offered a more conservative view in 1663, consisting of a system of five innate "common conceptions" (*communes notitia* in Latin): 1) knowledge of God; 2) worship of God; 3) virtue and piety; 4) penance and detestation of sin; and 5) divine retribution in this world and the next. This system was rejected by the Scottish economist and historian David Hume (1711–1776). He denied any belief in "God" and in a "soul" because they cannot be logically defined. There is only measurable experience, "Empiricism—the theory that all knowledge is derived from sense-experience."[48] Religion is an illusion derived from fear of the powers of nature.

In Germany, the Prussian philosopher Immanuel Kant (1724–1804) pondered the various features of the Enlightenment and, after long reflections known as a "decade of silence," generated a "Copernican" revolution: just as Copernicus detected that the sun governs life on earth so the human mind detects whatever is known. But whatever is known, either by observation or by reasoning, is known in time and space which hide "a thing in itself." It can only be experienced as a "phenomenon—a fact or situation that is observed to exist or happen, especially one whose cause or explanation is in question."[49] Kant published his massive reflections in a trinity of books:

46. NOAD.
47. NOAD.
48. NOAD.
49. NOAD.

The Critique of Pure Reason, *The Critique of Practical Reason*, and *The Critique of Judgment*. In these works he contended that beyond phenomena there are "postulations," assumptions derived from reasoning discussions, but not rationally demonstrable, such as "God, freedom, and immortality." That is why human life should be governed by relationships that create a morality based on a "categorical imperative," reciprocity: "act according to the maxim whereby you can, at the same time, will that it should become a universal law." This is a "secular" version of the biblical "golden rule"—"You shall love your neighbor as yourself" which, however, is part of a double commandment that conditions the "love of neighbor," "You shall love the Lord, your God . . ." But Kant rephrased his "postulations" of mysteries at the end of his life. They are described on a plaque at his tombstone in his hometown Königsberg, Germany (now Kalinigrad, Russia): "Two things fill the mind with ever new and increasing admiration and awe, the more often and steadily we reflect upon them, 'The starry heaven above myself and the moral law within me.'"

In the maze of Enlightenment philosophy there was little, if any, room for a religion that was defined by the death and resurrection of Jesus. Controversy about the "truth" of Christianity was inevitable. It arose when an "enlightened" intellectual, Herman Samuel Reimarus, a teacher in Hamburg, Germany, shared "fragments" with the renowned writer and playwright Gotthold Ephraim Lessing who published them in 1777 as "Wolfenbüttel Fragments" (the name of a northern German town, Brunswig, with a famous library). The "Fragments" present a denial of traditional Christianity: Jesus was neither the "Son of God" nor a "Christ"; mediating salvation; his resurrection is a fiction concocted by his disciples after he failed as a political Messiah; and the "gospel" is a fraud. The controversy raged for about a year and has surfaced off and on ever since among scholars who are addicted to the "quest for the historical Jesus." Today, the addicts constitute "the Jesus Seminar" with about a hundred international members. In 1779 Lessing called for religious toleration in his play, "Nathan the Wise," in which three believers, a Christian, a Moslem, and a Jew become friends because the three popular religions (Judaism, Christianity, and Mohammedanism) represent a harmonious revelation with universal morality. The Catholic Church and the ever-present anti-Semites condemned the play.

Some German Enlightenment figures moved from cold-blooded reasoning to subjective "feeling" (*Gefühl* in German), a sense of wonder, intuition, and a bond with nature. Even a Lutheran bishop, Johann Gottfried

Christendumb

Herder (1714–1803), adopted this stance, together with the philosopher and lay theologian Johann Georg Hamann (1730–1788). They viewed Christianity in this manner, calling it a "religion of humanity" in close contact with the spirit of classical antiquity. This kind of attitude also guided the renowned poets and writers Friedrich von Schiller (1759–1805) and Wolfgang Goethe (1749–1832) who expressed their awe about the mystery of life sensed in Christianity; but they were not card-carrying Christians. They represent a "romanticism—emphasizing inspiration, subjectivity, and the primacy of the individual."[50] A popular Romantic fictitious Catholic autobiography from the pen of a German lawyer, Wilhelm Heinrich Wackenroder, typifies the overabundance of emotions combining spiritual and secular values, *Outpourings of an Art-Loving Friar (Herzensergiessungen eines kunstliebenden Klosterbruders, 1797)*.

Traditional Christianity was promoted outside of Europe by missionaries. Catholicism was successfully spread around the globe by Jesuits and other missionaries, in the Spanish and Portuguese colonies of Latin America, in the Caribbean; in Asia, mainly India and China. In Africa, the early Christian strongholds in the North, with St. Augustine's bishopric in the fifth century, were absorbed by Muslims in 648. Two centuries later, Christianity returned as part of the slave trade of Spanish and Portuguese businessmen. They invited Catholic missionaries to southern and western Africa. There were enormous travel hazards. Many missionaries died at sea before reaching their remote destinations. Protestant Missionaries began work in South India, with a center in Tranquebar and in the Caribbean Islands, with a small church in St. Thomas. France had established a strong colony in Rio de Janeiro, Brazil, competing with Spain in foreign trade. In North America, the French established a settlement in Quebec, Canada, and when England defeated them in a battle outside the city in 1729, French Catholics and Anglicans lived in separate cultures. In the South, England created the territory of "Virginia"—named after "the virgin queen" Elizabeth I (whose celebrated virginity is questioned by reports of affairs). English immigrants also established a bridgehead in Plymouth, Massachusetts, where Puritan pilgrims dreamed of a kingdom of God in "New England." The Lords of Baltimore, George Calvert and his son Cecil, founded Maryland as a haven for British Catholics who began to arrive in 1634. Dutch immigrants established a Calvinist Reformed church in New Amsterdam (now New York). Soon, the maze of spirituality and

50. NOAD.

cultures expanded in the "new world," moving from East to West, crossing a seemingly endless "new frontier." This phenomenon of growth is called "denominationalism." The designation combines faith and money—two decisive features of American Christianity. A "denomination" is both "the face value of a banknote" and "a recognized autonomous branch of the Christian church."[51]

The spread of Protestant denominations was conditioned by open, geographic space. When there were differences of opinions, dissatisfied members of a denomination simply moved on and, like ranchers, created their own denominational brand. As Calvinists, Puritans were Bible centered, but without a belief in verbal inspiration, and they believed that God works through a "covenant" whose political reality is a commonwealth or nation governed by biblical guidelines. Baptists, on the other hand, believed that one becomes a Christian by a free personal decision, that each congregation is independent, and that church and state must be separated. Quakers were pacifists. They and the Baptists were not tolerated in Massachusetts. Neither were solitary idealists like Anne Hutchinson who had the guts to question the work of some Puritan clergy who refused to cooperate, certainly not with a woman. So she assembled women for private discussions, asserting that the Holy Spirit worked through grace, not through Puritan law. Threatened with persecution, she went to New York where she was killed by Indians in 1643. Puritan Schadenfreude saw divine providence at work in the event. Another dissenter, Roger Williams, founded the city of Providence in Rhode Island in 1636 and welcomed the Baptists who were not tolerated in Massachusetts. But he criticized the pacifism of the Quakers because national self-defense was part of his "democracy." In 1681, a rich Quaker in England, William Penn, used a land grant from the British king (who owed money to Penn's father) to create a "holy experiment" in the "new world," later known as "Pennsylvania" (Penn's woods," from the Latin *sylvae*, "woodland'). The Quakers were univocal in their condemnation of slavery, the great scandal of early American culture.

By 1640, about twenty-thousand Puritans had settled in Massachusetts, guided by the "Cambridge Platform" of 1648 with a Congregationalist polity and the teachings of the Westminster Confession. Harvard College had been founded in 1636. Worship was conducted in "meeting houses" with the sermon as the main event. The biblical "covenant of grace" had to be affirmed by every parishioner. But the second generation of Puritans

---

51. NOAD.

successfully lobbied to have their children baptized as church members without such an affirmation. So the Puritans compromised with a "half-way covenant": baptized children were accepted as "half-way" members and were not admitted to Holy Communion until they made their public testimony. This compromise and "Sabbath-breaking" led Puritans to find a scapegoat, "the witches of Salem." Women were tried in court for strange behavior, ranging from teen-age hysteria to trumped-up accusations by chauvinistic husbands. Trial, torture, and death marked the infamous Salem witch-craft trial of 1692. Hysteria and casuistry killed more than twenty women. A strong guilt-trip by a patriarch of Puritanism, Increase Mather, stopped the terror. The guilt-trip continued until 2001 when the Massachusetts legislature proclaimed all the accused "witches" innocent. Today, the terrible event is marketed as a tourist attraction, "America's Bewitching Seaport with a Little History at Every Step." The son of Increase Mather, Cotton Mather (1663–1728), was the theological star in the New England colony. He had no sense of Christian modesty and promoted everything he did, especially his many publications; he hardly ever had an unpublished idea in his mind and claimed to have conversations with angels. German "Pietists," especially Moravians, settled in Pennsylvania. Zinzendorf spent some time in Philadelphia founded by Quakers in 1682.

An English parallel movement to German Pietism was "Methodism," a designation probably derived from the methodic spiritual discipline of its founders, the Anglican priests and brothers John and Charles Wesley. Ever since their studies in Oxford, they pursued a strict schedule of study, worship, and care for the poor. John did an unsuccessful stint as a missionary in Georgia, then experienced a conversion at a Pietist Moravian meeting in London, and began preaching in the open air to the chagrin of the Anglican bishops. By 1740, he had organized disciples in "bands, classes, and societies." His brother Charles composed many popular hymns, and George Whitefield, an early disciple, conducted sensational revivals. They quickly spread to America and initiated the "First Great Awakening" between 1700 and 1750, masterminded by George Whitefield. By 1795, a Methodist denomination was established, known for its successful tackling of the social ills caused by the "Industrial Revolution—the rapid development of industry that occurred in Britain in the late eighteenth and nineteenth centuries, brought about by the introduction of machinery, the use of steam power, the growth of factories, and the mass production of manufactured goods."[52]

---

52. NOAD.

Methodism prevented the spread of the Social-Communist revolution on the continent to England by providing the political soil for the growth of the Labor Party, the political protector of the poor working-class. In America, Methodism was driven with great success by horsepower, "Circuit Riders," who started and maintained a strong Christian mission, beginning with revivals in 1700. Their most sensational agent was George Whitefield. He visited virtually every populated place in England and America; he addressed crowds of several thousand people nearly every day for over a month, speaking without notes like a famous actor, and he did all that without any long interruptions for thirty-three years. Benjamin Franklin, who refused to join any church, admired Whitefield because he could be heard by thirty-thousand people at one time—proven by Franklin as one of his scientific "experiments."

The revivals caused apprehension among leaders of established churches. But the "awakening" was defended by the first renowned American theologian, Jonathan Edwards (1703–1758), a Yale-educated pastor in Northampton, Massachusetts, who became famous through his sermon "Sinners in the Hands of an Angry God." He also tried to propose a happy medium in writings that combined Protestant (Calvinist) and Enlightenment notions, focusing on human sin, divine glory, and the beauty of nature. But as a pastor, he could not let go of the Puritan custom that only card-carrying converts ("professedly regenerate") should participate in Holy Communion. So the famous "liberal" theologian was fired by his congregation—*theological* compromises do not always shape practical, *pastoral* work. Edwards withdrew to a a small congregation in the wilderness town of Stockbridge. There, he produced his significant theological writings, defending the doctrine of original sin. In 1757, he became President of Princeton College in New Jersey, but died of smallpox after a few months. His son Jonathan, Jr. spread the "Edwardsian" point of view.

The revival was successful among Baptists in the south, and, like in England, battled social ills, even slavery though only for a brief period and not everywhere. Some small black churches were established with white help in the 1770s. A peculiar event illustrates the political power of the revivals: In 1775, colonial soldiers in favor of independence from Britain heard their chaplain praise George Whitefield when they stopped near his burial place in Newburyport, Massachusetts. They went to his tomb, opened the coffin, and took his clerical collar and wrist bands from the skeleton as symbols of inspiration for their cause. In this peculiar manner, the revivals pointed to spiritual freedom from sin and to political freedom from British colonial tyranny. Puritans and "Republicans," the architects of the Constitution of the United States in 1787, could see eye to eye as patriots, except in Canada where loyalty to the British crown prevailed.

The faith of the "founding fathers" of the United States was grounded in a practical "deism." Benjamin Franklin mused that any improvement of the human race has a better chance without religion, and Thomas Jefferson reduced his respect for the Bible to his own version of a Unitarian faith.[53] The founders contended that government should not adopt any religion—a conviction written into the First Amendment of the Constitution. On the other hand, the "pursuit of happiness," declared to be a basic human right in the "Declaration of Independence" in 1776 was not granted to slaves. But odd Christian groups were tolerated, like the "Shakers," led by Mother Ann Lee (1736–1784) who believed in the equality of sexes but prohibited sexual relations. She taught her commune of celibate men and women to believe that everyone would be saved, known as the doctrine of "universalism." "Shaker furniture," simple and practical, made the group known world-wide. Within the broad spectrum of early American Protestantism the spirit of liberty was perceived more in the Bible than in creeds, with the problematic assumption that the Bible is simpler.

The American Enlightenment that shaped the revolution of 1776 was dominated by the Scottish school of "common sense" headed by Thomas Reid (1710–1796) and others. They radicalized the "empiricism" of their fellow-countryman David Hume by insisting that "truth," must be based on a real, subjective experience. Reid used the example of a "centaur" (a Greek mythological figure with the head, arms, and torso of a man but with the body of a horse): a centaur is not "real" because one cannot experience a horse or a human being in such a manner. Princeton College and the Yale Divinity School propagated the "school of common sense" which left little, if any, room for Christianity.

The "Second Great Awakening" (1795–1810) injected a considerable measure of hot piety into the growing American culture with its cool, rationally "enlightened" character. Interdenominational and inter-racial camp meetings at Cane Ridge, Kentucky, for "the conversion of sinners" became media events because of electrifying features like dancing, laughing and even barking—perhaps releasing emotions repressed by Puritan discipline and the hard effort to survive on a farm or a ranch in the "wild west." In the

---

53. Above, 126.

South, the wakening was propelled by Baptists, Methodists, and Disciples of Christ (founded in c. 1807 by a former Presbyterian and native of Ireland, Alexander Campbell, who revived early Christian life and advocated unity). In the East, the New England Presbyterian Lyman Beecher and others institutionalized the second awakening through special interest-groups, such as the American Board for Foreign Missions (1810), the American Bible Society (1816), the American Sunday School Union (1824), the American Tract Society (1825), and the American Society for the Promotion of Temperance (1826). Two principal leaders emerged, the Methodist Francis Asbury, and the Congregationalist Charles Finney. Asbury made "circuit riding" a virtual addiction, directing missionaries to "go [ride?] into every kitchen"; he himself crossed the Appalachian Mountains more than sixty times! His goal was the conversion of individuals for the sake of improving human society—no slaves and no hard liquor. After a dramatic conversion in 1821, Finney organized revivals in major cities with sermons demanding repentance at the "anxious bench," a designated place near the mass meetings where Finney dealt with the condition of individual souls; often combined with "protracted meetings" at night for several weeks. This was a new form of the medieval private confession before a priest, but with quite different features; Finney became known for confronting sinners with his "penetrating gaze" as a means of contrition.

Revivalists and Bible-quoting "evangelicals" dreamed of a "Christian Protestant America," extending west to reach every soul, even in territories with a sparse population. Peter Cartwright (1785–1872) was the model of the tireless Methodist circuit rider in Indiana, Illinois, and Iowa. He ran for Congress against Abraham Lincoln, and preached more than 100,000 sermons. Magazines spread the "good news" of the Bible, the best of all good books, and inter-denominational mid-week Sunday Schools began to teach the weekly Bible lessons—a tradition continued today during the summer vacation, known as "vacation Bible school." Christian political parties emerged from the revivals in the camp meetings. Party names reveal their political ambitions: a "Liberty Party" for the liberation of slaves; an "Anti-Mason Party" against the "Free Masons"; and the peculiar "Know-Nothing" or "American Party."[54] These parties indicate an enduring close tie

---

54. So named because when asked about the party, individual members responded, "I know nothing." "American" refers to patriotism, assumed to be lacking in Roman Catholic immigrants because they were controlled by a foreign power, the papacy. Given such characteristics, this party is quite "un-American" in its refusal to reveal its purpose and in its religious intolerance.

between religion and politics—a significant mark of American life despite the constitutional separation of church and state.

In Canada, Roman Catholicism remained the dominant religion. The British ruled with benign neglect and never enforced Anglican Protestantism. On the contrary, the English parliament approved the establishment of a Catholic hierarchy in 1850 despite strong Protestant complaints about "papal aggression." Catholic-Protestant hostility was quite common and triggered violence here and there. Presbyterians and Methodists settled in the Atlantic Provinces, Nova Scotia, and Prince Edwards Island. In Ontario, various denominations mixed with Anglicans, ranging from mainliners (Congregationalist and Disciples of Christ) to outsiders (Mormons, Plymouth Brethren, Millenarians). There was much agreement about the need for individual conversion and social harmony. Christian unity was quite visible in the foundation of the University of Manitoba in 1877; it combined three denominational colleges, Anglican, Catholic, and Presbyterian (and Methodist in 1881).

In 1857/58, a "businessmen's awakening" occurred in the United States. Its principal leader was Dwight Lyman Moody (1837–1899) who moved from his native New England to Chicago where he was attracted to the "Young Men's Christian Association" (YMCA, founded in London in 1844) and its ecumenical, interdenominational work of spiritual formation. Moody offered a standard Christian message, calmly and plainly, dressed like a businessman, without any of the emotional acrobatics of revivalist preachers. Foreshadowing modern advertising, he summed up his message in "Three R's: Ruin by Sin, Redemption by Christ, and Regeneration by the Holy Spirit." A Bible Institute, Summer Mission Conferences, and a Student Volunteer Movement became instruments for the realization of his vision, "the evangelization of the world in this generation." This enthusiastic, yet naïve, commitment echoed earlier, similar calls for a global Christian mission, especially by the English Baptist cobbler William Carey (1761–1834) who was renowned for his work in India. He successfully propagated a world-wide Christian mission, beginning with his work in India. But sentimental Christian mission, the conversion of every heathen in the world, got suck in colonialism and proselytism—a conversion to European culture affected by the old habit of a union of church and state. This ideology is exemplified by the U.S. President William McKinley who viewed the war against Spain for the control of the Philippines in 1898 as an opportunity to "civilize and Christianize the Filipinos." One could even hear it said in the

Loose Ends

U.S. Senate that the war was God's assignment to the American people to lead in the regeneration of the world.

The bloody uncivil "Civil War" (1861–1865) divided "Protestant America" on the issue of slavery. A tiny minority "awakened" to the abolition of slavery, made popular through Harriet Beecher Stowe novel *Uncle Tom's Cabin* (1852). She was the daughter of the revivalist Lyman Beecher and the wife of a Congregationalist pastor. Abolition found some roots in the North while in the South it was regarded as a violation of "natural" law and of the biblical tradition. That tradition admonishes Christian slaves to obey their masters, and masters are admonished not to threaten their slaves (Eph 6:5, 9). In 1865, Tennessee confederate veterans founded an organization that used violence against abolitionists, the "Ku-Klux-Clan" (from the Greek *kuklos*, "circle" and old English "clan"). Once again, the cross became a symbol of violence and hatred. Abraham Lincoln, who never joined a church, rejected Christian claims that God was on one side of the civil war; he expressed the hope that God would protect the entire nation.

Any notion of a "Protestant America" died in the West where Catholics had a stronghold among Hispanic immigrants. Moreover, freelance Christians did not unite. Unitarians flourished in California. Revivals, religious pluralism, and geographic distance shaped inter-denominational spiritual traffic. What united Christians was a "civil religion—a mingling of ultimate allegiance to the universal standards of Christianity with the particular values of a person's nation, region, or way of life."[55]

After the war, African Americans created their own path in the maze of American religions: "colored" Methodist Episcopal and Presbyterian churches, with the first African American bishop, Daniel Alexander Payne; and independent churches, especially "Pentecostal holiness churches" mainly in the South. But the persecution of slaves continued, well documented as lynchings. A black Baptist educator, Booker T. Washington, established the Alabama Tuskegee Institute in 1881 where segregated slaves could attain professional skills based on realistic faith and morals—a way to integrate them into American society.

Millions of Catholics migrated to the U.S. in the last third of the nineteenth century from southern and central Europe, especially from Poland and Italy. In 1888, the construction of The Catholic University of America began in Washington, DC. Religious orders also increased; they created parochial schools. Greek and Russian Orthodox Christians immigrated in

---

55. Noll, *A History of Christianity in the United States and in Canada*, 331.

fewer numbers. Some Catholics pioneered a mission to Protestants with the objective of converting them "back to Rome." A convert in New York, Isaac Hecker, founded the Paulist Order in the 1850s for this purpose. But Hecker seemed to love the enemy too much. So the Vatican became suspicious and, after Hecker's death, issued a warning against "Americanism" in 1899, the tendency to alter Catholic teachings by adjusting them to "modern" views held by individuals without permission from the hierarchy. Cardinal James Gibbons, Archbishop of Baltimore, assured Rome that American Catholics would remain loyal members.

Protestant higher education became quite liberal by the end of the nineteenth century. New universities were established, imitating German state universities as centers of scholarship without any religious affiliation: Examples are Johns Hopkins, Duke, and Vanderbilt. Compulsory chapel was abolished at Harvard in 1886. The founding president of Cornell University, Andrew Dickinson White, analyzed the problem of religion and science in his popular book *A History of the Warfare of Science with Theology in Christendom* (1895); it showed how Christianity had stymied scientific advances.

Women made their mark as promoters of foreign mission and as protectors of family life from the "devil" alcohol. They founded mission societies for raising interest and money. When the prohibition of hard liquor began to surface as a political issue in the 1860s, the "Women's Christian Temperance Union" was formed in 1874 in Cleveland, Ohio, led by the Methodist Frances Willard. Evangelical Protestant men followed suit with the "American Anti-Saloon League" in 1895. They even received support from "dry" Catholics and together they successfully lobbied for the Eighteenth Amendment that prohibited "intoxicating liquor" from 1919 to 1933—a brief, problematic Christian intoxication of the Constitution, with interesting consequences such as car racing and "mob" business.[56] The media-hungry baseball star turned revival preacher Billy Sunday reveled in "booze" sermons against "hog-jowled, weasel-eyed, sponge-columned, mushy-fisted, jelly-spined, pussy-footing, four-flushing, Charlotte-russe Christians."[57]

---

56. "Rum runners" drove high-speed cars to deliver liquor from stills to underground dealers linked to the "mob," also known as "Mafia" (from the Sicilian *mfiusa*, "one who brags, or is a swagger"). There is also a direct link between "rum running" and NASCAR (National Association for Stock Car Auto Racing).

57. Quoted in *The Detroit News Tribune*, October 19, 1916.

Loose Ends

The mazy means and ways of Christian history created a confusing struggle between adherents to the old, traditional faith and the advocates of an enlightened Christianity. The struggle is well illustrated by the American schism of Fundamentalist revivalists and progressive rationalists. Fundamentalists irrationally clung to a literal interpretation of the Bible as the never-changing Word of God while rationalists viewed virtually all their new insights as divinely approved. Using the popular image of the church as a ship, it could be said that, instead of concentrating on sailing the high seas of history, the "church" lost its focus to stay on course by quarrels about it on a crowded deck. No one listened to the captain any more. They all made fools of themselves, no longer knowing where they would land. So the vessel began to look like passengers on a "ship of fools" who no longer know where they would land.[58] Or to use a land-locked symbol: the seeds for the growth of Christianity seemed to have fallen "on rocky ground" (Matt 15:5).

Faith on the Rocks

In 1799, the German Calvinist Reformed philosopher and theologian Friedrich Schleiermacher (1768–1834) published a small book that became a watershed in the history of Christian theology, *On Religion: Speeches to its Cultured Despisers*. It was the plough, as it were, that tried to open minds for a new theological field with a new crop of ideas presented in his systematic theology, *The Christian Faith* (1821–1822). Like a creative chef, Schleiermacher mixed the various Christian spiritualities of his day and served them in a new way as his theological specialty. But the basic ingredient of the "new" menu was an old dish, the notion of "feeling" (*Gefühl* in German), encompassing "consciousness." He was exposed to emotional piety when he began his higher education in a Pietist Moravian school, then spent some time for study at the University of Halle and worked as the chaplain at the Prussian royal court in Berlin where he encountered "the cultured despisers

---

58. The image of the church as a ship is found in early Christian catacombs and churches. The famous painting "Ship of Fools" by the Dutch artist Hieronymus Bosch (c.1490–1516) caricatures pleasure seekers, misers, sick, dying and people falling off the ship, caricaturing the state of the medieval church. The American writer Catherine Anne Porter published a novel with the same title in 1945, deliberately modernizing the message of the Bosch painting by portraying international passengers on a boat sailing from Mexico to Europe in 1931. The passengers range from decadent members of high society to poor refugees who are victims of tyranny.

of religion." Among them were "enlightened" rationalists and "romantic" poets, writers, and university professors who were colleagues at the new University of Berlin. In sermons and lectures Schleiermacher defined "religion" as the universal bond that unites humankind in an intensive "feeling," "a sense and taste of the infinite," an immediate and original emotional encounter with "God" as a person or impersonal being, pending one's imagination. In short, religion creates an awareness of an absolute dependence on a non-human universal power. In this sense, Schleiermacher used the insight of Immanuel Kant who had "postulated" a power beyond earthly life, sensed as "the starry heaven above and the moral law within." From this perspective, Christian theology belongs to the discipline of historical studies. Its core is the man Jesus who was more conscious of the "eternal" than any other man, indeed, he was so penetrated by a supra-human reality that he was described as a "divine redeemer." But the biblical stories about his birth and death are superfluous. Schleiermacher's historical conclusions have no room for a faith in Jesus as a "Christ," or as the resurrected "Lord" of believers waiting for his "second coming." He related his "feeling" about the Jesus to friends in an emotional description of Christmas Eve in 1805 in the form of a dialogue. It was inspired by a flute concert and exuded feelings that Schleiermacher attributed more to women than to men: an intuition of realities not subject to rational explanation, like music, poetry, and other, similar media—a chauvinistic Christmas celebration without a baby as the "Son of God."

Schleiermacher managed to persuade many minds that theology and philosophy became embedded in "subjectivism"—the doctrine that knowledge is merely subjective and that there is no external or objective truth."[59] Two eminent philosophers offered variations on the theme of "religion." In Tübingen, Johann "Gottlieb" (German for "lover of God"!) Fichte (1762-1814) saw the "eternal" experienced in the individual who was part of "a moral world order." In Jena, Friedrich Wilhelm Joseph von Schelling (1775-1854) regarded Christianity as the final stage of an evolution of knowing "God," but without any specific doctrines like the a "Son of God" or a "Trinity."

The mind who tried to work these views into a system was Georg Wilhelm Friedrich Hegel (1770-1831). A graduate of the University of Tübingen, he was an itinerant teacher until 1818 when he moved to Berlin. Like a gymnast on a trapeze, Hegel swung back and forth, linking up with

59. NOAD.

others who were catchers or manned the platforms from where the show started. He constructed an impressive, though quite controversial, dialectic that tried to demonstrate the need to move from "subjectivism" to "absolutism"—the "acceptance of or belief in absolute principles in political, philosophical, ethical, or theological matters."[60] Accordingly, all reality can be rationally perceived as a Trinitarian dialectic in history: specific "ideas" create a movement ("thesis") from which spring other ideas that create a counter-movement ("anti-thesis"), and finally end up in a cluster of new features, a ("synthesis"). This dialectic continues to the end of time. Applied to Christianity, there is a beginning in Judaism, challenged by (Greek) Hellenism, and merged into Roman Catholicism. In this way, finite subjective experience comes to know infinite absolute ideas and can construct a rational view of world history. But this view of a triune rationalism raises issues that are almost as complicated as the dogma of the Trinity. The examiners of Hegel's doctoral dissertation in Tübingen already noted deficiencies. "Hegelians" spilt over the issue whether "ideas" or "matter" are the decisive movers and shakers of history. "Right wing Hegelians" envisaged history as ruled by lofty, often religious ideas. "Left wing Hegelians" viewed decisive historical change as driven by "material" concerns. The most renowned Protestant church historian on the right was Adolf von Harnack (1851–1930) who advocated a return to the "original" Christian teachings (its basic "thesis") in a widely read tract titled *What is Christianity?* backed up by seven volumes of a *History of Dogma*. The most influential mind on the left was the atheistic economist Karl Heinrich Marx (1818–1883), a native Jew and a journalist who became convinced that historical change is driven by material conditions, especially the conflict between the rich and the poor. Marx "converted" the German capitalist Friedrich Engels to join him in drafting the famous *Communist Manifesto* of 1847, backed up by Marx's three volumes on the dangers of capitalism, *The Capital* (*Das Kapital*) of 1867. The rest is history, well known in the creation of global "Communism," anchored in the "Bolshevik" (from the Russian *bol she*, "greater") faction of the Russian Communist dictatorship from 1917 to 1989.

Schleiermacher's theology and its enhancement was dubbed "liberal"—a mild designation in the face of his disregard of the life, death, and resurrection of Jesus as historical events. Other radical liberals openly criticized, ignored, indeed mocked Christianity in the turbulent culture of the nineteenth century. It was marked by the political religious façade of

---

60. NOAD.

the "Holy Alliance" of 1815, staged by Austria, Prussia, and Russia. The alliance did little more than brag arrogantly about the demise of Napoleon. It was opposed by two political islands, England and the Vatican. Both did not want to be in the orbit of such a suspicious trio. Various national revolutions between 1848 and 1852, inspired by Marxists, only strengthened the monarchies because of a common fear that these "Communist" uprisings would replace the comforts of the ideological status quo of "God and country." Curious minds even adopted a philosophical pessimism, made popular by the curmudgeon among intellectuals, Arthur Schopenhauer (1788–1860). He saw nothing positive in Christianity and propagated the notion that the world consists of a blind force, "the will to live," which causes human conflicts. He invited his students and readers to replace Christianity with Buddhism as an escape from earthly suffering. The best state of mind is "Nirvanah [a Hindu word for 'being extinguished']—a transcendent state in which there is neither suffering, desire, nor sense of self . . . a state of perfect happiness."[61] Friedrich Wilhelm Nietzsche (1844–1900), the son of a Lutheran pastor, viewed Christianity as a global curse. A deteriorated mental state, said to be caused by syphilis, shortened his life. Known as "the grave-digger of Christianity," he bade farewell to the God of traditional theology and philosophy without, however, denying "a redemptive mission" in history: "God is dead. God remains dead. We have killed him."[62] As a cultural world-view, Christianity, became associated with the "natural" and the "romantic," expressed in the music of Ludwig van Beethoven (1770–1827) and Johannes Brahms (1833–1897). Richard Wagner (1813–1883) made German mythology his leitmotif, especially in his operas which inspired the National Socialists led by the mesmerizing racist tyrannical power of Adolf Hitler in the 1930s.

In the face of a dominant secularism, Roman Catholicism held its own through its spiritual uniformity and political existence as a tiny "nation," the Vatican. The pope was seen by many as the symbol of stability, stemming the

61. NOAD.

62. Quotation in *The Gay Science* (*Die fröhliche Wissenschaft*), 125. Nietzsche used the Persian prophet Zarathustra (*Zoroaster*) in his work *Thus Spake Zarathustra*, (1885) as a mystical missionary of redemption. Zoroastrianism was a religious movement in the sixth century BCE. It made a radical distinction between light and darkness as symbols of good and evil. Descendants of the cult are known today as "Parsees" (derived from "Persia") in India where they found refuge from Muslim persecution in the seventh century CE. A terminal mental illness stopped Nietzsche from offering any clear philosophical explications.

Loose Ends

tide of multifarious change. The Vatican used its political "concordats" to safe-guard the interests of the Roman Catholic Church. Catholic Hapsburg Austria consented in 1855 to repeal the religious freedom granted in 1741. Spain agreed to revive the dormant Inquisition. France granted the church full authority over parochial schools. A quarrel about "mixed marriages" in the German arch-diocese of Cologne (1815–1844) ended with a Catholic victory; a couple in a mixed (Protestant-Catholic) marriage still had to promise to raise their children as Catholics. Moreover, the controversy motivated more than one million pilgrims in 1844 to visit a famous relic in Trier (west of Cologne), "the seamless tunic" worn by Jesus on the cross and taken by the soldiers after the crucifixion (John 19:23–24). Strong popes managed to hold Italian socio-political critics in check and to preserve the political independence of the Vatican when Italy became a kingdom in 1861. Papal power triumphed in the "divinely revealed" dogma of Mary's "immaculate conception" in 1854 and in an "encyclical" with a "syllabus of errors" in 1864 which condemned eighty religious, scientific, political, and economic insights. The syllabus condemned many "modern" views, stubbornly adhered to medieval teachings, and rejected religious liberty by declaring the Catholic Church as the only authentic Christian church. Such arrogance was crowned with the dogma of papal infallibility in 1870 at the First Vatican Council (1869–1870).[63] The dogma granted the pope infallible authority without the consent of the church. Faith was on the rocks, with the "rock of Peter" as the center-piece. The dogma was the star missile in the silo in Rome—first used against those who opposed it! In 1871, the opposition, consisting of Catholic intellectuals, professors at German universities, and bishops from various countries met at a congress in Munich, Germany, and formed a reform church called "Old Catholic Church." Old Catholicism survived in small national and territorial churches.

Papal power also was effective in another struggle with the German empire, dubbed "the cultural struggle" (*Kulturkampf*) from 1872 to 1879. It was a classic struggle between two powers with elitist claims: Prussia and the papacy. The Prussian Chancellor Otto von Bismarck tried to impose laws curbing Roman Catholic power: no statements regarding politics from pulpits; no Jesuit order and permits for other religious orders; and no other but "civil" marriage ceremonies. When bishops and clergy resisted, Prussia imposed fines and prison sentences. In 1873, Pope Pius IX responded with an encyclical that declared the legislation null and void, and it ordered

---

63. Above, 52.

all Catholic clergy to disobey under penalty of excommunication. A vocal German majority supported the pope. Bismarck escaped an assassination attempt by a Catholic carpenter apprentice; and large crowds went on a pilgrimage to Lourdes, France, to invoke the Virgin Mary for revenge. The Roman Catholic "Center Party" won a majority of seats in the parliament. Catholics heard the noise of Thanksgiving Masses join the angelic choirs in heaven. In the wake of victory, the Roman Curia tightened its control of ecclesiastical teaching. Pope Leo XIII issued an encyclical in 1878, rejecting "godless" science and subjecting philosophy and theology to the medieval teaching of Thomas Aquinas. A group of European "reform Catholics" were severely criticized for engaging in innovative, critical biblical studies. Their scholarly writings were condemned as products of a dangerous "Modernism." Pope Pius X condemned it as a "heresy" in an encyclical of 1907. In 1910, all clergy, heads of religious orders, and teachers in seminaries and universities had to swear an "Anti-Modernist Oath" that declared miracles as true, and prohibited any questioning of Catholic doctrines. Militarist Prussia was defeated by the papal "church militant."

Some European Protestants found refuge from secularism in a romantic awakening fed by Pietism and patriotism. Schleiermacher's call for religion as "feeling" was revived in Prussia where intellectuals at the new University of Berlin led a movement stressing religious toleration, love of country, and even of "God." A young Lutheran "Schleiermacherian" pastor, Klaus Harms, used the three-hundredth anniversary of Martin Luther's call for reform (in the *Ninety-Five Theses* of 1517) in 1817 as a reveille for a religious awakening. But his confessional Lutheranism only grabbed a few minds rather than large crowds. When the Prussian king, Frederick William III (1797–1840) used the same anniversary in 1817 to order a union of Lutherans and the (Calvinist) Reformed through a common liturgy, the old ghost of Eucharistic hostility raised its ugly head again. Lutherans insisted on their view of Holy Communion as the sacrament of Christ's "real presence" (over against the Calvinist version of "spiritual presence"). A brief but bitter controversy over the new "liturgy" (*Agende* in German) resulted in the formation of a separate "Evangelical-Lutheran Church in Prussia" after the king's death in 1840. Even Schlermacher found himself in such conservative company because he opposed the royal order for union as an abuse of political power. Saxon conservative Lutherans felt threatened by the events in neighboring Prussia. In 1838, about twelve hundred emigrated to Missouri in the United States and founded the Lutheran Church-Missouri

Loose Ends

Synod, still alive and well today, but shunning other Lutherans. Conservative Lutheranism found an intellectual home at the University of Erlangen. Since the name is also the verb "to seek," a word-play soon appeared—"Seek your salvation in Erlangen" (*Suchet das Heil zu Erlangen*). A graduate of Erlangen, Johann Wilhelm Löhe (1808–1872), organized a "neo-Lutheran" center in the small Bavarian town Neuendettelsau, with a church using high liturgy, a hospital, and schools with deaconesses as the labor force. A mission society connected with Lutheran immigrants in America. But towards the end of his life, Löhe succumbed to the infectious theological "rabies" of millenarianism, with apocalyptic speculations about the end-time. Friends covered up his "heresy" by burying him dressed in his conservative liturgical vestments—an attempt to soften the verdict on Judgment Day?

The Erlangen theologian Adolf von Harless (1806–1879) is credited with propagating a brand of inflammatory theology about "orders of creation." Nation, the white race, family, economy, and even war were viewed as divinely willed orders, leading to such prejudicial ideologies as ethnic nationalism and racism, especially in twentieth-century Germany. It made theology regress into a peculiar ethics. Some church historians did massive research in the history of doctrine (*Dogmengeschichte*). Others became known for their research in the history of religion (*Religionsgeschichte*). All these enterprises constituted a "cultural Protestantism" (*Kulturprotestantismus*).[64] At the University of Heidelberg, the Lutheran church historian Ernst Troeltsch (1865–1923) presented a history of Christianity from the viewpoint of social ethics in his tome *The Social Teachings of the Christian Church*.

German Protestants tried their hands in politics an public "works of love." Some became quite patriotic in Germany in the Covenant of German Protestants in 1909. Others created an "inner mission" (as a partnership with "foreign mission"), organizing schools or deaconesses and shelters for the homeless and unemployed. The "inner mission" movement rallied around Pastor Fredrick Bodelschwingh, a playmate and friend of the Prussian Emperor Fredrick III who financed the care for the sick and the poor in the 1870s. A seminary trained pastors for such work, continued by the son of Bodelschwingh who linked the need for welfare with government agencies after World War II in 1946. Similar efforts were made in Scandinavia.

---

64. A designation coined by the Lutheran theologian Albrecht Ritschl (1822–1889) who advocated a "theology of moral value" in his major work *The Christian Doctrine of Justification and Reconciliation*. This kind of Protestantism existed from 1860 until the end of World War I (1918), stressing patriotism and German culture.

Christendumb

In England, High, Low, and Broad Church Parties appeared. The Broad Party helped to spawn the "Oxford Movement" in the 1830s and 40s, led by the Anglican clergyman John Henry Newman and the Oxford professor Edward Pusey. They published "Tracts for the Time" against the secular Enlightenment, calling for a return to early Christian values. Newman became convinced that these values were best preserved in Roman Catholicism. So he converted and was rewarded with a cardinal's hat. Pusey did not go as far and faded away. Instead of strengthening Anglicanism, the Oxford movement brought Roman Catholicism back to England. Broad Church Oxford professors tried to unite Anglicanism but offended many by trying to adjust theology to liberal views that wanted to reconcile Christianity with natural science in a series of rather arrogant "essays and reviews" in 1860. The status quo seemed to please the majority in The Church of England. Major changes were regarded as offensive dissent. When it occurred, it quickly deteriorated into radical esoteric movements like the "Irvingians," followers of a millenarian Scottish revivalist, Edward Irving, who claimed to be an angel charged with a commission to create seven final congregations (as suggested in Rev 1:4) and send "twelve apostles" into all the world until 144,000 converts were assembled for the final trek into heaven (Rev 7:4). On the continent, Irving attracted some believers who, however, joined another radical Anglican clergyman, John Nelson Darby (1880–1912). He gathered followers in America, promising them a "secret rapture out of this world" (according to 1 Thess 4:16–17 "to meet the Lord in the air") before the final judgment if they denounced the institutional church.[65] A Methodist pastor, William Booth distributed a tract titled "The War Cry" which outlined a "military" campaign against all sins, led by him as "general" and others as "officers" under his command. But his "salvation army," as he dubbed it, did more harm than good with forced conversions and sloppy social work. The Calvinist "Free Church of Scotland," known since 1847 as "United Presbyterian Church," remained in the main stream, working well with other churches.

Some continental European Protestants went with the flow of culture in The Netherlands, in Switzerland, and in Scandinavia, adjusting to religious toleration and, in the case of Denmark, creating a "folk church" pioneered by the multi-talented churchman Nikolai Frederik Severin Grundtvig (1783-1872) who fused Lutheranism and Danish folk culture into a lively national church that liked to sing his many hymns in a popular hymnal. He

---

65. Quotation from Eric W. Gritsch, *Born Againism: Perspectives on a Movement*, 18.

also served as a member of the Danish Parliament. The most unusual mind of the nineteenth century was also a Dane, the young writer Soren Kierkegaard who, like a lonely screeching seagull, felt "sick unto death" after breaking off his engagement with Regina Olsen in 1840. He poured his pain and despair into novels and treatises that accused the institutional church of hypocrisy and made him the "father of a religious modern existentialism" a century later. In Sweden, a Bible-thumping movement drew many lay people into pious study groups. Members were called "readers" (*laesar* in Swedish); they also spread in Norway (part of Sweden until 1905). A Norwegian farmer and businessman, Hans Nielsen Hauge, led an "awakening" that called for better morals in government and industry. He served time in jail and had to work in a salt mine for preaching in the street, prohibited by Norwegian law. Some groups migrated to Latin America where Germans established enduring Lutheran churches, especially in Brazil.

In the United States religious liberty created a doctrinal mixture of foreign and home-grown faiths. By 1890, white Protestants of British background dominated (c. 52 percent), followed by Roman Catholics (c. 26 percent), black Methodists and Baptists (c.13 percent), Lutherans (c. 4 percent), and Eastern Orthodox (c. 1 percent).[66] New theological and scientific insights shook the biblical foundation of a majority of denominations. Biblical criticism questioned many naïve assumptions lumped together in the notion that the Bible is the carrier of eternal truths transmitted by inspiration to its authors. The "theory of evolution" in Charles Darwin's sensational book *The Descent of Man* (1871) challenged the biblical doctrine of creation. The Presbyterian Seminary in Princeton, New Jersey, became a bulwark against anything that challenged the "inerrant" Bible. Two professors, Chares Hodge and Benjamin B. Warfield, went to bat for it in their journal *Biblical Repertory and Princeton Review*. In 1881, they declared that God dictated the biblical texts to their authors. The General Presbyterian Assembly adopted the Princeton stance in 1910. Contrary opinions were rejected; several professors were dismissed. In 1922, the renowned Baptist teacher at the Union Theological Seminary in New York and regular guest preacher at the First Presbyterian Church in New York, Harry F. Fosdick slammed the Fundamentalists in a sermon printed in *The Christian Century*, "Shall Fundamentalists Win?" Threatened with censure, he became pastor at the Park Avenue Baptist Church. Hectic controversies finally moved the General Presbyterian Assembly to reject Fundamentalism in 1925. Fosdick

---

66. Noll, *A History of Christianity in the United States and Canada*, 361.

became the interdenominational minister at Riverside Church in New York when it was built by the Baptist business magnate John D. Rockefeller in 1931.

The conservative Bible movement became known as "fundamentalism" through the publication of *The Fundamentals* between 1910 and 1914. Two wealthy oil barons and CEOs of the Union Oil Company in Los Angeles, the brothers Lyman and Milton Stewart, donated $300,000 to the literary enterprise led by the millenarian preacher of the Moody Church in Chicago, Amzi Clarence Dixon. This fusion of business and religion was like the medieval fusion of church and state, pope and emperor. Now it was a fusion of corporate wealth and the defenders of an infallible Bible. Dixon created a committee and established the "Testimony Publishing Company." It hired sixty-four authors from England and the United States to "prove" the biblical truth of five "fundamentals:" 1) the literal inspiration of the Bible; 2) the virgin birth of Jesus; 3) his death as atonement for all sins; 4) the bodily resurrection; and 5) the truth of the miracles of Jesus. Three million copies were sent free of charge to Protestant pastors and lay leaders throughout the world—a deliberate anti-Roman Catholic gesture. It was grounded in the desire to create a "Protestant America" through the conversion of Jews and the rejection of Catholics as "citizens" of a foreign power, the Vatican.

World War I (1914–1918) revealed the cultural captivity of Christianity, especially in Germany. The Lutheran chaplain at the Prussian court preached a sermon on the biblical passage "If God is for us, who is against us?" (Rom 8:31). He made it clear, to the delight of Emperor William II, that God was on the side of Germany. Other preachers urged parishioners to stir up the spirit of hatred as an expression of patriotism. The most renowned Protestant scholar, Adolf von Harnack, composed the official solemn call for war by the emperor, and the popular theologian Reinhold Seeberg drafted the "Declaration of University Professors of the German Empire" in 1914, contending that there is no difference between the spirit of German scholarship and Prussian militarism. The four-hundredth celebration of the Reformation (1517–1917) made Martin Luther's hymn "A Mighty Fortress is our God" virtually a second national anthem, with pictures portraying him as a battle hero dressed in iron armor. Non-German European Protestants and Roman Catholics stayed neutral, with some papal critique of Eastern Orthodoxy in Serbia where the assassination of Archduke Franz Ferdinand of Austria had caused the war. German Protestants stood with the "fatherland" even after its military defeat. By 1921, the old "territorial" fusion of church and state in Germany was replaced by "church councilors" (*Oberkirchenrat*) who negotiated with the state tax system for support. The religious education in public schools was controlled by the cluster of territorial churches, Protestant and Catholic.

In the United States, the war created tensions with German immigrants as "enemies." Some American Lutherans prayed publicly for a German victory. Occasionally, German books were burned. Members of a Baptist church in Oklahoma refused to celebrate Easter because they viewed it as "a German heathen custom!" Some parochial German schools were closed. The frontier mentality created some violence: interruption of worship services, forced kissing of the American flag, and even some cases of pastors who were tarred and feathered. "Ignorance breeds more contempt than familiarity." The revivalist Billy Sunday quipped, "If you turned hell upside down you'd find 'Made in Germany' stamped at the bottom of it."[67] But on the whole, Lutherans supported the American war effort with a network of social services ranging from care for soldiers to post-war efforts of reconstruction, sponsored by the National Lutheran Council in 1918. The hope for peace and Christian unity had been expressed by a single churchman, Nathan Söderblom (1866–1931), the Lutheran archbishop of Uppsala in neutral Sweden. He had made an unsuccessful "Appeal for Peace" in 1914 and became the head of the Swedish branch of the World Alliance of Churches for Promoting International Friendship. In 1917, Söderblom managed to gather about thirty delegates from neutral countries in Uppsala. The conference intensified ecumenical movement, beginning with a Universal Conference of the Church of Christ on Life and Work in Stockholm in 1925, the sixteen-hundredth anniversary of the Council of Nicea (325–1925); about six hundred delegates from thirty-seven countries and ninety-one churches attended. In 1927, a World Conference on Faith and Order in Lausanne, Switzerland became the final structure for the World Council of Churches in Geneva in 1947. It took two horrible world wars to get a substantial portion of churches and denominations together for cooperation.

The lunatic fringe of Christianity saw in the ecumenical movement a betrayal of Christ and the Bible. In 1919, a "World Conference on Fundamentalism" in Philadelphia tried to unite the movement. The main target of Fundamentalists was Charles Darwin. In 1925, "The Bible Crusaders

---

67. Nelson, *The Lutherans in North America*, 398.

of America" appeared with the slogan "Back to Christ, the Bible, and the Constitution." Business corporations, the governor of Florida, and many tracts called for political action against "unchristian science." The Florida millionaire George F. Washburn spent a small fortune to lobby for a Constitutional Amendment "to make America Christian again." He also offered to pay for public debates with the "agnostic" enemies of the Bible. The famous "monkey trial" of a biology teacher in a high school, in Dayton, Tennessee in 1925 made the fundamentalist issue a global media event. But the trial fizzled out. John T. Scopes was found guilty of violating the state's anti-evolution law and was fined $100. The defense had been in the hands of the liberal lawyer Clarence Darrow, matched with the prosecuting attorney William J. Bryan, a Fundamentalist who had been the losing presidential candidate against William McKinley in 1896. The trial was portrayed in the classic 1960 film *Inherit the Wind*—an appropriate title for the trial. Scopes accepted a scholarship to the University of Chicago to study geology, a subject he researched and taught throughout the remainder of his life.

A popular annotated Bible combined Fundamentalism with millennialism. The *References Bible* (first edition in 1909, final edition in 1919) was published by a Tennessee lawyer, Cyrus Ingerson Scofield, a veteran of Robert E. Lee's defeated army in the Civil War. After the war, Scofield became a Congregationalist minister in Dallas, Texas, where he succumbed to the siren song of the disciples of Darby who taught the resurrection of his disciples through a "secret rapture." The Scofield Bible offered a view of world history in seven stages: 1) the age of innocence (Adam and Eve); 2) the age of conscience (the covenant after the Fall); 3) human government (Noah and the flood); 4) the age of promise (God and Abraham); 5) the law of Moses (ending with the crucifixion of Jesus); 6) the age of grace (for converted Jews and Gentiles); and 7) the fullness of time (millennium of Christ and restoration of the Davidian kingdom (with Jesus as the "new David"). The seven ages are strictly "Christian," assuming either a conversion or rejection of Jews. This belief-system is called "dispensationalism—belief in a system of historical progression and plan of salvation."[68]

68. NOAD. Made popular in the 1970s in the best-selling book of the millenarian evangelist Harold ("Hal") Lee Lindsey, *The Late, Great Planet Earth*. He predicted that the world would end in the 1980s, occasioned by the "Antichrist" embodied in Communist Russia. Twenty-eight million copies were sold before they were quietly withdrawn in the 1990s. A film version appeared in 1979, narrated by Orson Wells. Lindsay continually revised his predictions. In 2008 (August 8 in *Time* magazine) he identified President

Loose Ends

Scofield's millenarian fundamentalism was combined with a "Pentecostal revival" based on an unusual event on December 31, 1899 described by the founder of a Methodist College in Topeka, Kansas, Charles F. Parham. He taught a Bible course on the phenomenon "baptism by fire" based on the Pentecost story (Acts 2:3–4, the fiery tongues of the Holy Spirit move the apostles to preach). The spiritual gift of "speaking in tongues" (1 Cor 11:10) is called "'Glossolalia' [from the Greek *glossa*, 'tongue' and *lalein*, 'speaking')—the phenomenon of (apparently) speaking in an unknown language, especially in religious worship."[69] Parham claimed that at the New Years' Eve meeting with students, one of them spoke "in tongues" and others spoke in foreign tongues, including Chinese. *The Kansas City Times* reported that twenty-one languages had been spoken in subsequent revival meetings. Parham moved his school to Houston Texas, where he trained twenty-five students as missionaries. His street preaching drew large crowds. A black convert from Louisiana, who became the pastor of a black Baptist church in Los Angeles, began to speak in tongues and attracted others who became known as "Holy Rollers." They used an abandoned Methodist church for their "services." A report by *The Los Angeles Times* made the group a tourist attraction. They also claimed that the devastating earthquake of April 18, 1906 was a sign of perdition for those who refused to repent. Thousands of curious tourists and anxious Christians made a pilgrimage to the "Holy Rollers" and spread their "Pentecostal spirit" almost everywhere in the country; the American love for religious revivals received a powerful impetus. A lone Lutheran tourist from Norway tried to spread the Pentecostal experience. But it went over like a lead balloon among self-satisfied, relaxed Scandinavian Lutherans. In 1914, three hundred Pentecostal delegates gathered in Hot Springs, Arkansas and established their own denomination, the "Assemblies of God." Disagreements about the Trinity echoed the old Greek Orthodox belief about the independent power of the Holy Spirit (it does *not* proceed from the Son, as the Nicene Creed affirms). Some remained in the Church of the Nazarene that had been founded in 1907 and rejected "speaking in tongues" in favor of a Jesus-centered faith and life. Others followed particular emotions, visions, or just a wild hint and did everything from scratch. One of them endured as the first radio-evangelist: "Sister Aimee" (Aimee Elizabeth Semple McPerson). She established her own denomination in 1927; she used the radio

---

Barak Obama as the "Antichrist."

69. NOAD.

as a tool of evangelism; and she published her visionary theology in books and in a monthly periodical, *The Crusader*, and in a weekly newspaper, *The Bridal Call*. Her biography reads like a bizarre adventure novel, combining spiritual and secular motifs.[70]

Millenarians bequeathed to future generations of Bible thumpers peculiar mathematical speculations about the end-time. The classic case is the chronology of a Baptist preacher from Vermont, William Miller. He arrived at his date for the Last Day through calculations based on Dan 8-9 and on the day-equals-year analogy of the Irish bishop James Ussher (1581–1656) used by readers of the King James Version of the Bible. The bishop dated the events described in Dan 9 in the year 457 BCE. The seventy weeks in Dan 9:24 added up to CE 33, the year of Christ's death; and the 2,300 years of Dan 8:14 added up to 1843—the day of the end. When nothing happened, Miller and his disciples moved to Battle Creek, Michigan, where they established a "Seventh-Day Adventist Church" in 1863—using the Jewish "Sabbath": as the holy seventh day. It took the "Millerites" two decades to swallow their eschatological pride and abandon their boss's mistake. Such behavior earned revivalists in general the nickname "immediatists" who desire to "tune in, turn on, and drop out."

Sober, rational theology prevailed in mainline denominational seminaries and in graduate schools. Scholarly ties to Europe were maintained. The American counter-part to Adolf von Harnack in Germany was the church historian Arthur Cushman McGiffert (1861–1933) at Union Seminary in New York. The Baptist theologian Shailer Mathews (1863–1941) advocated the modern critical theology at the University of Chicago. The Jesuit John Courtney Murray (1904–1976) tried to steer a middle course between solid theology and a "modernism" feared by the Vatican. But the Bible dominated the literary market in many translations. "Over 2,500 different English-language editions of the Bible were published in the United

---

70. A native of Canada, she grew up Methodist, received the "baptism by the Holy Spirit" in 1908 from a revivalist, Robert Semple, married him and joined him on a mission to China. She had a baby; her husband died shortly after their arrival. Hardly twenty years old, she returned to the United States, married the salesman for a grocery firm in New England and divorced him when he refused to join her own mission. She moved to Los Angeles and built her "mission" on a vision of Ezek 1:1–28, depicting four angelic creatures—a man, a lion, an ox, and an eagle, the "perfect gospel" for "body, soul, spirit, and eternity." She called her denomination "Four Square Gospel." In 1931, she married a third time, a singer named David Hutton. In 1944, she died of an overdose of the sedative Seconal. Her lavish funeral was photographed by *Life* magazine. Her second husband, McPherson, became the CEO of the denomination.

States between 1777 and 1957."[71] African Americans cherished "the good book" as a message of liberation from slavery. Stories of Christian immigrants and novels on Christian themes became best-sellers. Ole Rölvaag wrote a moving account of a Norwegian family settling in Dakota (*Giants in the Earth*, 1929); Willa Cathers described Roman Catholics in the Southwest (*Death Comes for the Archbishop*, 1927). Emily Dickinson (1830–1886) published more than one thousand poems. The role of the church in the lives of African Americans was depicted in Zora Neale Hurston's *Their Eyes Were Watching God* (1937). Religious struggles oozed from the works of Nathaniel Hawthorne (*The Scarlet Letter*, 1850) and Herman Melville (*Moby Dick*, 1851). Mark Twain satirized church life in *Huckleberry Finn* (1885), and William Faulkner modernized biblical figures (*Absalom, Absalom!*, 1936, and *Go Down Moses*, 1942).

The crash of the stock market in 1929 produced hard times for American Christians. Protestant influence declined, but Catholics became popular through socio-political endeavors: A Catholic, Al Smith, ran for president in 1928, and Dorothy Day created the Catholic Worker movement to deal with the Depression. Young Catholics in Canada worked for renewal, among them the future Prime Minister Pierre Elliott Trudeau. (1960).

The small missionary enterprises of the eighteenth century expanded into a global mission in the nineteenth century. The medieval combination of church and state emerged again in the economic greed of European colonial powers, such as England, Germany, France, and Spain. They, and big business in the United States, combined religious and economic interests. Missionaries became partners in a steadily increasing global economic exploitation. In 1792, the British Baptist cobbler William Carey established an ambitious Mission Society "to preach the gospel to every creature," beginning in the largest British colony, India. The enterprise was copied world-wide, and he became known as the "father of modern mission."[72] But global missions were dominated by colonialism and proselytism. The World Missionary Conference of 1910 began to separate the propagation of the Christian faith from political and economic interests and called for an "ecumenical" (from the Greek *oikumene*, "the inhabited earthy") mission

---

71. Noll, *A History of Christianity in the United States and Canada*, 401.

72. Scholarship has shown "that this is a misunderstanding." So judged by a renowned historian, Stephen Neill, *The History of Christian Missions*, 222.

that would also be an ecumenical movement, uniting churches at home and abroad.

World War I brought the demise of imperial rule embodied by Austria, Prussia and Russia. As a result, numerous political promoters struggled for domination. Democratic compromises emerged. The new super-powers were Communist Russia in 1917, headed by Joseph Stalin, and German National Socialism ("Nazism") in 1933, led by Adolf Hitler and aligned with Italian fascism linked to Benito Mussolini. It took World War II (1939-1945) to overcome Nazism and fascism; a "cold war" with Communism ended its tyrannical rule in Europe (1945-1991). Russian Orthodoxy survived in exile, underground, and as a partner with the Communist government during the war against Germany. (Priests blessed weapons and prayed for victory of "mother Russia"). A few small denominations (Lutherans, Baptists, and others) survived as religious minorities. Roman Catholicism negotiated a "concordat" with the Hitler regime in 1939, guaranteeing mutual neutrality. But the ink was hardly dry when Hitler ignored the agreement. In 1937, Pope Pius XII responded with an encyclical drafted in German for wide distribution, "With Burning Concern" (*Mit brennender Sorge*), calling for passive resistance. It was drowned in Nazi propaganda. Some clergy were jailed for anti-government activities.

A Protestant (Lutheran and Calvinist-Reformed) majority in Germany joined the massive support for Hitler as the self-proclaimed providential "Leader" (*Führer*) of a new age and a new race. Already one year before Hitler became Chancellor, church leaders supported him in a movement called "German Christians" (*Deutsche Christen*), pledging support as "a church of the realm" (*Reichskirche*), headed by a bishop appointed by Hitler. Their "platform" linked Martin Luther's "heroic German piety" with the new policies of race and patriotism as logical extensions of the sixteenth-century Reformation. Two elite Lutheran theologians, Paul Althaus in Erlangen and Emmanuel Hirsch in Bonn, played into Nazi hands with a call for a halt of all German ecumenical work with Christians in the countries that claimed victory over Germany in World War I. The Nazi government seduced Christians with the claim that it supported a "positive Christianity," meaning religious freedom except when national security is threatened. But such security was advocated from the beginning of Nazi rule which propagated its own racist, anti-Semitic, and mythological "religion." The alleged ideological threat to security was Jewish capitalism.

Loose Ends

When Hitler appointed a presiding bishop, a small group of pastors resisted, led by the naval hero Martin Niemöller, a submarine commander in World War I and renowned pastor in Berlin. The group met at Barmen as the "Confessing Church" (*Bekennende Kirche*). In a "Declaration," they denounced the "German Christians," asserted the gospel of Jesus Christ as the highest authority, and repudiated the "false teaching" about special providential leaders. Hitler tightened his hold on the church by demanding an oath of allegiance to him in 1938. As state employees, pastors had to sign the oath; most of them did. Those who did not received no salary; younger clergy were drafted into the armed forces. The new Germany had no military chaplains. Only a few church leaders stayed the course of resistance, among them the young theologian Dietrich Bonhoeffer who joined the conspiracy to assassinate Hitler. When it failed in 1944, he was executed. Niemoeller became a prisoner in a "concentration camp," with Hitler's order not to kill him. When Nazi Germany occupied Denmark and Norway, church and state refused to obey his "puppet government. The Lutheran archbishop of Norway, Eivind Berggrav called for armed resistance in 1941. Hitler's attack of Russia in the same year prevented a blood-bath in Norway. Finland chose an alliance with Hitler against Russian threats.

In 1945, German Protestant church leaders offered a public declaration of penance in Stuttgart. But the dark cloud of Communism had already begun to darken Christian life in the Russian Communist satellite, the German Democratic Republic in the East. But this time, German Protestants were united in their resistance. Relations between East and West were maintained, despite the notorious Berlin Wall of 1961, and parishes served as centers of critical discussion of politics, a camouflage for underground resistance. Eventually, Communist pressure dissipated in the context of a "soft revolution" that removed the Berlin Wall and the structures of international Communism in 1989. By 1991 a reunited Lutheran-Reformed church functioned again as a free church. Among the heroes of resistance outside of Germany was the Hungarian Lutheran bishop Lajos Ordas (1901–1978) who survived Nazism and Communism, with only limited support by his church. A World Council of Churches had been established in 1947 to unite Christians around the world. National councils followed suit, exemplified by The National Council of Churches in the United States in 1959. Even Roman Catholicism joined the effort of reform in the Second Vatican (1962–1965). It was set up by the very untraditional Pope John XXIII who wanted to "open windows" to the world. Although some fresh air entered the Vatican, subsequent popes did not keep the windows open. Even the popular Pope John Paul II (1978–2005) did not pursue proposed reforms, though he spent much time trying to make his church look attractive in the world. Only "ecumenical dialogue" became an enduring feature, but any major break-through is still in the future.

Post-war Christianity made news in the United States when predictions of church growth dominated in the 1950s and a "charismatic" (from the Greek *charisma*, "gift of grace") renewal began to sweep through the country in the 1960s. Population growth after the war spread optimism for church growth; many families looked for a "church home" to match the home purchased to pursue the "American dream," usually in the suburbs. Catholics and Southern Baptists grew most rapidly. Presbyterians, Lutherans, and Congregationalists merged into larger church bodies. The notion of a "Christian (Protestant!) America" again ruled many optimistic hearts and minds. What The National Council of Churches had declared at its first convention in 1950, "A Christian America in a Christian World," seemed to become a reality. Moreover, psychological peace through Christian faith was heralded in the first of many books on "self-help," Norman Vincent Peale's, best-seller *The Power of Positive Thinking* (1952)—satirists responded with "St. Paul is appealing, Peale is appalling," and Billy Graham followed with *Peace With God* (1953) He also became the spiritual "guru" (from "teacher" in Hindu and *gravis* in Latin, "weighty") of the high and the mighty, with mass meetings for the ordinary "hoi polloi" (Greek for "the many").

The "charismatic" movement of the 1960s swept over the country, targeting traditional mainline Protestant churches (mainly Episcopalian, Lutheran, Reformed, and Roman Catholic) which were viewed as boring and lifeless. Large graduate schools and universities were also affected ("Glosso-Yalies" at Yale University). Like many American innovations, the movement began in California, in Van Nuys, where the quiet, conservative Episcopal rector and native of London, Dennis Bennett, suddenly spoke "in tongues" at a prayer meeting in 1959. The congregation complained to the bishop who transferred Bennett to a poor, dying Episcopal parish church in Seattle, Washington. There, Bennett's charismatic ministry attracted a massive following which numbered two thousand in 1968, among them many non-Episcopalians. News spread that the wife of an affluent executive of the Lockheed Aircraft Company had spoken in tongues and organized a "Blessed Trinity Society" to honor the neglected Third Person, the Holy Spirit. Its "wings" now became linked to the wings of Lockheed because well-paid executives joined the "society" and made substantial financial contributions. A minister of the Assemblies of God, Ralph Wilkerson, assisted the society in establishing "charismatic clinics" where clients could nurture and refresh their revivals. Wilkerson used Trinity money to transform a musical theater in Anaheim, near the Walt Disney resort, into a church in the round, "Christian Melodyland." The movement spread east and established a center in Plainfield, New Jersey, with a *Logos Journal* in 1971. Charismatic motifs were exported to London, England, with a "Fountain Trust" of volunteers and a "Renewal" magazine. A widely publicized conference of charismatics was staged at the Royal Albert Hall in London, with an address by the American Pentecostal evangelist Oral Roberts, Catholic charismatics appeared at the University of Notre Dame, staged conferences, and in 1975 held a conference in Rome, representing fifty countries through ten thousand delegates. Pope Pious VI blessed them and appointed a cardinal to promote cooperation between "enthusiasm and institution." The movement declined after about two decades but continued in various churches. Similar experiences were recorded in Africa, Asia, and South America, often with close ties to native religious customs.

Almost parallel with the charismatic movement was Christian participation in the revolutionary struggles related to "civil rights" in the United States. Faith moved into political action, pushing for civil rights and an end to the Vietnam War. Non-violent "freedom riders" joined "conscientious objectors" in the streets. The civil rights movement gained momentum when the young Baptist preacher Martin Luther King, Jr. led a bus boycott in Montgomery, Alabama (1955–1956). "The Southern Christian Leadership Conference" employed King's strategy of non-violence (influenced by the Indian "revolutionary" hero Mahatma Gandhi, 1869–1948). White racists used bloody violence to prevent the rise of civil rights. But the charged prediction "We Shall Overcome" became a reality in the Civil Rights Act of 1964. It could not have been passed without the leadership of King and other clergy. He was assassinated in 1968 when the Vietnam War (1955–1975) was hotly debated with violence in the streets. Again, Christian participation in the anti-war movement made a difference.

In Canada, a "quiet revolution" by Catholics in Quebec made the news in the 1960s. French-speaking Catholics advocated a "free French Quebec," supported by President Charles de Gaulle during a visit in 1967. But economic and linguistic motives outflanked Catholic religious concerns.

Christendumb

Hindsight suggests that the eighteenth-century philosophical Enlightenment initiated the demise of the "medieval synthesis," breeding fear, and replaced it with a joyous secularity, propelled by hope. But subsequent generations were unable to sustain the optimistic climate of opinion generated by enlightened rationality. Hope was soon threatened by dark clouds exposing future generations to dangerous storms. Christians began to wonder whether the "dark" Middle Ages had returned in other ways, yet still spreading their well-known features of tyranny, exemplified by racism, fascism, and Communism. A horrible world war, with its abominable Holocaust, overshadowed astonishing scientific achievements, such as the exploration of outer space, resulting in a landing on the moon. Christians became confused. Faith, "the rock of ages," began to crumble in a peculiar "age of rocks." It needed to be refreshed and strengthened like a drink in need of ice—"on the rocks."

Back to the Future

Christianity is defined by its history as a movement of believers driven by hope in a future leading to the end of time and the second coming of Christ. It is an eschatological (end-time) movement, beginning and ending with Christ in a never-ending future with God. This promise is the core of true "evangelism"—the spread of the "good news" (*euangelion* in Greek, also the linguistic root for "angel—"gospeling"). Any good and necessary change, refreshment, and reform is a wake-up call to recapture the attention to the future. Such wake-up calls are usually made by "church fathers" who recapture the original sense for the fulfillment of Christian life in the future, not in the past or present. These church fathers are sagacious and careful theologians, quite distinct from the multitude of fear-mongers who offer sensational calculations about the end-time, usually using symbolic biblical numbers like 1,000 (*millennium* in Latin), or 7 (analogous to the seven days of creation). They are known as "Millenarians," "Adventists," and "Left Behind" merchants.[73]

73. Two best-selling authors, Tim LaHaye (1926–) and Jerry B. Jenkins (1946–) have become rich through a series of Bible prophecy novels about a "secret rapture" (published 1995–2007), avoiding the terrible Judgment Day for those who are "left behind." The radio host for "Christian families," Harold Camping, predicted the dates for a "rapture" of followers into heaven on May 21, 2011, followed by the destruction of those "left behind" and the world on October 21, 2011. The religious hoopla made much money. "Secret rapture," above, 166.

Between the two world wars (1918–1939) the Christian love-affair with "religion" a la Schleiermacher cooled quite a bit. "Religion" did little to oppose the Nazi-ideology in Germany, topped by the horrible anti-Semitic holocaust, or the atheistic propaganda of Communism, marked by ruthless tyranny. Now calls were heard for the biblical "gospel" as "the power of the future" shaping the present. Joking students chose three "B" theologians (the first letter of their family name) as most influential on a Sunday morning in church: 1) Karl Barth in the pulpit, calling for an unconditional Christ-centered faith; 2) Rudolf Bultmann in a pew, trying to discern what is historically and biblically correct in Barth's message; and 3) Emil Brunner at the open church door attempting to explain to outsiders what was going on inside.

Karl Barth (1889–1968) was the decisive critic of nineteenth-century liberalism with its stress of "religion." A native of Switzerland, he studied for the ministry in Bern, Berlin, and Marburg. He became the pastor of a (Calvinist) Reformed parish in the small Swiss town of Safenwil in the German-speaking part of Switzerland. Well trained in the liberal tradition of Schleiermacher, he failed to attract parishioners to a Christian life as a universal religious sentiment embodied in a "cultural Protestantism." Desperate, Barth began a personal Bible study and discovered that, compared to his theological preparation for parish ministry, the good, old book introduced him to "a strange new world." Since the apostle Paul offers a comprehensive Christian worldview in his Letter to the Romans, Barth decided to write a commentary on it as the basis of his preaching. It turned out to be the death knell for the burial of the reigning liberal Protestant theology. Barth contended that the nineteenth-century version of the Christian faith had little, if anything, to do with the original "gospel" depicted by Paul. Barth employed a radical dialectic, spiked with the paradoxical language of the lone Danish nineteenth-century theologian Soren Kierkegaard, to make his case for change. An "infinite, qualitative distinction" must be made between the God-ness of God and humanity. God is "the Wholly Other" without any "point of contact" (*Anknüpfungspunkt* in German) between divine and human entities. There is an "impassible gulf" which is only bridged by the divine self-revelation in Jesus Christ. First published in 1919, then amplified in 1922, the *Commentary on Romans* struck like a bombshell. It has been lauded as the antidote to Schleiermacher's *Speeches on Religion*.

Christendumb

Barth was called to Germany to teach theology at Göttingen, Münster, and Bonn. Opposition to the Hitler regime, guiding the drafting of the "Barmen Declaration" of the "Confessing Church" in 1934, and refusing to give the Hitler salute, "Hail Hitler" (*Heil Hitler*, with a raised right arm) ended Barth's career in Germany. Dismissed, he went to his native Basel, Switzerland. There, he argued his cause in a monumental, voluminous *Church Dogmatic*, in a new journal titled *Between the Times* (*Zwischen den Zeiten*), and in lectures and seminars at the university. For decades Barth's opinions on virtually everything could be heard from Basel since he traveled only to very few places (to Geneva for helping to organize the World Council of Churches in 1947 and to Rome for an evaluation of Vatican II in 1962, with an extension to the United States for lectures at Princeton, New York, Chicago, and San Francisco).[74] Even Roman Catholicism acknowledged Barth's ecumenical significance; Pius XII (1939–1958) called him the most important theologian since Thomas Aquinas. The Swiss Catholic theologian Hans Urs von Balthasar (1905–1988) became a good friend, known for his love of music, art, and literature.

Barth's wake-up call is grounded in the simple, clear proposition that all of life must be centered in Jesus Christ who will take his followers from this world to a never-ending life with God. The voluminous *Church Dogmatics* explicates this proposition by redefining traditional theological topics, beginning with creation and ending in eternal recreation. The doctrine of John Calvin's controversial "double predestination" is a case in point: the only knowledge about God's wrath and love is God's incarnation in the death and resurrection of Jesus Christ in whom all of humanity is condemned and saved. Any assumption of a timeless divine judgment before the Christ event is unreal.[75] All knowledge of God is Christ-centered. There is no "natural theology" but only a "theology of the incarnate Word." That is why theology is best articulated in prayer and praise. Barth's theology calls to mind the image of the pilot of a primitive plane in bad weather, relying "on a wing and a prayer." Barth "flew," as it were, into each day with a Bible meditation, accompanied by the music of Wolfgang Amadeus Mozart whom he viewed as the leader of the heavenly symphony of angels. Then, he continued working on his lectures. Teams of graduate students and doctoral

---

74. The visit to the United States was a public media event. Barth was featured on the cover of *Time* magazine on April 20, 1962 (also the unmentioned birthday of Adolf Hitler!) as the most influential Christian theologian in modern history.

75. Original doctrine above, p.130.

candidates worked on special issues treated by Barth in his dogmatics. His simple piety and sagacious theological reflections were mixed with a dry, self-critical sense of humor.[76]

Rudolf Bultmann (1884–1976), a New Testament scholar in Marburg, wrestled with the problem of how one can combine a modern world-view, marked by electricity, radio, and many other changes, with faith in the gospel imbedded in a world of spirits, miracles, and a flat world. In 1941, he put his concerns into a lecture that caused an uproar, "The New Testament and Mythology." It called for a "demythologizing" of the gospel. Bultmann used the very controversial distinction of "reality" and "myth" advocated by the German existentialist philosopher Martin Heidegger (1889–1976) in the context of a complicated dialectic of "time" and "being," obscured by linguistic definitions: the flow of time is to be understood as "history" (*Historie* in German) in the sense of objective verifiable events; and as "story" (*Geschichte in German*), in the sense of a subjectively experienced reality. Both become "truth"—as an unquestionable datum (communicated by research), and as an overwhelming message (delivered in a sermon). The resurrection of Jesus, for example, is a "story" whose existential impact makes it "true" by faith. But it is not "history" because it lacks scientific evidence. Politics also played a role. Bultmann opposed the Hitler regime; Heidegger supported it.[77] But his program of "demythologizng the New Testament" created an intensive controversy that included also Catholics. Some were convinced that Bultmann had defined the resurrection of Jesus as "myth" and demanded a heresy trial. But Bultmann affirmed the power of myth as a mind-changing reality in the form of "proclamation" (*kerygma* in Greek). Unsophisticated minds are changed by hearing the "gospel," and sophisticated ones remain unchanged through historical-critical "proof"— "penance" is a "change of mind" (*metanoia* in Greek, Matt 3:2, "Repent, for the kingdom of heaven has come near"). Consequently, what is proclaimed

---

76. Barth wrote a letter of thanks to Mozart in heaven: *A Letter of Thanks to Mozart*, (Eugene, OR: Wipf & Stock, 1986). When asked to summarize his theology, Barth quoted a popular Sunday school song he learned from his mother, "Jesus loves me, this I know, for the Bible tells me so" (Quoted in Charles M. Cameron, "Karl Barth the Preacher," *Evangelical Quarterly* 66/2 [1994], 103). When annoyed about his critics, he frequently declared, "Well, they might as well be 'Barthians'" (intimating that only Christ should have disciples).

77. Bultmann did not make too much political noise in his support of the "Confessing Church" and was not drafted into the army—the punishment of pastors and professors. A hip problem prevented his draft, and he managed to keep his teaching position. Heidegger was a member of the Nazi party and not a card-carrying Christian.

is as real as the result of historical-critical analysis. "Faith comes from what is heard, and what is heard comes through the word of Christ" (Rom 10:17). Christ is "the word become flesh" (John 1:14). That is why an illiterate grandmother has the same faith as a sharp New Testament scholar. But the heated debate about "myth" left little, if any, room for common sense. Only after two decades did the Lutheran church in Germany change Bultmann's "heretical" image and acknowledge him as a faithful Lutheran theologian. After his death, on his one-hundredth birthday in 1984, a national Lutheran church paper summarized Bultmann's career with the headline, "From Ecclesiastical Bogeyman to Pious Teacher."[78] Once again, another case of poisonous rabies of senseless debate had to be overcome.

Emil Brunner (1889–1966), like Barth, rejected the liberal theology of Schleiermacher, as the pastor of the small mountain parish Obstalden, near Glarus. But when he criticized Barth for his total separation of "nature and grace" (in an essay so titled in 1934) Barth responded with a brief "No!" (*Nein*) and ignored him for the rest of his life—probably the only time when a renowned professor behaved like an angry boy in a playground. Brunner continued to be on Barth's side in his polite, modified way, summarizing his position in a three-volume dogmatics. Teaching in England, in the United States, and in Japan, he ended his career with a critique of the institutional church under the heading "the misunderstanding of the church." Brunner offered a verdict popular among sectarians: institutionalized faith quenches genuine spiritual life.

Barth's influence remained strong in many circles of the world-wide church. But few theologians became strong disciples. Among them is the German Reformed theologian Jürgen Moltmann (1916–), known for his "theology of hope." It had strong political undertones and found disciples in Europe and in the United States, especially after Barth's death in 1968. Some of them became "theologians of liberation," concentrating on the plight of the poor, especially in Latin America. The Catholic theologian and parish priest Gustavo Gutierrez worked in the slums of Lima, Peru. Bishops adopted his advocacy expressed in the phrase "preferential option for the poor." He and others also called their efforts *praxis*—"the divorce between theory and practice of Marxism which ensued under Stalinism."[79] This definition was rejected by the Vatican because of its relation to atheistic Communism. "Liberation theology" extended to South Korea in the

---

78. Reblin, "Vom Kirchenschreck zum frommen Lehrer," 35.

79. NOAD.

1970s where Presbyterians tackled the plight of "the ordinary people" (*minjung*), refugees from the north and people struggling for a decent living. Like Methodism in eighteenth-century England, the movement helped to speed the way toward freedom and material success. In South Africa, the racist politics of "apartheid," totally supported by the South African Dutch Reformed Church, encountered strong critics in the activist Nelson Mandela and in the Anglican priest Desmond Tutu; by 1994, South Africa was "liberated." In 1995, surprising penance for condoning slavery moved the largest Protestant denomination in America, the Southern Baptists, to accept African Americans as equal Christians.

In 1965, at the end of the Second Vatican Council, Roman Catholicism entered into ecumenical dialogue with Protestants, motivated by the "opening of windows" by the council fathers. A cardinal called Martin Luther "a common teacher" (*gemeinsamer Lehrer*) in 1970.[80] The formal Lutheran-Catholic Dialogue was used as a model in many other dialogues. Lutherans and the (Calvinist) Reformed finally dialogued successfully about the divisive issue of Holy Communion. "It is not the *mode*, but the *consequences* of the presence of Christ in the Supper that should be foremost on the common agenda."[81] They finally enjoyed mutual Eucharistic hospitality. Many Protestant churches followed suit. But the Vatican stubbornly declared that the Roman Catholic Church is the "true" church. One could hear the popular slogan in the halls of the World Council of Churches "Doctrine divides, life unites." Global Christianity agreed to feed the hungry and cure diseases, but without visible, spiritual unity.

In 1968, Pope Paul VI began an enduring struggle against changing sexual morality with his encyclical *Humame Vitae* ("Of human life"). The key issue was unconditional rejection of any kind of abortion, accompanied by a rejection of homosexuality. But the right to abortion was granted in the United States in 1973 (in the *Roe v. Wade* judgment of the Supreme Court). Protestant leaders of "old time religion" in the United States were upset by the banning of school prayer in 1962. As one irrational opponent put it at a rally, "Do we now have to pray with our kids at home?" The conservative

---

80. German address of Johannes Cardinal Willebrands at the Fifth Assembly of the Lutheran World Federation in Evian, Switzerland: "Gesandt in die Welt," *Lutherische Rundschau* 20 (1970) 459. To remove Luther from the list of "heretics" (as some Catholic lay leaders suggested) would be a nightmare of legalese, given the complexities of Canon Law.

81. Quoted in Eric W. Gritsch, *A History of Lutheranism*, 245. Agreements in 1973 in Europe and in 1989 in the United States.

"evangelicals" also rejected abortion and became strange bed-fellows with Catholics on this issue. Eventually, popes and bishops also had to face the massive, moral deterioration of celibate priests who had succumbed to the sin of pedophilia, a very expensive sin because its victims were silenced with large sums of money. By 1980, evangelicals, led by Oral Roberts and others, had united with Republicans to elect Ronald Reagan as President, even though he hardly ever went to church.

Schleiermacher's view of religion again made a come-back couched in a modern new dress through the work of the German-American theologian Paul Tillich (1886-1965). Teaching at the inter-denominational Union Seminary in New York, then at Harvard University, he attracted a large following with the notion that human life is "on the boundary" marked by faith as the "ultimate concern" for God as "the ground of being." Such language in sermons and in a three-volume dogmatics seemed to fit the American mood of the second half of the twentieth century, looking for rational cohesion. Two (Calvinist) Reformed theologians, Reinhold Niebuhr (1892–1971) at Union Seminary and his brother H. Richard Niebuhr (1894–1962) at the Yale Divinity School were critics of this American mood. Reinhold Niebuhr called for a "Christian realism" to detect and fight socio-political sins; his brother Richard denounced self-righteous denominationalism. In 1984, a "Tillichian," Carl E. Braaten, and a "Barthian," Robert W. Jenson (both Lutherans) advocated an "evangelical-Catholic" stance in a massive Lutheran dogmatics, in collaboration with others; Jenson published his own *Systematic Theology* in 1999. Scandinavian Lutherans concentrated on "motif-research" in Lund, Sweden, tracing enduring Christian motifs, exemplified by Anders Nygren's study of "love" (erotic self-love, *eros* in Greek and non-erotic self-less love, *agape* in Greek). An International Congress for Luther Research, founded in 1956 and meeting about every four years, included a strong Roman Catholic faction since 1964. The German Jesuit Karl Rahner (1904–1984) became the ecumenical theological voice of Roman Catholicism. It has found its strongest ecumenical expression in the work of Otto Hermann Pesch who taught at the Protestant University of Hamburg and in 2010 published his views in a massive dogmatics with the subtitle "based on ecumenical experience" (*aus ökumenischer Erfahrung*).

Schleiermacher, Barth, and Tillich continued to shape theological minds. If they had anything in common it was entertaining gossip about women. Schleiermacher dated two married women in Berlin (one at a time) and, when one affair became known, he left the city for two years.

Barth had a student assistant living and working with him for thirty-five years, Charlotte von Kirschbaum, who became a member of a "household of three," causing a scandal in the family and among many disciples. But Charlotte was buried alongside Barth and his wife. Tillich was a well-known womanizer. His second wife published accounts of his affairs (which often included her). *Time* magazine (October 8, 1973) published an obituary titled "Paul Tillich, Lover."

In the 1960s, Protestant denominations intensified the struggle about the issue of homosexuality, especially same-sex marriage. Biblical Fundamentalists tried to quote it out of existence, citing the death penalty prescribed in Lev 21:13—a very selective reading of Jewish law in the light of other peculiar culinary laws, like the prohibition of eating water animals without fins and scales (Lev 11:12). Mainline denominations experienced defections. The Anglican Communion, known for its dignified pose, endured some bitter struggles when homosexual bishops came out of the closet. But political liberation from racist tyranny in South Africa and elsewhere prompted leaders like Bishop Desmond Tutu to view homosexuality as a matter of ordinary justice. Other changes were less dramatic. Sunday liturgy was rocked by secular music, and the custom of cremation reduced final commendations to "ashes." Church membership keeps declining, and ecclesiastical bureaucrats try to find missionary advantages with "dismembership" (not "active" with obligations, but voluntary). "State churches" in Europe lose members who no longer want to pay a church tax.

Calls for a return to the "simple" life of the first generation of Christians are heard again at the beginning of a third millennium of Christianity. Authority (from the Latin *auctoritas*, "origination") is established by reverence for beginnings. Some groups cling to a restitution of the earliest Christian ways of life, exemplified by Mennonites and others. Roman Catholicism claims to preserve the earliest tradition in the "apostolic succession" of popes. But the "infallibility" of this claim, codified in a dogma in 1870, encountered much opposition within and outside of Roman Catholicism. Protestants are planning a world-wide quincentenary of Martin Luther's *Ninety-Five Theses* (1517–2017) which called for a return to the gospel without "indulgences." The gospel remains the "good news" of a new life with Christ in a never-ending future. That is why Christianity, in its core, is an eschatological movement, end-oriented. "Now I know only in part; then I will know fully, even as I have been fully known (1 Cor 13:12).

A Serious Epilogue

AT THE END OF any honest narrative of the history of Christianity one is always bewildered, indeed annoyed, by the difference between the meager evidence of "intelligent" faith[1] and a massive "dumb" impiety. One can, of course, never be smart or wise enough to transcend "dumb" Christendom. For Christianity is also part of human history dominated by "Murphy's Law—a supposed law of nature, expressed in various humorous popular sayings, to the effect that anything that can go wrong will go wrong"[2]—or that Christians will never be smart enough to be faultless witnesses. On the planet "Earth" nobody is "perfect" (from the Latin *perficere*, "to complete something")—"free from any flaw or defect in condition or quality; faultless."[3] This state of affairs has been summarized by philosophers and theologians in the notion of "evil."[4] To "live" is always in some way "evil" ("live" spelled backwards!).

Evil is part of Christian existence, evident by delusions of grandeur about heaven and earth. Some Christian minds assume that they can outsmart even God. This kind of grandeur increased with the long waiting for the end of the world by those who "have tasted the goodness of the word of God and the powers of the age to come" (Heb 6:5). But the original good taste, grounded in hope as anticipation of a life without evil, is often overwhelmed by the memory of bad times. So hope is replaced by fear, indeed

---

1. NOAD: "intelligent—often contrasted with *dumb* . . . from Latin *inter*, "between" + *legere*, "choose."

2. NOAD. Expressed in 1949 by Edward R. Murphy Jr. (1918–1999). He was a major in the U.S. Air Force with combat experience in the Pacific theater of World War II. After the war he worked on crew safety systems, including the "Apollo Project" for the landing on the Moon in 1969.

3. NOAD.

4. "Evil" is derived from Old English *yfel* and its modern cognate "over." It is also rooted in the German for "over" (*über*) and for "calamity" (*Übel*). Both roots indicate transgression. "Evil" is also "diabolical" (from the Greek *diaballein*, "to set things apart by throwing them," "to confuse"). As a noun (*diabolos* in Greek), it is "devil."

sometimes paralyzed by doubt. Consequently, old mistakes are repeated by anxious and impatient minds. But Christian faith must attempt to curb fearful dumbness with hopeful intelligence in order to survive in the mean, meantime between Christ's first and second coming.

What follows is a lesson of history, focused on vigilance as an indispensable ingredient of intelligent faith on the historical trail of Christianity, with its innumerable human foibles. Naïve, "dumb," Christians must be replaced, or at least shepherded, by "intelligent" ones who know how to maintain the spiritual strength to stay on course to the salvation promised by Christ. The course is complicated because it is mapped by two interwoven interims, the time between personal birth and death and the time between Christ's first and second coming. That is why the first Christians called themselves people of "the Way" (Acts 24:14) to a future "where righteousness is at home" (2 Pet 3:13), "strangers and foreigners on earth" trekking to a destination where God "has prepared a city for them" (Heb 11:10). But evil lurks everywhere in the masks of confusion, delusion, and illusion. It may be compared to a motion picture which lures viewers into illusions of comfort, or instills fear through threatening illusions. The reality of life outside the theater is cleverly veiled by an optical illusion on a screen in a dark place.

The Bible associates evil with loneliness. God tells Adam, "It is not good that the man should be alone; I will make him a helper as his partner" (Gen 2:18). But the partner, Eve, becomes the mother of the "original sin" which is inherited by every human being. Its origin is couched in the biblical story of Eve's temptation to play God (Gen 3:5)—the most dangerous human pastime. Note the juicy features of the story (Genesis 3).[5] While Eve relished the splendor in the garden of "Eden" (Hebrew and Sumerian for "delight"), a crafty, chauvinistic serpent curled up to her and asked, "Did God say, 'You shall not eat from any tree in the garden?'" Eve replied that God had prohibited eating the fruit from a tree "in the middle of the garden," indeed had commanded not to touch it on penalty of death. Slyly, the serpent probed Eve's curiosity, saying, "You will not die; for God knows that when you eat of it *your eyes will be opened and you will be like God*, knowing good and evil" (Gen 3:4–5, italics added). Eve rose to the bait, ate the

---

5. There are two creation stories: 1) Gen 1–2:3, the creation week; 2) Gen 2:5–25, the Garden of Eden. Genesis 2:4 is the literary bridge connecting them. Scholars contend that the second story is older. Note the difference in the discernment of nudity: "Adam and Eve were both naked, and were not ashamed" (2:25). But after their sin they covered their nudity with fig leaves (3:7).

A Serious Epilogue

forbidden fruit, and shared it with Adam. But now the tables turned. When their eyes were opened, they saw no trace of any divinity but the human reality of being naked (usually a less attractive state than being well-dressed). Ashamed and embarrassed, they made loin clothes from fig leaves and hid themselves from God among the trees. When God flushed out Adam, he, like a hen-pecked husband, pleaded ignorance and blamed Eve for the "sin;" and she blamed the serpent! No "mea culpa," ("my fault"), no confession. So God punished the spineless trio. The serpent was degraded to a humiliating crawling life marked by human enmity; Eve was condemned to endure the pain of child bearing and being under her husband's thumb; and Adam was sentenced to hard labor for life, being "dust" and returning to dust after death. Moreover, God exiled the couple to a place "east of Eden" where they had to fend for themselves and experience evil as deceit and violence in the murder of their son Abel by his brother Cain (Gen 4:1–16). But God remained their gracious creator promising redemption in a future "paradise" (from the Greek *paradeisos*, "a royal park"), with permission to eat the fruit from a "tree of life " (Gen. 3:22), an image of Christ (Rev 2:7).[6]

The image of the serpent as a symbol of evil changes radically in the Bible. It becomes a symbol of salvation from death during the exodus of the people of Israel from Egypt. When poisonous serpents frightened the people, Moses was told by God to make a bronze serpent, and anyone who was bitten survived by looking at it (Num 21:9). This symbol of salvation is continued in the story about a meeting by night between Jesus and a Pharisee, Nicodemus, who wanted to know how to be born again (John 3:1–21). Jesus told him that it happens when the Holy Spirit descends from above and, like the wind, "blows where it chooses." "But you do not know where it comes from or where it goes" (John 3:8). When Nicodemus asked, "How can these things be?" Jesus answered, "No one has ascended into heaven except the one who descended from heaven, the Son of Man.[7] And just as

---

6. The biblical story of original sin, the Fall, is depicted by artists and writers. Michelangelo Buonarroti (1475–1564) painted it on the ceiling of the Sistine Chapel in Rome. In 1667, the exit from the garden of Eden and the redemption of humankind were portrayed in the ten books of the classical poem by John Milton *Paradise Lost*. The Brothers Grimm's fairy tale *Snow White and the Seven Dwarfs* is a counterpart to the biblical story, a caveat to children of all ages against pride and prejudice embodied in vanity. It leads to deceit and violence (the wicked stepmother), first encountered in the murder of Abel by his brother Cain. Ernest Hemingway (1899–1961) wrote a novel, *The Garden of Eden*, published posthumously in 1986.

7. The "Son of Man" is a Semitic designation for humanity. It is used in the New Testament as a title for Jesus, "the Messiah and the Son of the living God" (Matt 16: 16).

Moses lifted up the serpent in the wilderness, so must the Son of Man be lifted up, that whoever believes in him may have eternal life" (John 3:14). The serpent as a symbol of healing and salvation is also an image used by ancient Greek and modern medicine in the mythical figure of Asclepios, walking with a snake-entwined staff; and in the logo for modern medicine, showing a serpent curled around a staff.

Jesus used this image of the serpent to identify the most necessary ingredient of the mission entrusted to the disciples, advice of how to survive in the mean meantime before his second coming. He also used three other animals as symbols of the hardship of the mission. "See, I am sending you out like *sheep* into the midst of *wolves*; *so be wise*[8] *as serpents* and innocent[9] as *doves*" (Matt 10:16; italics added). The mixed metaphor of animals draws attention to the danger of the mission. Sheep, as symbols of being "dumb" are quickly devoured by wolves who symbolize radical persecution. "Brother will betray brother to death, and a father his child, and children will rise against their parents and have them put to death; and you will be hated because of my name. But the one who endures to the end will be saved" (Matt 10:20–22). If the apostles behave only like doves, cooing with love and joy on roof-tops, they represent a naïve, child-like faith, as a response to the gift of the Holy Spirit (symbolized by a dove at the baptism of Jesus by John the Baptist, Matt 3:16). But doves also symbolize "dumb" children without any education for survival, unprotected in a hostile environment. Doves do not survive long in a hostile environment of fowl hunters. Those who know, know that most fowl can be shot at close range while making love.

Jesus called for the protection of a warm, dove-like spirituality by a cold-blooded, serpentine wisdom. Christian life in this world needs the dialectic of "dovehood" and "serpenthood," usually associated with worship (doxology) and education (catechesis). "Serpenthood" in its medical sense points to a life-long struggle with evil for survival. Like the practice of medicine, it must prevent, diagnose, and cure disease as best as possible. In the Christian context of interim existence, the cold-blooded, serpentine diagnosis of evil by the best doctors of theology is essential. The diagnosis must concentrate on the most dangerous aspect of evil, the temptation of "playing God"—idolatry. Its most common manifestation is the "holy" use

---

8. *Phronimos* in Greek, "wise" in the sense of being "*bright*" (not "dumb"), intelligent, clever, alert"—serpentine faculties no longer used for evil purposes but for good ones, symbolized by medical care. See also above, 2 n. 1.

9. *Akeraios* in Greek, "innocent" in the sense of being "pure, unmixed, uncorrupted"—"*dumb?*"

of ego-power, ranging from capricious claims ("Me-ism"—"what you have belongs to me") to uniformity maintained at all costs ("fathers" of all stripes claiming to know best what is good for everyone in the "fatherland"). The enduring challenge of spiritual formation is the unmasking of evil through reality checks and the sharing of the analyzed results with those who are unable or unwilling to face evil as an inevitable reality of everyday life. Like in medicine, precise diagnosis, based on findings and symptoms is the key to a prognosis. It needs "intelligent" practitioners: sharp, cold-blooded, "serpentine" minds, trained to choose between "wise" and "innocent" care—"from Latin *innocent*, 'not harming,' from *in*, 'not' + *nocere*, 'to hurt.'"[10] More often than not, a second opinion is needed. Example: a teacher was unable to teach because of fear. A lengthy psychiatric analysis offered the diagnosis, "You have an inferiority complex that paralyzes you in the classroom. Find another occupation." The teacher was advised by a good friend to get another opinion. A lengthy analysis offered the diagnosis, "You do not have an inferiority complex. *You are inferior.*" Now the teacher could teach again, though not as well as many others, but well enough to make a living. Sometimes, analysis causes paralysis.

Baptism commits every Christian not to be "dumb" in an evil world, but to be vigilant in the face of evil and to unite with other Christians in vigilance, struggle, and perseverance. Like emergency teams of doctors or firefighters, they should be with other members of the "church militant" in the task of "exorcism" (so called in the Middle Ages, from the Greek *exorkizein*, "to adjure," "drive out" an evil spirit). The liturgy of baptism testifies to that.[11] First, the candidate pledges to "renounce all the forces of the devil" (in infant baptism adults stand in until the candidate "confirms" the pledge as an adult in a liturgy of "confirmation"). Then, the candidate confesses his/her faith in the words of the Apostles' Creed as an indication that one is not alone in the struggle. Finally, the candidate is "sealed by the Holy Spirit" as the main combatant (Jesus promised it as an "advocate' [*parakletos* in Greek, "comforter," "defender"] in John 14:16). Baptized Christians are grounded in an enduring reality check that prevents them from the "dumb" glory of trying to realize the kingdom of God on earth. They must learn again and again to shun the temptation of being "dumb" earthly wiseacres and remain eschatological wise-crackers—to mock the

---

10. NOAD.

11. The liturgy is virtually the same in all churches. For example, "Holy Baptism" in the *Lutheran Book of Worship*, 121–25.

devil with a gallows humor about the "banality of evil,"[12] and move from their bondage to sin to "the freedom of the glory of the children of God" (Rom 8:21). Intelligent, serpentine, cold-blooded vigilance is the price of freedom—also from being "dumb."

The history of Christianity reveals a dangerous neglect of "serpenthood" in favor of a sentimental, childish preference for "dovehood." The apostle Paul delivered an exemplary call for a realistic dialectic of "serpenthood" and "dovehood."

> We must no longer be children, tossed to and fro and blown about by every wind of doctrine, by people's trickery, by their craftiness in deceitful scheming. But speaking the truth in love, we must grow up in every way into him who is the head, into Christ, from whom the whole body, joined and knit together by every ligament with which it is equipped, as each part is working properly, promotes the body's growth in building itself up in love. (Eph 4:14–16)
>
> Let your speech be gracious, *seasoned with salt*, so that you may know how to answer everyone (Col 4:6; emphasis added)

If such advice is taken seriously the rest of the history of Christianity might not be as dumb as the Christian story of the past two millennia—and Christians might once again become the "salt of the earth."

---

12. See Hannah Ahrendt, *Eichmann in Jerusalem. A Report on the Banality of* Evil.

Timetable

1–700 CE

c. 4–14	Birth of Jesus.
45	Paul begins missionary travels.
c. 50	Apostolic Council of Jerusalem.
64	Emperor Nero burns Rome. Persecution.
70	Destruction of Jerusalem after Jewish revolt.
c. 200	Neo-Platonism. Bishop of Rome gains power.
250	Persecution makes martyrs "saints."
312	Conversion of Emperor Constantine Toleration.
325	Council of Nicaea. Nicene Creed.
300	Anthony, "Father" of monasticism.
336	First Christmas.
380	Christianity becomes an enforced state religion.
400	Apostles' Creed. Augustine.
410	Rome conquered by Goths. Pope Leo I.
432	St. Patrick's mission to Ireland.
480	Benedict, "Father of Western monasticism."
500	Incense introduced in worship.
534	Justinian Code. Canon Law.
580	First church bells in France.
587	Visigoths converted in Spain.
597	Benedictine monastery in Canterbury.
622	Mohammed and Islam.
700	Boniface's Mission to Germanic tribes. First Easter eggs.

Timetable

700–1400 CE

720	Controversy about images (icons).
725	Boniface fells "holy" oak and converts Germanic tribes.
800	Charlemagne (Charles the Great), Holy Roman Emperor.
850	Jews in Germany. "Yiddish" spoken.
904–11	"Pornocracy" in Rome.
993	First "canonization" of saints.
1054	Schism of East (Greek Orthodox) and West (Roman Catholic).
1095	First Crusade. Jerusalem conquered.
1100	Beginning of scholastic theology. Anselm of Canterbury.
1150	Paris University founded.
1200	Franciscans and Dominicans. Thomas Aquinas.
1204	Sack of Constantinople.
1215	Fourth Lateran Council.
1232	Inquisition.
1268–71	Papacy vacant.
1302	Bull "Unam Sanctam": no salvation without a pope.
1305–78	Pope resides in Avignon, France.
1348	Bubonic Plague (Black Death).
1378–1415	Two popes (Rome and Avignon, France).

1400–2012 CE

1400	Hussites Renaissance, and Humanism.
1415	Council of Constance. Pope John XXIII deposed.
1450	Gutenberg printing press.
1453	Turks conquer Constantinople.
1492	Discovery of America. Catholic mission.
1517	Martin Luther's "Ninety-Five Theses."
1521	Luther condemned by church and state.
1525	German peasant revolt suppressed. Radical Reformers.
1527	Reformation begins in Scandinavia.
1529	"Protest" at Diet of Speyer.
1530	Augsburg Diet and Confession.
1534	Henry VIII of England becomes head of the church. Jesuits.

Timetable

1541	John Calvin reforms Geneva.
1545–63	Council of Trent. Roman Catholic reforms.
1555	Peace of Augsburg.
1559	Elizabeth I. Anglicanism. Puritans.
1618–48	Thirty Years' War. Peace of Westphalia. Enlightenment.
1620	New England Puritan Protestants.
1791	First Amendment and Religious Freedom in the U.S.
1800	Schleiermacher's theology. Foreign mission. Revivals..
1854	Dogma of Mary's immaculate conception.
1870	Vatican I. Dogma of papal Infallibility. Old Catholics.
1910	World Missionary Conference in Edinburgh. Beginning of the Ecumenical Movement. Roman Catholic "anti-modernist" oath.
1914–18	World War I.
1920	Karl Barth's theology.
1933	Struggle under the regime of Adolf Hitler.
1939–45	World War II.
1947	World Council of Churches.
1962–65	Vatican II. Roman Catholic Dialogues.
1989	Collapse of Communism.
2000	End-time speculations.
2017	500th anniversary of the Reformation (1517).

Bibliography

Ahrendt, Hannah. *Eichmann in Jerusalem. A Report on the Banality of Evil.* New York: Penguin, 2006.
Arnold, Gottfried. *Impartial History of the Church and Heretics (Unparteiische Kirchen- und Ketzergeschichte: vom Anfang des Neuen Testaments bis auf das Jahr Christi 1688).* Franckfurt am Mayn: T. Fritsch, 1699–1700.
"Billy Sunday Fights the Devil." *The Detroit News Tribune.* (October 19, 1916).
Bremer, Thomas. *Cross ad Kremlin: A Brief History of the Orthodox Church in Russia.* Translated by Eric W. Gritsch. Grand Rapids: Eerdmans, forthcoming.
Calvin, John. *Institutes of the Christian Religion.* Edited by John McNeill. Philadelphia: John Knox, 1993.
Cameron, Charles, M. "Karl Barth the Preacher." *Evangelical Quarterly* 66:2 (1964) 103.
Carroll, James. *Constantine's Sword: The Church and the Jews—A History.* New York: Houghton Mifflin, 2001.
The Catholic Encyclopedia. 17 vols. New York.; Encyclopedia, 1917. Online: http://www.catholic.org/encyclopedia/.
Chesterton, G. K. "Essay on St. Thomas." *The Spectator* (February 27, 1932) n.p.
Descartes, Rene. *Principles of Philosophy.* Whitefish, MO: Kessinger, 2010.
Flannery, Austin, ed. *Vatican Council II.* Newport: Costello, 1981.
Gritsch, Eric W. *The Wit of Martin Luther.* Minneapolis: Fortress, 2006.
———. *Born Againism. Perspectives on a Movement.* Minneapolis: Fortress, 2007.
———. *Toxic Spirituality: Four Enduring Temptations of Faith.* Minneapolis: Fortress, 2009.
———. *"Professor Heussi? I Thought You Are a Book": A Memoir of Memorable Theological Educators (1950–2010).* Eugene, OR: Wipf & Stock, 2009.
———. *A History of Lutheranism.* 2nd ed. rev. Minneapolis: Fortress, 2010.
Kant, Immanuel. *The Critique of Practical Reason* Cambridge: Cambridge University Press, 1997.
Life Magazine. "Martin Luther." (1997) 11–25.
Lindsay, Hal. *The Late, Great Planet Earth.* Grand Rapids: Zondervan, 1970.
Luther's Works. 55 vols. Edited by Jaroslav Pelikan and Helmut Lehmann. Philadelphia: Fortress, 1955–1986.
Marty, Martin E. *The Christian World: A Global History.* New York: Modern Library, 2007.
Marx, Karl. *Critique of Hegel's Philosophy of Right.* Edited by Annette Jolin and Joseph O'Malley. Cambridge: Cambridge University Press, 1970.
McBrien, Richard P. *Lives of the Popes.* New York: Harper, 2006.
Munro, D. C. *Translations and Reprints From the Original Sources of European History.* Philadelphia: University of Pennsylvania, 1912.

Bibliography

Neill, Stephen. *A History of Christian Missions.* Edited by Owen Chadwick. 2nd edition. New York: Penguin Paperback, 1986.

Nelson, Clifford E., ed. *The Lutherans in North America.* 2nd ed. Philadelphia: Fortress, 1980.

Nietzsche, Friedrich Wilhelm. *The Gay Science (Die fröhliche Wissernschaft)* Translated by Walter Kaufmann. New York: Vintage, 1974.

Noll, Mark N. *A History of Christianity in the United States and in Canada.* Grand Rapids: Eerdmans, 1992.

"Paul Tillich". *Time* (March 16, 1959) n.p.

Reblin, Klaus. "Vom Kirchenschreck zum frommen Lehrer." *Die Zeit* 34/5 (August 17, 1984) 35.

Ritschl, Albrecht. *The Doctrine of Justification and Reconciliation.* Whitefish, MO: Kessinger, 2006.

Santayana, George. *The Life of Reason, or, The Phases of Human Progress.* New York: Scribners, 2006.

Schaff, Philip and Henry Wace. *The Ante-Nicene Fathers.* Vols. 1–3. Bel Air, CA: Cosimo Classics, 2007.

———. *The Nicene and Post-Nicene Fathers.* Vols. 1–7. Bel Air, CA: Cosimo Classics, 2007.

Smith, Charles M. *How to Become a Bishop Without Being Religious.* New York: Doubleday, 1965.

Steinsaltz, Adin. *The Essential Talmud.* 30th Anniversary Edition. New York: Random House, 2006.

Stendahl, Krister. "The Apostle Paul and the Introspective Conscience of the West." *The Harvard Theological Review* 56 (1963) 199–215.

The Use of the Means of Grace. Chicago: The Evangelical Lutheran Church in America, 1996.

Weber, Max. *The Protestant Ethic and the Spirit of Capitalism.* Translated by T. Parsons. London: Routledge, 2002.

www.ingramcontent.com/pod-product-compliance
Lightning Source LLC
Chambersburg PA
CBHW030111170426
43198CB00009B/580